The Art of Media Disinformation
is
Hurting the World and Humanity

Democracy

What the West can learn from China

Through the Eyes of an Outcast Journalist

Wei Ling Chua

The purpose of this series of books based on factual comparisons is not only aimed at exposing media disinformation, but to enable civilisations to learn from each other's merits.

ISBN: 1493546449
ISBN-13: 978-1493546442

Table of Contents

About This Series of Books

This is the first of a series of books on the issue of media disinformation and how it is hurting the world and humanity'. It is an evidence-based analysis supported by actual examples, events and incidents. My intention is not to demonise any country, but to highlight the indoctrinated disinformation and agenda-based imperialist "journalism" relentlessly pursued by the morally corrupt and ethically bankrupt mainstream Western media (hereafter, will be referred to as 'mainstream media').

The issues of democracy, freedom, human rights and good governance are not as simple and straightforward as we are told by the mainstream media. Western democracy is by no mean a solution to all human problems. There are good reasons behind everything that occurs in each country beyond the selective and distorted information circulated by the mainstream media.

There are good reasons why life was better off for the average Iraqi under Saddam Hussein, the Afghani under the Taliban, and the Libyans under Gaddafi, than the respective puppet regimes installed by Western governments through violent means. There are good reasons why there was little or no sectarian violence under Saddam Hussein, the Taliban and Gaddafi, yet this has become a daily routine after Western "humanitarian" intervention.

There are good reasons why the majority in Syria - including the Christian population - supported the Assad government. There are also good reasons why the Kurds are fighting the Western backed rebels in Syria. As well, there are good reasons why Western economic sanctions and Western-backed anti-Assad terrorists (mainly from outside Syria) failed to overthrow the Syrian government after two years of relentless terrorism inside Syria, destroying 9,000 state buildings, taking the lives of more than 100,000, and displacing millions in the process.

There are good reasons why China managed to be the first human civilisation to overcome tribalism and become united people in 221BC; while most European countries could only achieve that in the last 150 to 500 years. There are also good reasons why the so-called "Han Chinese" is actually a mixture of a dozen or more ethnic groups with their own distinctive languages, traditions and cultures, and yet happily regard themselves as "Han".

There are good reasons why China was able to hold up as a nation over the last more than two thousand years despite periods of social turbulence and foreign invasions, while the Roman Empire has disintegrated into nothing more than a memory in the textbooks.

There are good reasons why China led the world economically for two thousand years prior to the Opium War in 1840, was able to revive itself after 1949, and is now likely to again become the world's largest economy within a decade or so.

There are good reasons why China married their princesses; built, modified, extended and maintained the Great Wall from dynasty to dynasty (exact length: 21,196.18km); used trade (e.g. Silk-Road) and a tribute system as part of their defend strategies instead of resorting to colonialism, exploitation and slavery, and were able to absorb many of their former invaders (e.g. Mongolians of the Yuan Dynasty and Manchurians of the Qing Dynasty) into their society without the kind of ethnic cleansing native populations have experienced in America, Australia, Canada and New Zealand.

Despite the wealth and military might of the US and NATO, there are good reasons why the world's most powerful military coalitions were unable to win the Korean War; were defeated in the Vietnam war, and again defeated in Afghanistan and Iraq by the weaker people who were willing to sacrifice their own lives with bombs strapped around their bodies. There are good reasons why state terrorism is no longer profitable and now unable to make Western countries any safer.

There are good reasons why American diplomats were killed, and CIA officers were unable to feel safe in Benghazi - the so-called heartland of the "Libyan Revolution" - after the death of Gaddafi.

Beyond the media rhetoric of being a brutal regime, there are good reasons why the Communist Government in China has consistently led the world in citizen satisfaction in a number of opinion surveys, including the annual American-based PEW survey, while countries under Western democracies are persistently receiving very low ratings in citizen satisfaction in the same survey.

For people who acquire their information solely from the mainstream media, this series of books is guaranteed to provide surprising insight about why, how and what has actually happened across the world.

Through the presentation of facts, people will realise that the current form of Western democracy is just an illusion, as the voting system is nothing more than the skeletal structure of a human body without blood and flesh. Genuine democracy can only be achieved through cultural reform, and a reform to the internal structure of a political and party system. The surprise is that the Communist Party of China (CCP or CPC) has successfully practised such a higher form of democracy and is in the process of perfecting the political process through the internal design of the party system and public administration.

I hope that, by seeking **TRUTH** from indoctrinated information, we will enable **TRUTH** to flourish across the world. Genuine equality, fairness and justice for the entire human race would then find its way to every corner of the world. Through the presentation of **TRUTHS** supported by sound reasoning, logic and evidence, I hope that the merits, wisdom and experience of every human civilisation - big or small - will find their way to enrich the world's civilisations.

Only through accurate information will the world's people be able to foster mutual understanding, respect and acceptance. Only through accurate information will the true aggressors and brutal governments be then scrutinised by the world's people and their own citizens. Only through accurate information will the world be able to understand in an objective manner the connections between the state of an economy, political stability, freedom, human rights, democracy, and good governance. The world's civilisations would then be able to overcome their xenophobic perceptions of each other and learn to adjust themselves for the common good of the planet, the environment and the survival of humanity. Peaceful coexistence among mankind would then be a step closer.

Despite such being my intention, the evidence I present in this series of books will no doubt upset some within the Western society as many of these people are brought up to believe that they are culturally more humane and superior to the rest of the world. Through the repeated use of the term 'Western values' in the mainstream media, Western societies seem to regard their governments' ongoing military aggression across the globe - which have resulted in the deaths, injuries and displacement of millions - as 'humanitarian intervention'.

There are good reasons why the word "discovery" was used in school textbooks when Columbus set foot on America, and Cook on Australia, as if the original residents in those territories were not human beings and had to be "discovered" by a higher being.

The power and ability of the well-funded propaganda machine in the West in dictating the world's opinion on a variety of issues can never be under estimated. I can only hope that people will exercise objectivity to examine the accuracy of the information I present in this series of books. People are welcome to question me if any part of the information is inaccurate at wchua62@gmail.com.

Through exploring a series of topics such as democracy, human rights, freedom, minority policies, corruption, good governance, terrorism, culture of indoctrination, media control, censorship, political dissidents, NGOs, and certain highly distorted historical events such as the so-called Tiananmen Square "massacre", "free" Tibet and China's one-child policy, I hope that my evidence-based analysis will inspire a movement to boycott the agenda-based imperialist mainstream media for the common good of mankind.

It is very easy to tell lies, but a lot harder to prove a lie, especially when the lies are generated through a well-funded multibillion-dollar industry that controls what editors should accept, and what journalists should write through the workings of the market economy. In particular, many such rumours are generated by the US government and corporation-funded NGOs, academics, writers, journalists and career "dissidents" who have profited from exaggerating an incident or simply making up stories to stir social dissatisfaction and hatred against their targeted governments under the coordination of the mainstream media. Proving the existence of such a complex propaganda network is a challenge that this series of books seeks to explore.

I started to explore the issues of media disinformation in 2008 with dozens of articles published on the Internet. I began to spend time since the beginning of 2012 to consolidate my thoughts and research into an over four hundred thousand word manuscript. The initial idea was to write 15 chapters, but in the process of putting my thoughts into one book, I have uncovered new angles, new research methodologies, new evidence and resources to empower my analysis. As the manuscript has expanded to 38 chapters with thousands of documentations, citations and references and become too costly to produce, I decided to restructure the content and break down the manuscript into a series of books published in instalments under the title: 'The Art of Media Disinformation is Hurting the World and Humanity', and their respective subtitles.

The following subtitle is the first of this series:

Democracy – What the West can learn from China

Coming soon:

Tiananmen Square "Massacre"? – The Power of Words vs. Silent Evidence

The Untold Story – Chen Guangcheng & US Government

[Note: There should be at least 10 instalments in this series of books. All the instalments will carry the latest information and examples. The subtitles may change at the time of release.]

Introduction

After decades of ideological propaganda, it is now a widely held view that Western democracy is the ultimate goal of human civilisation, the aspiration of people around the world. The term "democracy" seems linked to all that is positive: good governance, prosperity, human rights, civil liberty, equality, social harmony, the rule of law and the legitimacy of a government. As a result, wars could be justified in the name of promoting democracy; and even governments that consistently enjoy high ratings in opinion polls among their people - higher than Western democracies receive - are considered illegitimate and labelled as a "regime". Ironically, democratically elected governments with anti-America sentiment such as Putin's administration in Russia and Chavez's government in Venezuela have been branded as autocratic and denounced as well. In the absence of monetary rewards to encourage deeper thinking and information in the news media about the achievements of other cultures (see 'Money Talk', one of the coming instalments for a detailed analysis), Western societies appear to have submitted themselves to the tunnel vision summed up by Winston Churchill: "Democracy is the worst form of government except for all those others that have been tried."

While believing that they live in an open society, the Western public is among the most misinformed people on the planet. The daily beaming of celebrity scandals and lifestyles and negative news and images of war, conflict, poverty and suffering on every TV screen (including fabricated stories and images, as will be illustrated throughout this series of books in the upcoming instalments) has successfully created generations of people with a false sense of superiority about their society and political system.

It can rightly be asked if the current form of Western democracy is the true goal of human civilisation. Should people be content with Churchill's decades-old assertion that there aren't better alternatives?

In reality, Western democracies are in serious trouble, facing an unprecedented level of debt, unemployment, political corruption in the form of political donations, advertising and lobbying, and social dissatisfaction. It is the Western political system that requires urgent reform, or risks a revolution from the 99% -- its people -- in the foreseeable future.

Evaluation of Chinese and Western political systems in theory, structure, process and performance

Let the figures do the talking

PEW Research question: *'How satisfied are you with the country's direction?'* [1]

Table below: Percentage of citizens satisfied with the country's direction (PEW survey 2002 – 2012)

Note: best to view the table below horizontally on Kindle.

Country\Year	2012	2011	2010	2009	2008	2007	2006	2005	2002
China	82%	85%	87%	87%	86%	83%	81%	72%	48%
Germany	53%	43%	39%	43%	34%	33%	29%	25%	31%
Britain	30%	32%	31%	21%	30%	30%	35%	44%	32%
USA	29%	21%	30%	36%	23%	25%	29%	39%	41%
France	29%	25%	26%	27%	29%	22%	20%	28%	32%
Japan	20%	25%	20%	25%	23%	22%	27%	-	12%
Italy	11%	-	-	-	-	16%	-	-	24%
Spain	10%	15%	22%	21%	50%	51%	50%	51%	-
Greece	2%	-	-	-	-	-	-	-	-
Canada	-	-	-	51%	-	47%	-	45%	56%
South Korea	-	-	-	10%	13%	9%	-	-	14%
Australia	-	-	-	-	61%	-	-	-	-
Sweden	-	-	-	-	-	66%	-	-	-
Netherlands	-	-	-	-	-	-	-	49%	-
Czech republic	14%	-	-	28%	-	23%	-	-	36%
Hungary	-	-	-	6%	-	-	-	-	-

PEW Research Center's Global Attitude Project is a nonpartisan 'fact tank' in Washington. The Center began to ask the question: 'How satisfied are you with the country's direction?' in dozens of countries in 2002. The table here, which I compiled from the annual PEW data since then, indicates that the Chinese are much more satisfied with their government than citizens of Western democracies. Unfortunately, PEW does not survey or publish data annually for all countries on their website, so, for example, data for Italy, Greece and Australia were not available in some years.

Nevertheless, we can still observe that prior to 2005 the Chinese government received only 48% in the satisfaction survey in regard to the country's direction (which was still higher than most Western democracies in that year with the exception of Canada at 56%). However, since 2005, the Chinese government has decisively led the world with an approval rating as high as 87% while most Western countries receive a mere 30% and below. Though there are many reasons for the upward trend in citizen satisfaction towards the Chinese government, the main ones include the economy, and the responsiveness of the government towards the collective voices of the people. We will get into these issues later on. In the meantime, one should note that even Asian countries that have adopted Western-style democracies, such as Japan and South Korea, have received very low scores in the PEW survey. Now, let's have a look at a few other surveys that tell the same story.

Tony Saich's Survey 2003 – 2009 ('Chinese governance seen through the people's eyes')

www.eastasiaforum.org/2011/07/24/chinese-governance-seen-through-the-people-s-eyes/

Percentage of citizens relatively satisfied or extremely satisfied with government
(Author's own surveys 2003-2009)

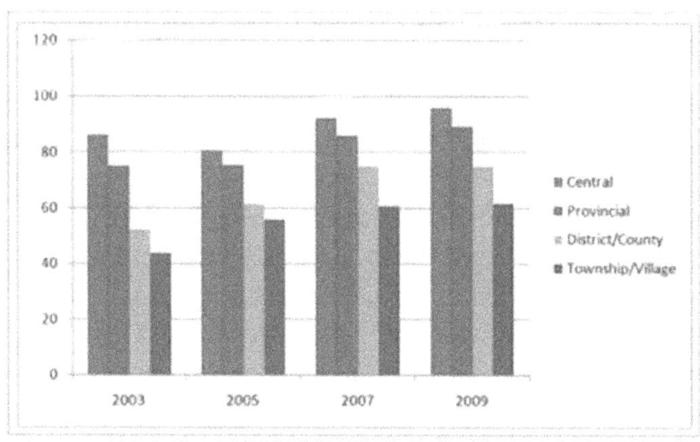

Tony Saich is Professor and Director of the Ash Center for Democratic Governance and Innovation at the Kennedy School of

Government, Harvard University. The above chart is a screenshot from Professor Saich's *article* on the East Asia Forum (24 July, 2011). Interestingly, Saich broke down his survey into four levels of government: Central, Provincial, District/County and Township/Village. The results demonstrate an upward trend in people's satisfaction across all four tiers of the Chinese government from 2003 to 2009. The Central government enjoyed the highest level of citizen satisfaction (approximately 86% in 2003, 80% in 2005, 91% in 2007 and 95% in 2009), whereas the lower the level of the government, the lower the level of citizen satisfaction. Nevertheless, it is important to point out that the overall level of citizen satisfaction across all four tiers of the Chinese government is on an upward trend. That means each level of the Chinese government has improved their performance over time. [2]

Unfortunately, I have to draw to the reader's attention the reality that - information that is in favour of the Chinese government - such as the above named Tony Saich Survey and the PEW survey - are rarely reported by the mainstream media. Despite the fact that there is a very high level of citizen satisfaction for the Chinese government, we have being told year on year by the news media that the Communist Party is a brutal regime, hated by the people, and has a problem with its legitimacy.

The latest is from the US government-funded "dissident": Chen Guangcheng (the blind "lawyer"), who reportedly posted a video to the US government-funded ChinaAid, called for, "China's next generation of leaders to implement political reform, or else face a violent end to the Chinese Communist Party rule." (Radio Free Asia, 3 December, 2012)[3] Weeks later, Chen was reported making similar statements to the Associate Press: "China's system is doomed," (The Australian, 29 January, 2013)[4] and again on 4 February, 2013, to the US government-funded Voice of America (VOA) that, "the Chinese government had lost its legitimacy."[5] It is worth noting that before Chen left China for the US several months ago, his complaints had all been local (see an upcoming instalments, 'The Untold Story - Chen Guangcheng & US Government', for details of how the US government recruits these so-called "dissidents" to smear against the Chinese government with the coordination of the Western media). However, over the last few months, the blind man began to attack the central government in every interview by the Western media. He appeared to be "well-informed" despite his blindness. It would be reasonable for one to wonder if the so-called "free" education extended to Chen at the New York University, the book deal, and the bestowing of the so-called "human rights" awards were not for free after all. Chen had obviously worked very hard for all those "freebies" that he appeared to spend more time on smearing the Chinese government than studying.

Other Surveys:

An NBC News/Wall Street Journal survey (11, 13-14 March, 2010) revealed that the American Congress enjoyed only a 17% approval rating, and that 50% would "vote to defeat and replace every single member of Congress, including their own representative."[6]

PEW survey (15 December, 2011) indicated that "just 20% of voters say they would like to see most members of Congress re-elected in the next congressional election. Two-thirds (67%) think most members of Congress should be replaced. This exceeds - by double digits - previous highs set in 2010, 2006 and 1994." [7]

Washington Post-ABC News poll (12 - 15 January, 2012) showed that 84% of Americans disapprove of the job Congress is doing. Only 13% of Americans approve of how things are going after the 112th Congress' first year of action.[8]

Gallup Poll (8 February, 2012): "Congress' job approval at new low of 10% - Republican and Democrats equally negative".[9]

Gallup Poll (11 January, 2013): "Congress begins 2013 with 14% approval."[10]

As one may observe from the above surveys, there are consistently very low levels of citizen satisfaction towards the performance of the American politicians and the Congress. The number of Americans wishing to replace the entire Congress with new faces is at an upward trend year on year - in the 2011 survey, only 20% of respondents would like to see most members of Congress re-elected. The job approval rating towards the Congress is at a historic low and in a downward trend at only 10% in February, 2012.

One would wonder why such depressing year-on-year survey figures have failed to compel the mainstream media to look for answers as to why citizen satisfaction has gone so low in America. The reality is that the entire political system in America is at a stage of stagnation and decline without much pressure from the news media calling for reform. This is in sharp contrast to the situation in China under the leadership of the Communist Party where the culture of self-reflection and self-criticism, founded during Mao Zedong's era, has been rooted into the entire political establishment.

China will not follow the path of the West

The truth is that there are many flaws and deficiencies in the design and practice of Western democracies. The Chinese government is fully aware of these flaws and is determined not to repeat the mistakes made by the Russians and Eastern Europeans two decades ago.[11](see the upcoming instalment 'Tiananmen Square "Massacre"? - The Power of Words vs. Silent Evidence', for the details of a PEW survey about the shift in attitude towards democracy in the former USSR nations at the 20th anniversary of adopting a Western-style political system)

In January, 2013, the then-incoming Chinese Chairman Xi Jinping reiterated in a party meeting that China will not follow the path of the West and stressed the importance of adhering to the existing socialist political system and direction. He asserted the importance of pragmatism and the spirit of ongoing reform. This is an excerpt from Xi's speech:

> CPC members should always harbor the spirit of "cutting a road when [they] come to the hill and building a bridge when [they] come across a river ... forge ahead and explore boldly along the path. CPC members should deepen reform and opening up, make discoveries, innovations and progresses. Party members should be brave in analysing and responding to pressing problems that the public want solving and to promote innovation in practice, theory and institutional building." (CNTV, 5 January, 2013)[12]

It is in such a spirit of ongoing self-reflection and reform that China is able to defy all odds and put the country back in one piece; even after more than a century of Western colonial exploitation and military aggression that had effectively bankrupted the country with dozens of unequal treaties,[13] followed by decades of brutal Japanese occupation that resulted in the deaths of up to 20 million Chinese and the injuries of another 15 million by the time the

Japanese surrender in 1945 (68 years ago).[14] In addition, when the Western-backed dictatorial and corrupt regime in China led by the then Nationalist Party fled the mainland to the Chinese province of Taiwan in 1949, the Party emptied national treasuries across the country, including 650,000 pieces (3,000 containers) of ancient artefacts from the imperial palace in Beijing.[15] These antiques are currently in storage and displayed at Taipei's National Museum, the Chinese name of Taipei's National Museum is named after the imperial palace in Beijing, '故宫'. Consequently, mainland China was left with nothing except dire poverty and chaos at the time the CCP took over as government in 1949.

Under the influence of the Western media, many people think negatively about the CCP. However, no one can deny their achievements and contributions to the Chinese people since 1949. As examples, China has transformed from the 'sick man of Asia' to replace its former invader, Japan, as the world's second largest economy in 2010, and is likely to replace America as the world's biggest economy within a decade or so. Under the leadership of the CCP, China doubled its national average life expectancy from 36 years in 1949 to 71 in 2004.[16] Even at a time of dire poverty and technological backwardness, China managed to halt the threat and advancement of the American-led military coalition in the Korean War (1950 - 1953), and fully withdraw all its military personnel several years after both sides agreed to cease military hostility. In contrast, the US continues its imperial military presence in South Korea to this day.

China has also managed to overcome technological sanctions imposed by the West and have produced their own satellites, GPS system (Beidou), and space station. Today, China is not only the world's factory for consumer products, but also a powerful player in the field of high-end technology. Despite the US Congress's hysterical attitude towards Chinese corporations such as Huawei, a recent report (29 April, 2013) by wired.com revealed that, "the Pentagon is so starved of bandwidth that it's paying a Chinese satellite firm to help with its communication and share data," for their military operations in Africa.[17] China has also managed to tap into the satellite launching and manufacturing market by securing business from European, South American, and African nations such as France,[18] Nigeria,[19] Belarus[20] and Venezuela.[21] Its GPS system

(Beidou) is making inroads into neighbouring countries such as Laos, Brunei, Thailand, Malaysia, Vietnam and the Philippines, and is scheduled to cover the world by 2020.[22] China is currently leading the world in the technology and usage of high speed trains.

China's education system is among the world's most successful: according to the OECD, in the Programme for International Student Assessment (which tests students from 65 countries in reading, maths and science), Shanghai, China was number one in the world for all three categories. In comparison, America ranked 23rd in science, 25th in reading and 28th in maths. (Business Insider, 9 April, 2012)[23]

Katherine Morton, a Senior Fellow at the Department of International Relations (Australia National University) believes that the real economic miracle achieved by China is that, "China has managed to feed roughly 21 percent of the world's population on only 9 percent of the world's arable land." [24]

In the latest developments, China has just invented the world's fastest super computer, "almost doubling the speed of the US machine that previously claimed the top spot." According to The Australian (19 June, 2013):

> The semi-annual TOP500 listing of the world's fastest supercomputers, released on Monday, says the Tianhe-2 - a creation of the National University of Defence Technology in central China's Changsha city - is capable of sustained computing of 33.86 petaflops, or 33,860 trillion calculations, per second.[25]

Most importantly, one should note that China has achieved all of this without resorting to colonialism, slavery and the exploitation of weaker nations through violent means such as military aggression, covert operations and bullying in the form of economic sanctions. In sharp contrast to America and other NATO countries, China has not engaged in any wars in over three decades. There is not a single Chinese soldier stationed outside of China without the endorsement of the United Nations for peacekeeping purposes. Anybody with common sense would recognise that all these positive developments in China since 1949 could not have been achieved without a dynamic political system and a team of competent political leadership.

Unfortunately, the news media in the West does not see the merit of learning from the success of other cultures as inspiration for self-improvement; they have instead concentrated their resources on ideological propaganda to uphold their model of the "worst form" of government, and have continually neglected to address their own flaws at the expense of their citizens' ongoing frustration. The reality is that through ideological propaganda, the West has stuffed their ability to reform their malfunctioning and outdated political model.

Reasons why China will never copy the West

In 2003, China set up an institution (The China Party System Research Center, 中国政党制度研究中心) chaired by dozens of scholars and experts, charged with the responsibility of analysing political systems across the world in order to enrich and perfect the theory and functionality of their existing political system. Their research is based on, but not exclusively the following:

- The existing domestic and world literature, philosophies and histories of political systems
- Visiting political institutions across the globe including those in the US and Europe to observe and evaluate the functionality, procedures, strengths and weaknesses of systems
- Interview academics and politicians in the respective countries for an in-depth discussion with regard to emerging issues
- Holding forums both domestically and abroad to generate feedback and ideas
- An in-depth study of Marxism, Leninism, Mao Zedong's thoughts, Deng Xiaoping's theories, Jiang Zemin's concept of the Three Represents, Hu Jintao's scientific development outlook, harmonious development and inclusive growth, and traditional Chinese wisdom

It is in such a spirit that these academics publish their observations and findings in a variety of publications in China annually. I have read a lot of literature on the net, the Chinese media and hardcopy printed materials related to the Chinese political system, including a report I bought in Shanghai in 2010 titled 'The Theory and Analysis of Party System with China Characteristics' by the Central Socialism Institute - China Party System Research Center (2010). [Below is the a scanned image of the book cover]

This book consists of 530 pages and 580,000 words. The analysis includes the history of China's party system - the evolution, the theory and the structure; the relationships between China's party system and state power; collective decision making and internal democracy; the issues, challenge, criteria and structure of multi-party corporations and consultations; the emerging issues and difficulties facing the existing party system. The truth is that the CCP has been very honest and objective in comparing and analysing their political system with others. Unlike the indoctrinated culture of the West, the intention and focus of the CCP is for self-improvement instead of demonising others. Much of my analysis about the Chinese political system will be based on information in this book, and unless otherwise cited, will be supplementary material in support of my analysis.

China's political process is dynamic, progressive, and democratic, and is charged with the energy for ongoing adjustment with accordance to changing social and global conditions. I have no doubt that, once people understand how it works, the Chinese model will eventually be recognised by many in the world as a model for self-improvement. Comparing to Western democracies, the Chinese system is able to sustain scrutiny in theory, structure, process and performance.

Quality of political leadership

Contrary to the Western media's claim of a princelings system of succession, China has actually adopted a system of government operated by bureaucrats in which leadership succession is increasingly based on but not exclusively the following:

- A complex process of recruitment from across the country and training from young
- An ongoing training program to upgrade the personal quality of party cadres and bureaucrats
- Performance-based promotions beginning from grassroots level
- Individual ability and ethical screening
- Layers and layers of internal democracy through corrective decision making

On 23 March, 2012, a report by the US government (the US-China Economic and Security Review Commission Staff research report) titled 'The Chinese Communist Party and Its Emerging Next-Generation Leaders' had at least acknowledged that China has increasingly institutionalised the process of its leadership succession. According to the introduction and conclusion of the report, the selected cadres are "better educated than their predecessors; they have all gained experience in provincial government administration, and arguably have outlooks that are more technocrats and less ideological than earlier generations of CCP leader". [26]

The strength of such a political model is that experience in nation building can be passed on to future generations of leaders, so mistakes can be learned; planning is forward-looking with a long-term focus. In addition, policies and strategies can be adjusted with a high level of continuity, purpose and direction. After all, the task of providing social stability, education, employment, basic infrastructure, food, shelter and clothes to 20% of the world population within a landscape of 9.6 million square kilometres is a life-time job, and can only be achieved with long-term development strategies and good governance.

Former US Secretary of State Henry Kissinger said in a panel at the Woodrow Wilson Center that: "Each generation of Chinese leader … reflected the mission and the conditions of his period." The following are some excerpts from the Washington Post (9 October, 2012) on how Kissinger described the respective Chinese leaders:

Mao Zedong:

> A revolutionary, a prophet who was consumed by the objectives he had set and who recognized no obstacles in terms of feasibility. [Note: One of the examples mentioned by Kissinger was Mao "getting the United States to balance the Soviet Union".]

Zhou Enlai:

> The most skilful diplomat that I encountered, a man of extraordinary ability to intuit the intangibles of a situation.

Deng Xiaoping:

> A great reformer, I certainly met no other Chinese who had the vision and the courage to move China into the international system and ... in instituting a market system.

Jiang Zemin:

> Someone who spent most of his 12 years "restoring China to the international system.

Hu Jintao:

> The first leader that actually had to operate China as part of a globalized system.

Xi Jinping:

> The next generation faces a transformation over the next 10 years of moving 400 million people from the countryside into the cities. This will involve not just technical infrastructure problems but a change of values and also a change in the role of the Communist party ... He (Xi) will seek such enormous internal changes that it's unlikely that in 10 years the next generation will come into office with exactly the same institutions that exist today.[27]

One should note that, among the above named top Chinese leaders, none have a father in high office with the exception of Xi Jinping. However, Xi joined the Communist Youth League in 1971 and the Communist Party of China in 1974, and worked for 40 years from a village level to get to where he is today.[28] The following is how former Singapore Prime Minister, Lee Kuan Yew described Xi after a 40 to 60 minute meeting with him:

> Mr. Xi's experiences during the Culture Revolution, when he spent some seven years working on a farm after being sent down to the countryside like tens of millions of other young people, had made him a "thoughtful" man ... I would put him in the Nelson Mandela's class of persons. A person with enormous emotional stability who does not allow his personal misfortunes or sufferings to affect his judgement. In other words, he is impressive. (Time, 19 November, 2007)[29]

In a speech in 2012 calling for Australia to adapt an independent foreign policy from America, former Australian Prime Minister Malcolm Fraser openly applauded "the contribution China has made to peace and to prosperity worldwide". Mr. Fraser was also impressed by China's "stability and sense of purpose". (The Australian, 26 September, 2012) [30]

In sharp contrast to the competence and continuity of China's political leadership at each stage of nation building in the country's direction, Western political systems have failed miserably in cultivating competent people for the top jobs.

In 2008, weeks before attending the G20 summit, a leaked phone conversation between the then Australia Prime Minister Kevin Rudd and US President George W. Bush revealed that President Bush didn't even know what the G20 was. (The Telegraph, 3 November, 2008)[31] On 14th November, 2010, The Guardian published an article pointing out that the then just published George Bush memoirs - Decision Points - were nothing more than other people's cut and pasted memoirs. The following is an excerpt:

> Bush's account is littered with anecdotes seemingly ripped off from other books and articles, even borrowing without attribution – some might say plagiarising – from critical accounts the White House had previously denounced as inaccurate. The Huffington Post noted a remarkable similarity between previously published writings and Bush's colourful anecdotes from events at which he had not been present. Bush borrows heavily from Bob Woodward's account Bush at War, which the White House criticised as inaccurate when it was published in 2002. He also appears to take chunks from a book written by his former press secretary Ari Fleischer. [32]

In fact, after digesting the content in 'Decision Points', The Guardian's feature writer, John Crace, put up an interesting article on 15th November, 2010 titled: 'Digested read: Decision Points by George Bush'. In his article, Crace presented his personal knowledge of the true legacy of George W. Bush. The following excerpt from Crace's article is, as far as my knowledge is concerned, an accurate description of what the former US president really was:

> During the last days of my presidency I gave serious thought to writing my memoirs. Karl Rove suggested I get a ghost who could write proper sentences and restrict myself to key moments of my time in office that I could retell to my advantage ... Quitting drinking was the toughest decision I've ever made ... I was extremely proud when my father installed me as governor of Texas. During my time in office I managed to build a new ball park for the Texas Rangers and execute record numbers of mentally ill prisoners. I had no aspirations to higher office until God told me I had a duty to serve my country. "But Daddy," I said, "I haven't a clue what I'm doing." "That's precisely why you're the right man. Keep your mouth shut and appoint my friends to key jobs and you'll be fine." "And what if we lose the election?" "Your brother Jeb can fix things in Florida." [33]

The cruel reality is that President George W. Bush is not the only example of an incompetence character among the American political leadership. At a time of mounting national debt (US$16 trillion), high unemployment (8%), poverty (foreclosure, homelessness, rising cost of living, and hunger), and social distress (Occupy Wall Street protests), the 2012 presidential candidates, including the incumbent President Obama seeking a second term, continued their tradition of China-bashing so as to blame their biggest creditor for all the dismay in America. Instead of working out a possible reform to re-energise the US economy and foster mutual trust with China to attract more Chinese investment, both sides of politics were competing like school children to see who would be harder on their biggest creditor if elected. The news heading on the First Coastal News (5 October, 2012), 'Truth Test: Obama claims Romney is not tough on China', has appropriately reflected the childish behaviour of the presidential candidates in America.[34] Such cases of campaign rhetoric prompted China to protest earlier on with the China Daily (27 February, 2012) carrying a heading, 'China urges US politicians to be responsible', which noted that, "maintaining the development of China-US relations is a joint responsibility for the two countries."[35] Worrying about the possible damaging effect to US-China trade relations, Bloomberg (14 June, 2012) published an article pointing out the obvious, titled 'China-Bashing as Campaign Rhetoric Binds Obama to Romney'. [36]

In a recently published book 'Act of Congress – How America's Essential Institution Works and How It Doesn't', journalist Robert G. Kaiser, a first-hand observer of the legislative process that resulted in the 'Dodd-Frank Wall Street Reform and Consumer Protection Act' in the wake of the financial collapse in 2008 concluded that:

> Most members of Congress don't understand what they're arguing about.[37]

In the UK, the Institute for Government's report on 'the challenge of being a minister' proposed that, "ministers should face regular performance reviews in the same way employees do in every other profession." According to the report, "most ministers get just over two years to prove themselves in the job before being moved on," and that the high turnover rate was, "damaging the quality of government." The reality is that excessive turnovers "reduce a minister's capacity to build up the expertise and experience required". Due to such incompetence on the part of the British ministers, they have to rely heavily on bureaucrats to tell them what to do, so when the bureaucrats are as incompetent as themselves, the bureaucrats take the blame instead. This is an abstract from a report by The Independent (24 May, 2011) about the complaints of British ministers against their officials:

> Minister complained that too often submissions and draft correspondence was inadequate. "Correspondence is not given the attention it deserves with slabs of stale prose which is not handled by sufficiently skilled individuals," said one former minister. "It is not just because of failures to spell and use grammar. Too many civil servants seem too concerned to flesh out all the detail they know to pay attention to the impact of logic and narrative." Civil servants were also blamed for being "poor on briefing, on what lines to take, and on the drafting of speeches" which, they said were often "poor, undeliverable and have no narrative".[38]

The issue of political incompetence within the British government is so serious that an editorial on The Independent (18 September, 2012) titled 'Our governance has yet to enter the 21st century - Too often, ministers feel the need for an outside alibi before they take decisions' complained about the inability of British ministers to make their own decisions, and having to appoint outsiders for policy making. The following is an abstract from the editorial:

> Whatever the qualifications of those chosen, however, such appointments raise another question – one that goes to the heart of how Britain is governed today. If so many additional individuals and organisations are deemed necessary to policy-making, not just by the last Labour government, but by a Conservative-led Coalition, what are ministers and the country's thousands of civil servants actually for? [39]

The reality is that in Western politics, the outward appearance of a politician is more important than substance. A liar who delivers well-spoken speeches and will say whatever to inspire the masses, such as "YES, WE CAN … I will close Guantanamo Bay when I become the president", is more attractive than a knowledgeable person who tells the truth with a sense of responsibility. As a result, there is no lack of examples of celebrities being invited by political parties to become one of their high profile candidates. For example, Arnold Schwarzenegger, an actor and body builder, who became the governor of California in 2003 after he was asked to run for governor by the California Republican Party in March 2001.[40] The outcome for California under his leadership should not be a surprise to anybody; according to the Wall Street Journal (21 February, 2009):

> The Golden State leads the nation on economic and fiscal dysfunction, from the empty homes spread across the Central Valley to the highest state budget shortfall in the nation's history with a fiscal hole of $41 billion.[41]

Forgive me for saying this: the Western culture as a whole is generally rather individualistic; people think only for themselves. That is, individual achievement is bigger than collective interests. There is a total lack of moral values among many of those within the Western political system. As winning an election is the primary objective; the welfare of the nation and the people is secondary. In sharp contrast to the West, the Chinese culture is basically a corrective one. People who are able to make their way to the top of the leadership ladder in China are usually less individualistic with positive personal qualities. There is a tendency that these leaders will consider issues relating to the wellbeing of the Chinese nation and the people decades after their passing. The following is a scanned image of a 2009 book, which analyses the speeches and conversations of Chinese leaders on the issue of lifting the leadership qualities of bureaucrats and party cadres as a means to further improve public administration:

Professor, Daniel A. Bell (Tsinghua University), wrote an article on the Christian Science Monitor (24 July, 2012) titled 'What America's flawed democracy could learn from China's one party rule' with the following highlight:

> Democracy has its problems. The world – especially the US – could learn from China's 'political meritocracy.' Its one party selects leaders based on

> ability and judgement. They balance the interests of an entire country – and the world, not just finicky voters or big donors.

In his article, Professor Bell rightly links the culture of political meritocracy in modern China to the traditional Chinese culture, which dates as far back as the 'Spring and Autumn Warring State Period' (approximately 771 to 403BC), where the concept of meritocracy was "shared by the vast majority of the known thinkers" including Confucius, and the subsequent institutionalised "imperial examination system that put successful candidates on the road to fame and power." According to Professor Bell:

> Whatever the flaws of the system, it did provide a minimal standard of talent selection and allowed for a modest level of social circulation. The examination system spread to Korea and Vietnam and also influenced the development of civil service examinations in Western countries. In the post-World War II era, East Asian societies developed rapidly at least partly due to the sound decision-making of meritocratically selected political rulers. [42]

Francis Fukuyama, a Senior Fellow at FSI (Stanford University), rightly points out in the project 'What is governance?' that the assumption that "democracy is an intrinsic part of good governance and that more democracy means better quality government," is just "a theory that remains subject to more empirical testing". Fukuyama asserted in his analysis that, "one can think of many ways in which greater democratic participation actually weakens the quality of governance." This is the reason why President Andrew Jackson (1828) believed that "since his party won the election, he should get to appoint federal officials, and that there was no job in the US government that was so difficult that any ordinary American couldn't do it." According to Fukuyama,

> This was the beginning of the patronage system in the US, in which the federal bureaucracy was controlled by the two political parties and in which jobs turned over with every election cycle. This began to end when President Garfield was assassinated by a frustrated office-seeker, which led to the Pendleton Act in 1883 and the establishment of the first US Civil Service Commission. For the first time, bureaucratic appointments began to rely on examinations and professional credentials, something the Chinese had come up with more than 2100 years earlier.[43]

The truth is that the Chinese is the first human civilisation to overcome tribalism and form a united country in 221BC; while most European countries only managed to achieve that in the last 150 to

500 years. It is worth noting that the so-called "Han Chinese" is a mixture of a dozen or more ethnic groups with their own distinctive languages, traditions and cultures, and yet happily regard themselves as "Han". This explains a lot about the advanced thinking and philosophies on the part of the Chinese that many in the West have yet to fully comprehend. I will get into the detail of this when I address the issue of minority policy in China in a coming instalment.

Unfortunately, many Western critics of China acquire information about China solely through the strictly controlled agenda-based mainstream media that will tell anything but the TRUTH. Despite an enormous amount of literature in China about the political system and how it work, we can hardly find any Western journalists - including those living and working in China - telling us about the political system with accurate information, and instead go by the standard format of describing the communist government as a "brutal regime" hated by the people, or a "one-party dictatorship". This is just like brainwashing people across the world that Columbus "discovered" America and Cook "discovered" Australia, as if the original population in these territories were not human beings and had to be "discovered" by a higher being. The missed opportunity for civilisation to learn from each other's merits is a loss for the West.

Political succession

As mentioned earlier, China has institutionalised its leadership succession process, with people training from young, and promotion being based on performance and personal merits. If we examine the background information of the latest leadership team in China, it is not hard to realise that many of the Chinese bureaucrats, including the current Chairman Xi Jinping, have brought with them decades of experience working from grassroots to provincial level, before moving on to the national level. The process is painfully lengthy and only the very best can make their way as a candidate for election at the Communist Party National Congress, and the two sessions (lianghui) - namely the Chinese People's Political Consultative Conference (CPPCC) and National People's Congress (NPC) - for a final decision through a voting system. Contrary to claims such as so-called "princelings", and "Shanghai clan" by the mainstream media, the top seven in the new Chinese leadership are from different parts of the country, and are armed with the experience of serving in at least two provinces. In fact, Xi Jinping has been the only so-called "princelings" that has managed to make it to the number one position of the Chinese leadership hierarchy since the founding of the People's Republic in 1949. It is important to note that the size of the population and economy in each Chinese province can be larger than many European countries. As such, it is clear that the Chinese political system is by all means far more responsible in delivering experienced and competent people to the top job. [44]

Chinese leaders like Xi Jinping and his predecessor Hu Jintao did not handpick their ministers like the Prime Ministers of Australia, Britain and Canada. They are elected through layers and layers of institutionalised internal democracy that will evaluate their suitability based heavily on their proven personal performance, leadership skills, knowledge and personal merits instead of their sweet-talking skills, looks or personal charm. It is hard to imagine a know-nothing alcoholic like George W. Bush, a body-builder and actor like Arnold Schwarzenegger, and people with no or little work experience in public administration like Barack Obama even making it to the district/county level under the Chinese meritocratic political process.

In addition, the process of mandatory leadership renewal in China has allowed for the injection of new blood within the leadership structure that ensures stability, consistency and continuity in nation building with a long-term strategic focus. This is again in sharp contrast to the Western system where extremists, racists, actors, inexperienced and incompetent characters with the backing of major political parties, interest groups, princelings, and corporate money can serve in the Parliament and Congress for decades. From a simple search on Wikipedia with titles such as 'List of members of the United States Congress by longevity of service' and 'Members of the Australian Parliament who have served for at least 30 years', one will realise that there is no lack of people who have taken up valuable parliamentary seats for 30 to 60 years. Many of these parliamentarians lack prior experience working in the public sector. The negative effect of this is that the system not only fails to recruit experienced and quality people to the top jobs, but effectively deprives the nation the opportunity to inject new blood into the system. As a result, we have seen a downward trend in the membership of political parties in the West.

Take Australia as an example: both the major political parties - Liberal and Labor – are having problems retaining and attracting membership:

Dr. David Kemp, a former Howard government minister, issued an assessment in 2008 alerting the party about the drastic decline in membership. According to Dr. Kemp, "over the last two decades, the number of Liberal branches has dropped by almost 20% to 292, and the average age of a Liberal member is 62." Using the State of Victoria as an example, Dr. Kemp pointed out that membership of the Victorian party has fallen from a post-Whitlam peak of 33,000 in the 1970s to 13,000 today (The Age, 31 March, 2008).[45]

The Labor Party faces the same situation; in a letter to leaders of Premier John Brumby's dominant Right faction in 2009, former cabinet minister Dr. Race Mathews revealed that, "the party's national membership has plummeted to about 50,000 – down from about 370,000 immediately after World War II – and the average age is about 50." Dr. Mathews also disclosed that, "there are fewer than 13,000 ALP members in Victoria and most are inactive." (The Age, 26 January, 2009)[46] In November 2011, former Prime Minister Kevin Rudd further revealed that the membership of the Australian Labor Party had further dropped from 50,000 in 2007 to 35,000 in 2011 (Brisbane Times, 28 November, 2011).[47] With the infighting that occurred between the then former Prime Minister Kevin Rudd and the then Prime Minister Julia Gillard from 2010 to June 2013, the latest report by The Australian (28 March, 2013) disclosed that, "a third of Labor members have failed to renew their memberships in the past year, forcing the party to mobilise union officials to prepare for the upcoming federal election." [48]

From this, it is not hard to visualise the reasons for the drastic drop in membership of political parties in Australia; namely, the lack of opportunity for the younger generation, internal fractions and sectarian politics, with party elders dictating the succession process not based on talent but power play. The following excerpt from the last four paragraphs of The Age's report (31 March, 2008) highlights some of the issues:

> Dr Kemp said a key aspect to renewing the party was to revamp the membership structure to complement traditional branches, as the current forms of involvement were not suitable for all. For the 30 to 50 age group, it was not easy for parents to get to branch meetings, for example, and the Liberals needed to make the party more accessible, he said. "The branch is still an effective way of engaging many people, but clearly it doesn't appeal to all people," Dr Kemp said. Last month, former Prime Minister Malcolm Fraser warned that the Liberal Party would be doomed to opposition unless it undertook reforms, such as preselections being decided by a plebiscite of all members in an electorate. [49]

The reality is that even minor parties like the Greens also do not use democratic means to decide the party leadership. As such, it is ironic that, The Age, a notoriously anti-Chinese newspaper in Australia that often complains about the lack of democracy in China, actually went along with the Greens Party elder Bob Brown's decision in 2005 not to allow the wider party membership to choose their leaders. The following is an excerpt from The Age's article dated 12 March, 2012, expressing support for Brown's autocratic decision in 2005:

> In 2005, Brown insisted the national Greens party have a leader, a deputy and a whip elected by the party room - not the membership. That burst of professional pragmatism was then a novel concept for an aggressively egalitarian grassroots movement resistant to hierarchical notions such as leaders. Brown's belief was that the Democrats were rendered vulnerable by the structural instability created by a leader anointed (and torn down) by a restless, plotting, petitioning membership. History has proved him absolutely right. The Democrats are gone, and the Greens in 2010 eclipsed their high-water mark, with 11.76 per cent of the primary vote. [50]
>
> [Author's Note: Democrats used to emerge as a third force in Australian politics, but the party was later totally destroyed by their restless plotting, and petitioning members who fought against each other in an individualistic and selfish manner.]

So, the concept of democracy is not as simple as 'one man, one vote'. Despite the relentless rhetoric against other cultures, Western politicians do not believe in the judgement of their own party's grassroots members. Barry Jones, a former minister in the Hawke government from 1983 to 1990, put up an article on The Conversation (27 March, 2012) titled 'The decay of the political process' with this complaint:

> The major problem for the ALP is that it is becoming increasingly disconnected from the community at large, or even Labor voters. This is

> partly because of the oligarchic structure of the Party in which control has passed to a small group of apparatchiks, sometimes called the *nomenklatura*, which dominates state and national conferences, people whose livelihood depends on the party itself or affiliated unions ...The development of national factions constitutes, in effect, the privatisation of the party, with factional warlords engaged in carving up the assets, rewarding factional loyalty and promoting an almost feudal code of allegiance. Factions are essentially executive placement agencies. Elections offer voters relatively limited choices, like choosing between KPMG and PWC, two management teams with a convergent set of operating methods, who use the same techniques.[51]

One should note that Australia's population was about 7 million in 1945 and has since tripled to more than 22 million in 2012; yet, the memberships of both the major political parties are in dramatic decline by an absolute number. Thus, when we measure the ratio between the party membership to the entire population in 1945 and 2012, respectively, it is not hard to notice that these political parties have disconnected from the general population. As aforementioned, the average age of Labor Party members is 50, and Liberals, 62. The legitimacy of these political parties should be a cause for concern, as it is obvious that they are being controlled by a handful of sectarian dictators from within; they do not represent the people, and most importantly, they are highly corrupt and "engage in carving up assets, rewarding factional loyalty and promoting an almost feudal code of allegiance".

In contrast to the situation in Australia, although the CCP may not endorse a voting system at a provincial and national level, the party membership has increased from around 4.5 million in 1949 to over 80 million in 2012. As a ratio of the entire population of 450 million in 1949 and 1.3 billion in 2012, there is far more grassroots participation and opportunity within the Communist Party than the two major political parties in Australia. I will get into the details of the membership structure of the CCP later.

The illusion of choice

Perceptions can be misleading. The skeletal structure of a voting system in the West provides people with the illusion of choice and freedom. However, in reality, the Western public rarely has a genuine voice in their so-called "democratic institutions". The reason is simple: despite the so-called two party or multi-party systems, voters are generally only given the choice to select among the same few rotten political parties and politicians in each election. This explains why the number of Americans wishing to replace the entire Congress with new faces is at an all-time high; as mentioned earlier, only 20% of Americans would like to see most members of Congress re-elected in the 2011 PEW survey. However, during the 2012 election, 90% of House members and 91% of Senators who sought re-election were successful. (Bloomberg, 13 December, 2012)[52] One would wonder why.

In fact, the same situation is happening in Australia. On the eve of the 2010 election, The Sunday Mail-Galaxy Poll indicated that, "a majority of Australians think neither Labor nor the Coalition deserves to be elected." (Courier Mail, 18 July, 2010)[53] Not surprisingly, a year later, another survey in 2011 gauged the same response from voters (News, 27 April, 2011).[54] Sadly, in the upcoming September, 2013 federal election, Australian voters will again be left with no alternative but the two rotten political parties to choose from. The Age (6 May, 2013) reported the latest survey by Melbourne University under the heading, 'Poll looms, voters tune out in droves' with this highlight:

> With just over four months to go before the federal election, Australians have switched off, with more than a third having little or no interest in September's election. A national survey by Melbourne University also found most Australians believe the quality of leadership and the tone of debate is worse than usual. And 70 per cent lack confidence in the federal government, including almost half of Labor voters ... The results ... reveal a deeper disengagement with politics than usual and presents a challenge for political parties vying for public attention. The centre's senior research fellow, Dr Denis Muller, said the survey found that Australians were "pretty appalled" at the standard of politics.[55]

Ironically, not only will the Australian voters be facing the two major political parties they dislike in the upcoming election, but they will also be facing the two Prime Ministerial candidates that they consistently rejected in a number of opinion polls. For example, a Galaxy Poll in Queensland for the Courier Mail (26 November, 2012) revealed that:

> Two thirds of Queensland voters say neither Julia Gillard nor Tony Abbott understand their concerns ... only about a quarter say either federal political leader has a good understanding of the issues that affect the

> state ... "The problem for the federal parties is that the two leaders are considered to lack empathy with the concerns of voters and do not have a good understanding of the issues that affect Queensland," Galaxy chief David Briggs said. [56]

Earlier on, another survey revealed that Malcolm Turnbull was more than twice as popular as the current Liberal leader, Tony Abbott. (Sydney Morning Herald, 17 September, 2012)[57] However, as the Liberals are also a political party controlled by party elders and internal sectarianism, Malcolm Turnbull, despite his popularity and talent, stood no chance in challenging Tony Abbott, a former Roman Catholic priest.

The truth is that Western democracy in its current form does not represent the will of the people. It is the big corporations and wealthy interest groups who are able to spray money around that dictate who becomes the Member of Parliament or Congress, the President, or Prime Minister. Without the endorsement of these big corporations and the wealthy with political donations and advertisements (a staggering US$6 billion in the 2012 US presidential election alone[58]), one would have no voice in the media, no money in hiring professional campaign staff, and no money setting up an election office or holding a large-scale public rally, so no voter would have the chance to hear your name and your policy. We will get into the details later on.

In the meantime, one should note that in a capitalist democracy, the mainstream media is very much controlled by a handful of big corporations. If an ideology presented in a public activity is different from the capitalist doctrine, it will receive no coverage at all. For example, during the anti-Wall Street protests in America, what the Western public did not see on their TV screens were the images of protesters erecting Chairman Mao posters calling for socialism in America (see screenshot below):

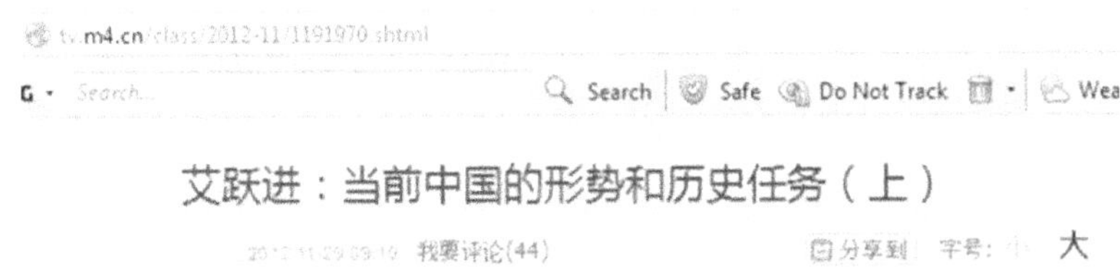

In fact, a similar situation has happened in Australia, with public rallies in Sydney in 2012 calling for the Australian government to adopt the Chinese public housing policy, as seen in the photo below from the Trotskyist Platform newsletter. This was not reported by the Australian media as well.

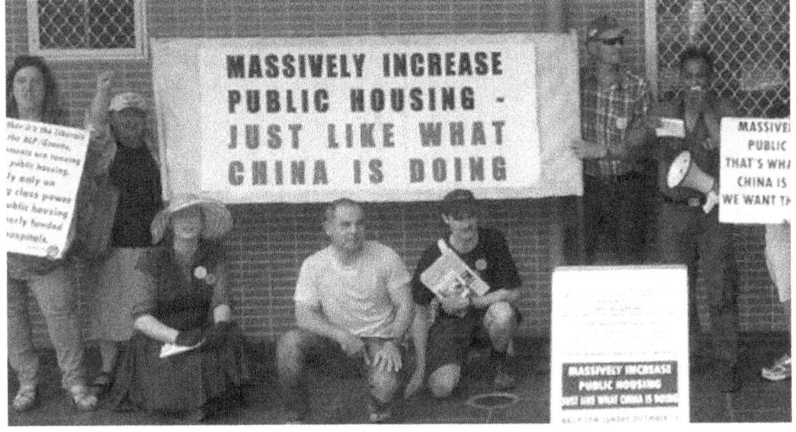

I remember clearly the day in 1999 when the Macau people were celebrating their return to their mother country – the People's Republic of China - after centuries of Portuguese colonialism; there were six to eight Falun Gong practicians protesting on the streets of Macau, such images were immediately broadcasted worldwide as evidence of Macau people protesting against the Chinese rule.

At a time of financial hardship in America, with many people losing their homes and jobs, and more than one million homeless children between 2009 and 2010 alone, we learn from Aljazeera (27 June, 2012) that, "more than 50 cities across the country have adopted laws that make it illegal to sleep, sit, beg or share food in public areas."[59] [Note: such new laws were designed to crackdown on the Wall Street protest movements, the details will be in the next instalment.] Ironically, in the land of "equality", the elected politicians are more equal than others: while the nation is in austerity with spending cuts to every sector, a Washington Post (7 March, 2013) report revealed that, "US lawmakers won't have their US$174,000 salaries affected by across-the-board government spending cuts into effect this month." This is due to the existence of a law designed to protect the income of lawmakers.[60]

Since the 2008 Global Financial Crisis, we have hardly seen any Wall Street criminals being prosecuted by the political and judicial system in the US. Instead, the ones being arrested, pepper-sprayed, beaten up and prosecuted have been peaceful Wall Street protesters. One needs just to Google the terms 'Wall Street protest and police brutality', and then click on the terms 'videos' and 'images', located at the top left hand side of the page to learn that many images of police brutality were from YouTube and other individual blogs - not the mainstream media. As a result, not many people in the West notice the level of police violence against protest movements in America.

In a recent article on the Global Research, Dr. Paul Craig Roberts, former Assistant Secretary of the US Treasury and former Associate Editor of the Wall Street Journal, pointed out that, "New York City has experienced a 73 percent increase in homelessness, while the net worth of the city's mayor has risen to $27 billion." [61]

At a time, when the country is burdened with US$16.4 trillion worth of debt, it was reported that President Obama was having a vacation in Hawaii that cost American tax-payers US$7 million solely for his security arrangements (The Telegraph, 4 January, 2013).[62]

The individualistic and selfish nature of the elitist culture in the West is not exclusively American; the same situation is evident in Australia. For example, a report by Perth Now (21 December, 2011) titled 'Capital burnout: Canberra bosses are Australia's toughest' revealed that:

> The turnover of staff employed by Julia Gillard (Prime Minister), Tony Abbott (Opposition leader) and their parliamentary colleagues is three times the workplace average ... with a staggering 80% staff burnout in three years ... while their bosses celebrated a 32% salary hike last week, staff have been offered 3% as the government battles to bring the Budget under control." As a result of such pay rise, we learnt that Prime Minister Gillard enjoyed a A$90,000 pay increment while thousands of public sector staff who earn between A$40,000 to A$60,000 a year were allowed a mere 3% rise.[63]
>
> [Author's Note: Ministerial staffs in Australia often have to work overtime without overtime pay.]

Ironically, as if the 32% pay increment was insufficient, these democratically elected representatives continued to receive another 3% pay rise in just three months. As a result of these two pay increments, the following is what federal politicians are getting in Australia at a time of an unprecedented budget deficit, public sector retrenchment and government spending cuts:

> The increase means a backbencher will get an extra $106 a week, taking their salary to $190,550. Combined with the massive pay rise MPs received in March, the annual salary of a backbencher has increased by $49,640 compared with a year ago – about $1000 a week. Prime Minister Julia Gillard's salary rises by $14,430 to $495,430, meaning she is earning a whopping $129,064 more than she was a year ago – or almost $2,500 extra a week. Opposition Leader Tony Abbott receives a $10,267 increase, taking his annual salary to $352,517. Mr Abbott is an impressive $91,834, or $1766 a week, better off than he was year ago. (The Age, 4 July, 2012)[64]

In addition, only less than a year after such a dramatic double pay rise for the elected politicians, The Age's (1 June, 2013) federal political reporter Daniel Hurst reported the following parliamentary activity:

> The main parties have united to increase secrecy about the running of Federal Parliament, with a new law set to prevent revelations about some of the perks enjoyed by MPs. Three departments - with a total budget of

> $170 million - that oversee Parliament will gain a blanket exemption from freedom of information laws. The Gillard government claimed an "anomaly" had been found last year when Fairfax Media successfully obtained information about the travel, catering and clothing purchases of former speaker Peter Slipper. But even the departments involved admitted they did not need a blanket exemption. And the law has been rushed through the House of Representatives even though an independent review on the issue is expected to be released soon.[65]

Like communism, democracy is a great concept. However, any great ideology, without putting in place a series of measures to overcome the selfish and corrupt nature of human beings, is nothing more than a paper theory. In practice, the outcome can be rather dreadful. A Guardian/ICM survey (March, 2011) in five EU countries - Britain, France, Germany, Poland and Spain - reveals that, "people see a bleak economic future and don't think their leaders will deliver." The following is an excerpt:

> The result is a crisis in European democracy. While people are divided on the need for state spending cuts and the speed with which they should take place, very few in the five states surveyed trust their politicians to deal with the problems facing their countries – or even their honesty. Only 6% of people across Europe say they have a great deal of trust in their government, 46% say they have not very much and 32% none at all. Only 9% of Europeans think their politicians – in opposition or in power – act with honesty and integrity. The lack of trust in government is greatest in Poland and France, where distrust outweighs trust by a net 82 percentage points. In France, the net negative score is 78 points and in Germany 80 points. Only Britain breaks the consensus somewhat, with a net negative score of 66 points. Even fewer Europeans think their politicians are honest. In Poland, only 3% of those questioned agree; in Spain 8%; in Germany 10%; in France 11%; in Britain 12%. Overall, the percentage of those who think politicians are not at all, or not very, honest outweighs those who disagree by a massive 89 percentage points.[66]

CNTV (10 November, 2012) broadcasted a program titled: 'Theoretical groundwork for CPC leadership' with this emphasis:

> Practice is the sole criteria for testing truth.[67]

It is in the spirit of Mao's era of pragmatism and scientific approach towards seeking truths from practice that China was able to learn from past experiences and progress with time. The following is a scanned image of a 2008 publication by the CCP, titled 'In-depth learning and practice of Scientific Development – Answers to 100 Questions':

Compared to the genuine effort that the CCP has put into trying to perfect their public administration and good governance, the West should be ashamed of its indoctrinated approach towards their seriously flawed political system, with its ongoing media disinformation and smear campaign against others.

Moral responsibilities

The Western voting system does not ensure a caring government. However, they do result in politicians engaging in all kinds of ill-considered welfare promises and spending for the purpose of snatching votes. Many are nothing more than empty promises for the consumption of the media. The relationship between Western politicians and voters is nothing more than an exchange of favour. It is hardly driven by any moral values or responsibilities. Sadly, when everybody lies to win an election, the society seems to resign to the reality that the media hardly makes any effort to call for reform. The Stratfor, a high profile American think tank, published an article (31 July, 2012) titled 'The Election, the Presidency and Foreign Policy', which acknowledged that:

> The American presidency is designed to disappoint. Each candidate must promise things that are beyond his power to deliver. No candidate could expect to be elected by emphasizing how little power the office actually has and how voters should therefore expect little from him. So candidates promise great, transformative programs. What the winner actually can

> deliver depends upon what other institutions, nations and reality will allow him. [68]

Common sense will tell us that under such a political system, the level of public trust towards the American government cannot be high. A PEW survey for the period 1958 to 2013 reveals that only 26% of Americans trust their government in 2013.[69] Not surprisingly, Australia, as a Western country with a similar political system, also shares a similar experience. An annual trust survey, released by PR firm Edelman titled 'Trust in government and CEOs low in the 2012 Edelman Truth Barometer" found that:

> Just 33% of Australians 18 and over trust their government, with 60% responding that they do not have faith in their leaders to tell the truth. Amongst 'informed' respondents (high income, tertiary-educated Australians who are politically aware), however, the figure was higher, with those who trust government coming in at 47% (down 5% from last year). [70]

Sadly, given the consistently low level of public trust and satisfaction towards Western politicians; mainstream journalists and elites appear to still indulge in their "superior" political system, and will not question the legitimacy of a political party who fibs their way into power.

In fact, it is not hard to examine the superiority of a political system in a scientific way by determining the responsiveness of a government towards a certain incident or event. Deng Xiaoping famously put it this way: "Regardless if it's a black or white cat, the cat that catches the mouse is a good cat".

As natural disasters have adversely affected the livelihood of many people across the world, I believe that using examples of how China, Australia and the US government responded to a major natural disaster will be an objective way to distinguish the concept of good governance in theory and in practice.

Measuring good governance by performance

Australia:

In 2009, there were major bushfires in Victoria, which killed 173 people and injured 414, with 7,562 displaced. The list of damage to property is as follows:

> Over 3,500 structures destroyed, including 2,029+ houses, 59 commercial properties (shops, pubs, service stations, golf clubs, etc), 12 community buildings (including 2 police stations, 3 schools, 3 churches, 1 fire station), 399 machinery sheds, 729 other farm buildings, 363 hay sheds, 19 dairies, 26 woolsheds. [71]

The then Australian Prime Minister Kevin Rudd told Parliament: "Hear this from the Government and the Parliament of the nation. Together we will rebuild each of these communities – brick by brick, school by school, community hall by community hall." (Brisbane Time, 11 Feb 2009)[72] However, 14 months after the fire, a report by the Herald Sun (4 April, 2010) titled 'Slow and steady but no promise of winning race' pointed out the reality on the ground:

> Hundreds of people in the worst-affected zones are committing to rebuild after Black Saturday ... But progress is patchy in some areas, and statistics reinforce that it will be many years before the destruction is close to being repaired ... Just under 300 rebuilding permits have been issued for houses, sheds and commercial properties in Marysville and the surrounding triangle ... Locals believe as few as 50 houses are actually being rebuilt in Marysville while many permits are probably for sheds ... In the Kinglake Ranges, taking in Kinglake, Pheasant Creek and Toolangi, 361 building permits have been sought. There were 505 properties destroyed there on February 7 ... There were 117 permits sought for Flowerdale and its sister hamlet, Hazeldene, compared with the 225 properties destroyed. [73]

Few months after the bushfires, a Royal Commission of Inquiry setup to investigate the Victorian bushfires had the following findings:

> The tragically high death toll was caused by grossly inadequate emergency services, lack of fire warnings and the absence of any centralised evacuation plan ... The individual homeowners were left to decide by themselves whether they should "stay or go". (WSWS, 28 May 2009) [74]

The Inquiry's findings also revealed that (News Limited, 28 May 2010):

> None of those in command showed any real leadership. [75]

According to the Herald Sun (7 May 2010):

> Victoria's police minister and the state's three most senior police officers were all absent from the emergency nerve centre when most of the deaths occurred on Black Saturday. [76]

In addition, according to the WSWS (17 May 2010):

> The uncoordinated and chaotic division of responsibilities and functions of senior police and emergency services leadership points to the negligence of the state government of Premier John Brumby. It made no serious attempt to establish clear lines of command and communication inside the IECC prior to the devastating fires.[77]

As for the federal government, besides making some grand statements for the consumption of the media at the beginning of the bushfires, this seemed to disappear from the radar at the anniversaries. The state government of Victoria was left to fend for themselves about the delays in rebuilding, including schools in the bushfire-hit towns of Marysville and Strathewen (Herald Sun, 7 Feb, 2010). [78]

Two years after the Victorian bushfires, and a year after the recommendations made by the Royal Commission of Inquiry with regard to improving electricity safety, the federal Labor government was in dispute with the Liberal state government over the cost of implementing the Royal Commission's recommendations (The Age, 26 June 2011).[79]

Tragically, three years after the 2009 bushfires, five people committed suicide due to the trauma it had caused. This was how The Age (19 May, 2012) reported it under the title 'Ashes to Ashes: Forgotten fire town mourns again':

> In April, four locals killed themselves in a suicide cluster. Maybe five. The proof of the fifth, a woman in the still-charred mountain forest alone with a gun, is yet to be finally determined. The month felt to everyone like a dirty stain. Of the four, two languished in the Hume region's nearest psychiatric unit three hours away in Shepparton, isolated from their families. Another was a paramedic who recovered the dead during Black Saturday's grim aftermath. He killed himself on the Saturday before this crisis meeting. In the hours leading up to what happened, armed police surrounded his home. He was one of the town's helpers yet was so wounded - by pre-existing trauma compounded, his family says, by the fires - that he dramatically took his own life. "Black Saturday was just one aspect," says his father, a country New South Wales churchman. "It was one bad thing too many." Only the day before, Friday April 20, news reached town of one of the Shepparton suicides, a 26-year-old depressive man who was, a friend says, "deeply traumatised" by the scorched-earth chaos of Black Saturday where the heat was enough to melt glass. The community already knew of attempted suicides. Local welfare agencies have now revealed increased domestic violence, marriage breakdown and alcohol and drug abuse.

Despite obvious community distress and trauma in the aftermath of the bushfires, all three tiers of Australian government (federal, state and local) appeared to be unconcerned for the welfare of the victims. Although some of the local media in Victoria, like The Age, made an effort to follow the case each year, there was a lack of emotive language used to condemn the inaction of the elected politicians. In this instance, The Age instead ended their report by giving the state government the final say with a hollow statement:

> A Victorian government spokesperson concedes some bushfire recovery services are in a process of "sunsetting" but says the government "remains committed to supporting communities affected by the 2009 bushfires".[80]

The truth is that government inaction in assisting the victims of natural disasters is a common feature in Australia. The victims of the 2007 bushfires in Western Australia also suffered a similar fate like those of the 2009 Victorian bushfires. On 14 November 2012, WA Today filed a report titled 'Forgotten bushfire victims still in limbo' with the following description:

> Several residents affected by fires in Toodyay, Kelmscott and Margaret River since 2007 claimed a lack of compassion and financial assistance from the state government was exacerbating their grief and ability to move on, even in cases when the government had accepted responsibility. Many were still living in temporary accommodation because they could not afford to rebuild their homes, while businesses were losing tens of thousands of dollars in lost trade. Robyn Lewis said she was selling her home to help her parents June and Harry Fraser, who lost their house during the Kelmscott bushfire in January, 2011. Her parents, aged 80 and 90, have been living in her sister's lounge room for nearly two years because they have no income to top up the small insurance payout they received. Ms Lewis will use the proceeds of the sale of her home and their insurance payout to build on their Kelmscott land and the three would live in the new house. "We're just desperate to get them back home," she said outside the committee hearing. Ms Lewis said Kelmscott residents felt forgotten because they had not received any state government assistance, while victims of other bushfires had. The government claims it is not liable to provide compensation because it did not cause the fire, which was started by an off-duty police officer using an angle grinder. [81]

Again, one may observe that the report is by the local media in Western Australia. At a national level, hardly anyone will learn about the fate of those bushfire victims in Western Australia unless they are willing to read nightly from more than half a dozen

Australian newspapers on the net like myself. Like The Age in Victoria, WA Today filed the report without using emotive language to condemn the elected representatives (federal, state and local) for not doing much to help those in distress. The reality is that in a capitalist democracy, where profit is priority, the poor and the disadvantaged with no financial ability to pay for home and contents insurance are supposed to fend for themselves. The Australian government will only provide minimum assistance or nothing at all if possible.

America:

The same situation happened to the victims of natural disasters in America. Many people may still remember the 2005 Hurricane Katrina in New Orleans during which "the Bush administration dithered for 48 hours after the hurricane, leaving the folded city of New Orleans without help." (The Age, 31 March 2009) [82]

The flood "killed 1,464 people, and an approximately 200,000 people were evacuated from the Gulf Coast Region to Texas, Florida, Georgia and Washington, D.C. Of the more than 400,000 residents who lived in New Orleans prior to Katrina, approximately 350,000 lived in areas that were damaged by the storm." [83]

According to BBC (2 March, 2006), video footage shows that "President Bush had been warned on the eve of Hurricane Katrina that New Orleans' flood defences could be overcome" and "there was a risk to evacuees in the Superdome." However, "Mr Bush did not ask any questions as the situation was outlined to him." [84]

During the 2007 election campaign, the then Senator Barack Obama condemned the Bush administration for discriminating against the minorities in New Orleans by not offering sufficient assistance. This is an excerpt from a report by the Christian Science Monitor (3 October, 2012), with video footage of Obama's speech in 2007:

> In the speech Obama suggests that the Bush administration discriminated against hurricane Katrina victims by, among other things, not providing as generous terms for federal aid as Washington did to New York after 9/11 and to Florida after hurricane Andrew, because they were disproportionately minorities. That, he says, led to a "quiet riot" among US blacks in the storm's aftermath. He gives a shout-out of welcome to his then-pastor, the Rev. Jeremiah Wright. (The Rev. Mr. Wright's racially

> tinged rhetoric caused Obama to later renounce their association.) Overall, Obama delivered his words in a preacher-like style he has seldom used in other public forums. Conservatives say that is yet more evidence that in 2007 he was pandering to his audience. "He is whipping up fear and paranoia and hatred. This is the exact opposite of what a uniter does," said Daily Caller editor Tucker Carlson during a Fox News appearance on Tuesday.[85]

The question is: did Obama do more for the victims during his presidency since 2008?

At the 4th anniversary of the disaster in 2009, a report by the Brisbane Times revealed that it was due to the failure of the American government that a flood occurred in 2005:

> A US federal judge has ruled that the Army Corps of Engineers' failure to properly maintain a navigation channel led to massive flooding in Hurricane Katrina in 2005, a decision that could make the federal government vulnerable to billions of dollars in claims. [86]

Yet, as the current state of New Orleans suggests, not much has been done by the US government to rebuild the flood affected areas. Amnesty International released a report with the title 'The Facts: The Right to Return—Rebuilding the Gulf through the Framework of International Human Rights', which revealed that:

> "Despite the passage of almost four years, thousands of those internally displaced as a result of Hurricane Katrina who want to return to New Orleans are unable to do so ... More than 14,000 families living in metropolitan New Orleans are still receiving Disaster Housing Assistance Program (DHAP) vouchers which help them pay rent. These vouchers come with an expiration date, which was recently changed from March 2009 to September 2009. Only approximately 7,500 of these families may be eligible for Housing Choice vouchers, which gives them access to Section 8 housing. Once the DHAP vouchers expire, the remaining families face potential homelessness. The U.S. Department of Housing and Urban Development (HUD) acknowledges that at least 4,000 of those who do not qualify for Section 8 housing will have difficulty finding affordable housing."

This Amnesty report further explained the situation:

> "After Katrina, the federal government placed tens of thousands of families in trailers which were meant to provide temporary shelter. Today, there are approximately 3,400 families still living in trailers in Louisiana and Mississippi, 760 of which are in New Orleans. After being told that they would be evicted if they did not vacate their trailers by May 30, 2009, the trailer residents will now be given the option to purchase their trailers

> for $5 or less. Many of the FEMA trailers contain levels of formaldehyde, a carcinogenic toxin, which are 75 times the recommended maximum for U.S. workers. The federal government has indicated that trailers with elevated levels of formaldehyde will not be available for purchase. As a result, only 1,160 of the trailers currently being used qualify for purchase by these IDPs. HUD has not yet provided a clear indication of how it will supply the remaining trailers." [87]

One should note that the above Amnesty report did not contain emotional language (such as 'the American regime') against the elected politicians' inaction to help the victims. The mainstream media in the US were basically silenced from reporting the problems in New Orleans. The AlterNet, an independent web media, reported the situation on 10 September 2009, titled 'How Corporate Media Are Washing Away Katrina From America's Mind', with a detailed description of how CBS, MSNBC, NBC, New York Times, The Times, and CNN neglected to mention in their reports the hardship and problems still existing in New Orleans. [88]

Seven years after Hurricane Katrina, the Christian Science Monitor (24 February, 2012) published a report titled 'New Orleans' razing craze aims to clear way for post-Katrina recovery' with the following description:

> Mayor Mitch Landrieu has made razing and cleaning up 40,000 abandoned homes and properties – the biggest such inventory in the nation, besting Detroit – a cornerstone of his administration. His aim: to piece back together the racial and social mosaic that for centuries defined the gritty, buoyant city along the Mississippi River's crescent bend. The 2010 Census, conducted five years after Katrina, found that 25 percent of New Orleans residential addresses were vacant, and Mr. Landrieu's administration is now moving aggressively to tear down homes that are abandoned or deemed uninhabitable. Last year the city razed 1,589 decrepit buildings, up from 154 two years earlier, in an attempt to clear the way for redevelopment in neighbourhoods previously filled (and still partially filled) with poor and minority residents ... Five years ago, residents helped create a blueprint for rebuilding New Orleans known as the Unified Plan. It backed resettlement of hard-hit areas in poor, low-lying districts, partly in a bid to retain a diverse populace. But New Orleans is today in danger of becoming what residents expressly said they didn't want: a smaller, whiter, more upscale city.[89]

Racism and discrimination against minorities and the poor is a serious problem in many Western democracies, and this is partly due to the design of the political system. We will get to this later. In the meantime, one should note that there were quite a number of incidents of police brutality and atrocities of minorities after hurricane Katrina. Here are a couple of news headings and excerpts:

1) 'Policeman 'fired at wounded men' in aftermath of Hurricane Katrina' (Independent, 8 July, 2011):

> A policeman sprayed gunfire at wounded, unarmed people and repeatedly stamped on a dying man on a bridge in New Orleans in the aftermath of Hurricane Katrina in 2005, a court heard.[90]

2) 'Five New Orleans police officers sentenced in Hurricane Katrina killings' (Guardian, 5 April, 2012):

> Four officers, along with a fifth who helped cover up the 2005 crimes, are sentenced to between six and 65 years in prison ... The officers sentenced Wednesday are among 20 policemen charged over killings, assaults and the fabrication of evidence during Katrina ... Four New Orleans police officers have been sentenced to decades in prison over the killing of two people and wounding of four others fleeing the massive flooding of the city by hurricane Katrina. A fifth officer was sent to jail for his role in a web of fabrications to cover up the true circumstances of the shootings on the Danziger bridge in 2005. The shootings came to symbolise the behaviour of a police force regarded as out of control in the chaotic aftermath of the hurricane which claimed nearly 2,000 lives and flooded about 80% of New Orleans. The policemen were prosecuted in federal court after Louisiana state authorities declined to charge them. The federal investigation revealed a coverup that involved planted evidence, invented witnesses and falsified police reports that prosecutors said exposed a culture of corruption and a code of silence in the New Orleans police department.[91]

As one may observe from the above examples of the Australian and American governments handling a major natural disaster, so-called 'Western democracies' did not ensure a caring government at all. The skeletal structure of a voting system is meaningless, as it fails to create a government that functions along the theoretical assumption of "from the people, by the people, and for the people".

Contrary to the stereotyped images of a ruthless and brutal Chinese regime propagated by the mainstream media, the way the Chinese government handled a nature disaster in 2008 will put to shame the governments in Australia and America.

China

The following is a report by the World Bank (4 December, 2012) about the challenges faced the Chinese government at the aftermath of the 2008 Wenchuan earthquake (Sichuan province):

> On May 12, 2008, an earthquake of magnitude 8.0 struck south western China, centered in Wenchuan County of Sichuan Province. As a result, more than 47 million people were affected; over 69,000 people died, 374,000 were injured, and 18,000 went missing. Public infrastructure, key government buildings and houses were severely damaged: 34,000 km of highway destroyed, 1,263 reservoirs damaged, 7,444 schools and 11,028 hospitals and clinics collapsed, and 5.5 million rural houses and 860,000 urban houses destroyed or significantly damaged. Sichuan and Gansu provinces were the hardest hit, with direct economic losses estimated at US$112.2 billion and US$7.1 billion respectively.

In spite of such destruction, four years after the earthquake, this is how the World Bank described the recovery:

> The Wenchuan Earthquake Recovery Project (2009-2014) is restoring and building high quality infrastructure and improving health and education services for residents in the areas affected by the devastating earthquake in 2008, laying a solid foundation for long-term economic and social development of participating cities and counties in Sichuan and Gansu provinces ... In order to plan for reconstruction in an efficient and effective manner, loss assessments, geological assessments and environmental assessments were conducted immediately after the earthquake. China's State Council issued the Overall Plan for the Post-Wenchuan Earthquake Recovery and Reconstruction which lays out the framework for all recovery and reconstruction efforts. Innovative mechanisms to secure the funds necessary to conduct these works, such as private-public partnerships, tax incentives, and the mobilization of public support are utilized thoroughly. The central government also set up a "twin assistance" mechanism by which affected counties are paired with a donor province responsible for offering financial and other assistance. The program also emphasized the non-structural aspects of building resilience in communities through better emergency preparedness and training programs ... Today, there is little sign of the devastation.[92]

In fact, at the third anniversary of the 2008 Earthquake, CNTV created a website with videos and photos of the massive reconstruction effort. The project was invested in by the Chinese government to help victims in all affected areas, which is on the same magnitude as the entire territory of France, or several smaller European countries combined:

http://cctv.cntv.cn/lm/storyboard/special/wenchuan_renconstruction/index.shtml

The speed and quality of the reconstruction has put to shame those Western governments who relentlessly demonise China over the issue of human rights year on year. What fascinates me is why such a massive humanitarian achievement by the Chinese government - let alone the world's history - wasn't reported by the mainstream media, Amnesty International, and Human Rights Watch.

For those who are interested to view more images of the reconstruction made by the so-called "brutal Communist regime" in China, another way to find the images is to Google 'Wenchuan and/or Sichuan earthquake reconstruction', then click on 'Images' and 'videos' at the top left hand side of the webpage. There are links to thousands of fascinating pictures showing the speed, scale and quality of reconstruction that changed the live of tens of millions of people in the quake affected regions. To view even more images, one could simply Google the net in Chinese such as '四川地震灾后重建'. It always puzzles me as to why on Earth Western journalists in China are so blind to any positive developments in China.

Below are the screenshots of four such images from the Internet as proof of the good work of the Communist Government in China; images that Western journalists have failed to show us:

www.dictall.com/news/2011-05/11/0039145.htm   wenchuan earthquake

Three years after quake, new towns rise in SW China

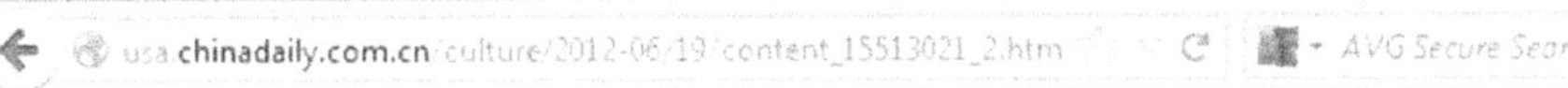

What excited Liu most are the bird's-eye views of the new homes and schools built in the affected areas. The Rebirth of Our Land features 30 aerial photos taken three to four years after the disaster.

"It's really dramatically changed and is in sharp contrast to the devastating images of the first album," Liu says.

english.peopledaily.com.cn/102774/8239702.html 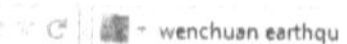

Life rebuilt from ruins: 5 years after Wenchuan earthquake (6)

(People's Daily Online) 13:46, May 10, 2013 Share

From the perspective of a good story under the topics of humanity and good governance, I believe that this kind of story should be widely reported across the world, so as to inspire the world's governments to do the same for their citizens in times of natural disaster. However, what the Western media has done over the years is to make use of some disgraceful people like Ai Weiwei, who made themselves very rich by colluding with a US government-funded network of people within China and overseas to instigate hatred against their own government. (See the upcoming instalment 'Money Talk' for information on how the US government and corporations reward people who smear against their targeted governments)

One should remember that the 2008 earthquake in China was of magnitude 8.0. It was a lot stronger than the 2011 earthquake in Christchurch, New Zealand at 6.1, and that resulted in many modern buildings collapsing. A report by The Guardian (9 February, 2012) revealed that at least one of the collapsed buildings that killed 115 people did not meet construction standards. This is how The Guardian reported it:

> A six-storey building that collapsed and killed 115 people during last year's New Zealand earthquake did not meet construction standards,

> according to a government report. The report, which called it "technically inadequate", was contested by the building's designer. The Canterbury Television (CTV) building in Christchurch collapsed during the magnitude-6.1 earthquake on 22 February. It accounted for nearly two-thirds of the quake's 184 victims. New Zealand's department of building and housing found in its report that the CTV building did not meet minimum requirements when it was built in 1986 and would fall far short of the latest standards. The report is the first to find construction flaws in a building that collapsed during the earthquake.

In fact, given the intensity of the quake at 6.1, many buildings that met Western construction standards also collapsed or at least partially collapsed. This is how The Guardian put it:

> Three previous reports on buildings that at least partially collapsed found they were built to requirements but failed due to the intensity of the quake. The findings could open the door for legal claims by victims' families.

As one may observe from The Guardian's report, one of the collapsed buildings was a high profile television building, and yet its structure was found substandard under the supervision of the supposedly high standard Western building approval process. The earthquake was only at a magnitude of 6.1, and yet "three previous reports on buildings" that met construction standards also "at least partially collapsed" because "they were built to requirements but failed due to the intensity of the quake".

One should note that the report by The Guardian came without emotional language that would condemn the New Zealand government. They even gave the designer of the building a voice in their report with the following statement:

> The report, which called it "technically inadequate", was contested by the building's designer.[93]

However, when the Western media - including The Guardian - reported about the Chinese earthquake, they basically disregarded the fact that it was at a magnitude of 8.0, and that China was still a developing country after more than a century of brutal semi-Western colonisation and Japanese invasion which only ended a few decades ago. They totally ignored the destructive power of an earthquake at 8.0. Without the backing of any scientific evidence, they simply made use of some disgraceful individuals in the Chinese society like Ai Weiwei, who profited from smearing the Chinese government for the consumption of the Western media. For example, by raising his middle finger in front of a camera, posing nude on many occasions and simply giving a meaning to whatever he did, no matter how childish and unethical his acts were, as long as it was to smear against the Chinese government, the Western media loved it.

Such unethical behaviour included destroying a 2,000 year old artefact from the Han dynasty (if you believe the media's claims that it was from the Han dynasty) and auctioning the photo series for 50,000 pounds, [94] or paying others to do virtually all of his so-called artwork or making use of the grief of some parents to claim that the deaths of all 5,000 children during the earthquake were a result of corruption and shoddy construction (tofu schools). He made is seem like all the bad things that take place at every corner of China must be the fault of the Communist Party.

It is this kind of ongoing shallow and unproven negativity against China and the systematic censorship of positive news about the Chinese government that gives the Western public a false sense of superiority about their political system and their so-called "Western values".

In a recent incident in the CBD of Melbourne, Australia, a crack on a wall and a mere 102km/h winds were blamed for a wall's collapse that killed three people. (The Australian, 4 April, 2013) Like the buildings that collapsed in New Zealand after an earthquake of only 6.1, this incident also took place in a developed Western country right in the middle of a major city, but The Australian newspaper did not condemn the Australian government for failing to uphold building and maintenance standards. The following was how The Australian explained the incident in a calm tone:

> There is growing doubt that developer Grocon had a permit for the erection of the hoarding, with former lord mayor Trevor Huggard saying the incident had exposed "a gaping hole" in the maintenance and administration of derelict sites in Victoria.[95]

The above two examples of buildings collapsing in New Zealand and Australia demonstrate the fact that it is never an easy job for any government to effectively oversee every construction project at every corner of the country, including buildings within major cities. Therefore, it is unreasonable and unjustified to capitalise on the grievance of the victims of a major earthquake at an intensity of 8.0 to simply stir emotion and hatred against the communist government, let alone of a developing country. One should also bear in mind that if we measure the size of a country by population, China's is over 60 times Australia's and 240 times New Zealand's, which makes it even more unreasonable.

It is very easy to demonise a government, especially China's; a developing country with 20% of the world population (four times America's). If one wishes to see a country in a narrow scope using the techniques of the Western media, I can guarantee that no country will be able to come up clean. Thus, it is important for us to put into perspective how these governments would perform under similar situations, in order to have an objective assessment on the issues of human rights and good governance. A simple search on the internet or Wikipedia with terms such as "Collapsed buildings in the United States" and "List of structural failures and collapses" will allow us to explore the issue further with thousands of examples of buildings collapsing in the US and across the world.

Unfortunately, at the 5th anniversary of the 2008 Sichuan earthquake, the Western media still focused on the deaths of the 5,000 children with hardly anyone to tell us what the Communist Government had done for the people since the disaster. What follows are just a few examples showing what the Western media reported on the 5th anniversary of the Sichuan earthquake.

According to AFP, Ai Weiwei "tweeted a link to his work "Remembrance"- voice recordings of people reading the name of students who died in the earthquake, which he put at more than 5,000."[96] As AFP is a Western news syndicate network, the same report was immediately echoed across the world using the same headline 'China marks anniversary of killer Sichuan earthquake', with the content giving people the impression that all the dead children were the outcome of corruption and shoddy buildings.

The UK Telegraph ran a heading 'The Children Airbrushed from the story of China's devastating quake', and continued to blame the deaths of the 5,000 children on the "shoddily constructed buildings".[97]

The South China Morning Post, a Hong Kong based anti-China English newspaper from the British Colonial era did the same with this heading: 'The shame of Sichuan Tofu's schools'.[98]

[Author's Note: the so-called Ai Weiwei's tweeted link is to material he had already used to smear the Chinese government in previous years; it is simply a reuse of the same material for the convenience of the Western media to continue smearing the Chinese government at each anniversary of the event.]

Apparently, the five suicides in Australia at the 3rd anniversary of the Black Saturday bushfires in Victoria, and the inability of the tens of thousands of minority Americans and the poor to rebuild and return to their homeland in New Orleans seven years after Hurricane Katrina, were not stories worth reporting at all. Western elites in the media industry appear to care more for the wellbeing of the Chinese citizens than their own. What a selfless love!

An interesting 2007 video on YouTube titled 'China Army VS USA Army in real war', produced by apparently angry Chinese netizens, showcased a collection of contrasting images of unarmed Chinese soldiers physically helping victims of a flood in China, and fully armed US soldiers pointing rifles at the victims of Hurricane Katrina. This is just another example of the contrast in official conduct in both countries. Here are some screenshots from that video:

Screenshot 1 (below): US Army. The meaning of the narration is: 'Big brothers, be careful not to get your military boots wet.'

Screenshot 2 (below): US army. The meaning of the first narration is: 'should we name this picture as "children under the barrier of guns"?'

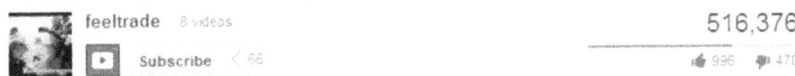

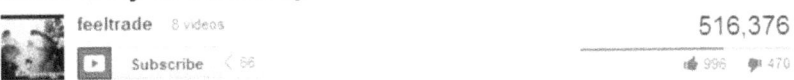

Screenshot 3 (below): US Army. Narration: 'Blocked by armed soldiers from leaving the chaotic and violent disaster region.'

Screenshot 4 (below): Unarmed Chinese soldiers having a rest.

Screenshot 5 (below): Chinese army. Narration: 'Chinese children in a flood zone.'

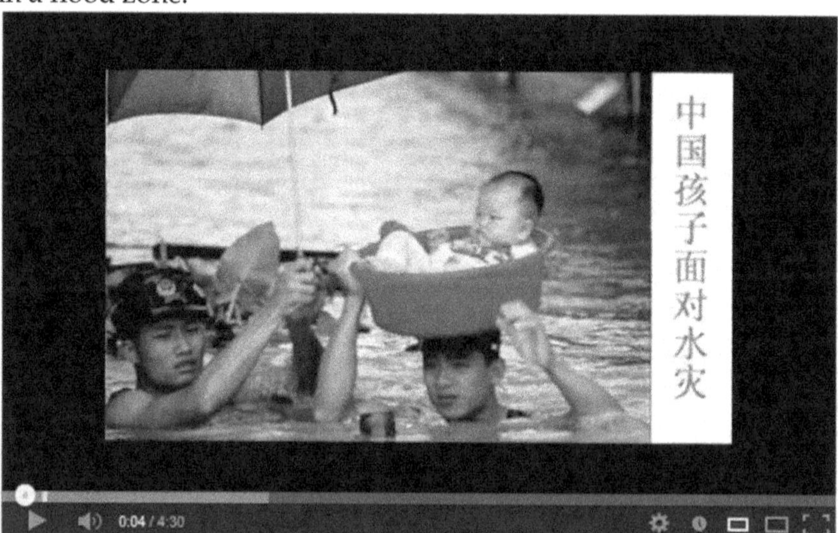

China Army vs USA Army in real war

The following is a screenshot of a rescue scene reported by a Hong Kong media during the 2008 Sichuan earthquake showing Chinese soldiers using their bodies to form a bridge so that the school children could safely cross a river. Unfortunately, these kinds of heart-felt meaningful stories from China will not be reported by Western journalists. Perhaps, to be more accurate, these kinds of materials will not be commissioned by the mainstream media.

Assessing 'democracy' through definition

The truth is that, through the systematic omission of any humanitarian achievements made by the Chinese government, such as aiding the tens of millions of victims of a natural disaster, the mainstream media has effectively promoted a false sense of superiority about their political system across the world. This is accentuated by the ongoing quoting of unverified, unscientific and baseless complaints made by a handful of unethical people like Ai Weiwei, Liu Xiaobo, and Chen Guangcheng. (I will explain in detail how these people have been recruited and rewarded by the US government in some of the coming instalments.)

When we attempt to give a definition to democracy, and match the actual behaviour and performance of Western governments and China based on a series of clearly spelt out values, we will discover that China is, in fact, more democratic in several aspects.

In a public lecture at the University of Western Australia on 7 August 2003, titled 'Ideas to save our withering democracy', Dr. Carmen Lawrence, former premier of Western Australia and Federal President of the Australian Labor Party in 2003, believed that when the performance of Western democracies are measured against a series of stated objectives, the political systems will unable to sustain scrutiny. The following is Dr. Lawrence's exact wording about democracy in Australia:

> When people at large are questioned about the key values of democracy, the vast majority agree about the need for free and fair elections, freedom of speech, equality before the law, active citizen participation and the protection of minority rights. These are the desiderata of modern democracies. When measured against these objectives, I believe we are falling short. Ours is a withering democracy.[99]

Therefore, when we compared the way China, Australia and USA handled a major natural disaster, and define democracy as "a government that listens to and responds to the collective voices and needs of the people", China is by all means more democratic than Western countries like Australia and America. The reality is that both New Zealand and Japan, as Western democracies, also performed badly in helping the victims of a natural disaster in their respective countries. News Limited's report (20 February, 2013) titled 'Two years later, Christchurch earthquake recovery remains slow' has this description:

> Christchurch is but one example of how even the wealthiest countries struggle to recover from large-scale catastrophes. In some cases, developing countries may be better off. Within two years of a 2004 tsunami, half the 100,000 permanent homes needed in Indonesia had been completed, and almost 700 schools had been built or repaired. But in Japan, nearly two years after the March 2011 tsunami flattened the northeast coast, few homes have been rebuilt.

News Limited then offered an excuse for developed countries, but didn't tell readers a thing about the humanitarian achievements of the Communist Government in China after the 2008 earthquake. The following are some of the given excuses:

> "Many people in developing countries don't rely much on governments, and even after a disaster, they just go ahead and do it," said Peter McCawley, an economist at the Australian National University ... "They often do it to low standards, but they just go ahead and fix it anyway." Conversely, disaster agencies in the First World have become "far too bureaucratic and tied up in rules," he said from Jakarta ... A major bottleneck in Christchurch is insurance. Most claims haven't been paid, as insurance companies and a government insurance fund that covers damage up to 100,000 New Zealand dollars tussle over who should pay for what ... Around 13,500 people have left the city since the earthquake ...[100]

New Zealander media Stuff (22 February, 2013) is more outright in its report with the following information:

> Less than a quarter of the worst-damaged homes have been repaired or rebuilt; the rate for lesser-damaged properties is about a third. Thousands of condemned houses are still to be torn down. Crucially, some residents have not received any money and still do not know when their homes will be fixed.

Stuff then moved on to tell of the suffering due to the lack of government support and difficulties in claiming insurance:

> Yes, the economy is healthy ... but on the ground, some people are still struggling. The case of people like Greg Mitchell is well known. You may not know him by name, but you have probably heard a story like his before. His insurer has told him his house is so badly damaged it must be rebuilt, but he still hasn't been paid out by the Earthquake Commission. Mitchell has filed three damage claims and EQC has to determine what damage happened when. If it finds no single event caused more than its liability cap of $100,000 damage, things will get even more complicated. "It is [frustrating]," he says. "You're not getting any further and you think 'why do I bloody bother?' I'll just sit back and in due time I'll get it, I suppose. I could ring up again today and it'll just be no different from last time and there won't be a cheque in the mail." Mitchell and wife Pauline are able to live in their cracked Brookhaven house, but there is resignation in his voice when he talks about two years of insurance inertia.[101]

One should note that none of these reports demonised the respective Western governments for not doing much for their citizens. In the capitalist democracies, such incidents appear to be an acceptable norm.

Objectively, the concept of good governance should be scientifically measured by the actual performance of a government under a similar set of conditions, and not a voting system. That is, it should be measured by the responsiveness of a government to perform, to deliver and to care for the collective voices of their citizens. The 2008 Sichuan earthquake affected areas are where many of the Chinese minorities reside, including a large number of Tibetan Chinese, and still, post-earthquake reconstruction investment was extended to all of them without discrimination. In addition, many of the reconstructed buildings were designed in accordance to the minorities' cultures and traditions.

The following screenshot from sina.com is one of the forty-six projects of reconstruction work in Sanjiang Town of Wenchuan County that was built in accordance to the culture of the minority population one year after the quake:

english.sina.com/china/p/2010/0926/341151.html

Photo taken on Sept. 25, 2010 show the houses rebuilt after the Wenchuan earthquake on May 12, 2008, in Sanjiang Town of Wenchuan County, southwest China's Sichuan Province. The forty-six projects of reconstruction work in Sanjiang were finished in September, 2009, under the help of Huizhou City in south China's Guangdong Province. The survivors in Sanjiang have resumed their daily lives. (Xinhua/Li Zuomao)

The following is another screenshot from indiandefence.com showing the erection of a new town two and a half years after the Sichuan earthquake:

The following is a screenshot of a newly built mosque on imgur.com:

I will explain in detail in one of the coming instalments 'The Untold Story - Tibet', about the background of self-immolations, and compare the treatment of minorities between China and the West in both ancient and modern times. The purpose of this series of books based on factual comparisons is not only aimed at exposing media disinformation, but to enable civilisations to learn from each other's merits.

Political beliefs and government responsiveness

One would wonder how a government under the so-called "one-party dictatorship" in the eyes of the West would outperform their own "democratic" government in caring for the wellbeing of their citizens at a time of a natural disaster. The answer is quite simple: the culture and beliefs of the Communist Party in China is more people-oriented than those of the capitalist elites in the West. It is also the distinction between the philosophies of communism and capitalism.

A report on the Christian Science Monitor (12 April, 2012) about a new indicator that measures 'social inclusion' (based on 15 variables like access to education, goods and jobs, and the perceptions of political freedom and government efficacy) was carried out in 11 Latin American countries and the US. Ironically, it found that America, the world's largest economy and the so-called leader of "democracy", ranked number 11. [102]

Like the annual outcome of the PEW survey, nobody should be surprised by the outcome of the survey in Latin America and the US. The personal beliefs and bias of the individuals within an institution will determine the ultimate behaviour of that institution. Something that often goes unnoticed at the entrance of zhongnanhai (中南海), the residential compound of the Chinese leaders in Beijing, is a five-word motto written by the late Chairman Mao, '为人民服务', meaning, 'Serving the people'. This is perhaps the only government in the history of mankind with such an official motto since its founding.

In a notable report to the CPC's 18th National Congress on behalf of the 17th CPC Central Committee, the then outgoing Chairman Hu Jintao reiterated that China will firmly "march on the path of socialism with Chinese characteristics and strive to complete the building of a moderately prosperous society in all respects."[103] Hu also pledged to keep improving the wellbeing of the Chinese people.[104]

Like his predecessor, the new Chinese leader Xi Jinping will continue to lead the country with the core value of putting the people first. At a press conference on 16 November 2012, Xi stressed that the mission of his government is to meet the desires of the Chinese people and ensure they live happily. The following is the exact statement:

> Our people have an ardent love for life. They wish to have better education, more stable jobs, more income, greater social security, better medical and health care, improved housing conditions and a better environment. They want their children to have sound growth, have good jobs and lead a more enjoyable life. To meet their desire for a happy life is our mission. [105]

Unlike the culture of lip service among Western politicians for their selfish short-term gains in an election, Chinese leaders never make statements they do not intend to fulfil. One needs just to examine the achievements of the CCP for the Chinese people since 1949 at each stage of nation building to understand their creativity, resourcefulness and determination to deliver a better life for their citizens on a massive scale. This was accomplished with limited resources, the enormous population and hostility from the West, including the imposition of economic and technological sanctions against China at various times in history. According to the World Bank (19 March, 2010):

> By working toward a better understanding of poverty and by tailoring efforts based on a rigorous system of monitoring and evaluation, China lifted more than 600 million people out of poverty between 1981 and 2004.[106]

In 2008, the World Bank presented a major overhaul of the estimates of global poverty, and concluded that, since 1981:

> China's poverty rate fell from 85% to 15.9%
> China accounted for nearly all the world's reduction in poverty
> Excluding China, poverty fell only by around 10%

As a result, the World Bank feels that, while China is on target to reach the Millennium Development Goals to reduce poverty and tackle various other issues, most other countries are not. (Global Issues, 12 November, 2011)[107]

As mentioned earlier, by comparing the responsiveness of the Chinese government and the so-called "democratic" governments of Australia, USA, New Zealand and Japan at a time of natural disaster, the evidence has consistently suggested that the concept of a caring government cannot be achieved through a Western-style voting system; it can only be achieved through the culture and beliefs of a political party. Like any human society, there are corrupt people within the CCP as well. However, the overall trend and achievements over the past decades has shown that the core value of 'serving the people' within the CCP has always prevailed. In contrast, for Western governments, bombarding the people with propaganda takes priority over tending to the needs of the people.

Hu Jintao once said (translate from Chinese):

> We must understand that the progressive nature of a political party and its status as a ruling party are not static and will forever be so. A progressive system at the time may not be so today. A currently progressive system may not be so in the future. [108]

It is in such a spirit that China's political system is in an active state of self-reflection and ongoing improvement. The way China introduces democracy is structured from the inside, and expands to the wider community. Their political processes are designed to accommodate for input from the community and interest groups, as well as to ensure quality decision making at each level of government. The ideology is to strike a balance between accommodating the diverse voices and the needs of the wider community without losing unity and the core direction of the nation. It is a political system based on reasoning, fairness and justice instead of the Western concept of 'majority-takes-all', whereby the 50.1% could ignore the rightful concerns of the 49.9%, particularly when ethnic minorities are involved.

The following is a scanned image of a 2010 publication by the CCP analysing the major issues and proposals outlined in a 2008 Party National Forum about ways to move forward with grassroots democracy within the CCP.

推进党内基层民主建设研究

One of the hundreds of responses from the 2008 National Party Forum outlined in the book is the need to lift the personal culture of party cadres and leaders through education on the concept of democracy. The party leadership is advised to listen to reasoning with an open mind, and the grassroots cadres are encouraged to actively contribute their opinions and suggestions. The CCP is engaged in an ongoing process of improving its internal communication channels to ensure that grassroots members can air their concerns, scrutinise the government's performance, and participate in finding solutions to problems facing their communities. The CCP believes that their grassroots members are closer to their respective community, and therefore, closer to the solutions to issues concerning those communities. Thus, there is a genuine desire to empower their grassroots members.

It was emphasized in the book that without quality people that practise democracy, the design of a democratic institution would not function as it is supposed to. The CCP do not believe in a Western-style voting system based on a simple 'majority-takes-all' because, as the book explains, the people come from a variety of interest groups and ethnic backgrounds. These groups, no matter how small, have their own unique needs and demands, so a simple 'majority-takes-all' political system fails to satisfactorily resolve the conflicts and needs of all within the community in a broader sense. In short, the CCP's emphasis on the process of communication with a variety of interest groups and ethnic minorities is based on reasoning, and emphasises that CCP members should culturally respect the needs of all in the country to uphold the CCP and community's expectation of equality, fairness and justice.

In practice, the CCP understands the concept of democracy better than the elites in the West. The following examples demonstrate that, besides having the skeletal structure of a voting system, the decision making process in the West can be rather autocratic and narrowly based when compared to China.

Chinese democracy vs. Western dictatorship

In Australia, under the leadership of the then Prime Minister Kevin Rudd (2007 to 2010), the key decision making was almost exclusively the business of a gang of four - the famously known 'kitchen cabinet'. Basically, the arrogant Rudd government did not trust the ability of all the ministers in his cabinet, and so formed a team of four, which comprised of himself and three other senior ministers: Deputy Prime Minister Julia Gillard, Treasurer Wayne Swan and Finance Minister Lindsay Tanner. (The Australian, 9 November, 2009)[109]

As an elected Prime Minister, Rudd was later betrayed by his ambitious deputy Julia Gillard with a sudden backdoor leadership deal. As a result of the powerful influence of a handful of powerbrokers within the Labor Party, the Australian people woke up one morning to see their elected Prime Minister weep in front of their TV screens after he was told by dozens of his colleagues that he was finished as Prime Minister. (Herald Sun, 25 June, 2010)[110] At the time, the Australian people didn't even know who was involved in the coup that overthrew their choice of Prime Minister in the 2007 election; the media then gave those people the title 'the faceless men'. The coup not only cost the Australian voters their choice of Prime Minister, but millions of taxpayer dollars. It was reported by the Courier Mail (12 November, 2010) that:

> Labor's faceless men delivered a $1.3 million bill to taxpayers when they dumped Kevin Rudd as prime minister – and the charges keep coming ... A further $5.4 million in payments have since been made to almost 100 ministerial staff who have walked out the door since the election of a hung parliament. Figures obtained by *The Courier-Mail* reveal that the cost of covering separation payments to Mr Rudd's personal ministerial staff following his dismissal in June, massive holiday pay amounts and the

> exodus of staff under the Gillard Government has come to almost $7 million. The payout covered senior advisers and office staff, when many chose to leave government rather than stay working under the new administration.[111]

Two years later, those behind-the-scenes Kingmakers - the 'faceless men' - still exercised their power at the expense of the Australia voters. The Australian (7 March, 2012) published a report titled 'Rare peek inside the factory of faceless men as Labor replaces loyalist with a legend' telling the story of how these faceless powerbrokers dictating who to be in power and who should be ousted. [112]

The reality is that the entire leadership succession process is highly corrupt and self-serving. On 12th September, 2010, a News Limited report titled 'Julia Gillard rewards the plotters' had the following information:

> Key coup plotter Bill Shorten, who helped convince Ms Gillard to challenge for the prime ministership, was made assistant treasurer and minister for financial services and superannuation - all key economic portfolios ... Ms Gillard denied she was rewarding the plotters directly, saying those promoted got there on merit ... She also singled out another plotter, Mark Arbib, for special mention. He has moved sideways in the outer ministry, losing employment participation and gaining indigenous employment, sport, social housing and homelessness. Ms Gillard said he gained "greatly increased responsibilities" Other key figures in the plot to oust Mr Rudd were Victorian senator David Feeney and South Australian senator Don Farrell, who won jobs as parliamentary secretaries.[113]

On 13 December, 2011, a report by The Age titled 'Gillard rewards her henchmen' had information of how Prime Minister Gillard strengthened her power base through a ministerial reshuffle:

> Prime Minister Julia Gillard has promoted her big backers in a ministerial reshuffle that aims to better sell the government's message and hold at bay Kevin Rudd's attempt to regain the leadership. Victorian right-winger Bill Shorten, who helped make Ms Gillard leader, is the biggest winner, moving into cabinet and the portfolio of Employment and Workplace Relations, a key policy battleground for 2012. He also retains Financial Services and Superannuation. Mr Shorten, a future leadership aspirant, declared: "I am absolutely stoked that our Prime Minister has given me this privilege. I completely and utterly support our Prime Minister." Mark Arbib, another right-wing factional player involved in elevating Ms Gillard, has been promoted to Assistant Treasurer, in changes that see Victorian left-winger Kim Carr forced to the outer ministry while two other left-

> wingers, Tanya Plibersek and Mark Butler, go into cabinet ... Mr McClelland has a cobbled together job of Minister for Housing, Homelessness and Emergency Management. His anger was obvious in his media statement about his achievements when he said the PM had "advised" he would be appointed to his new post. Cabinet has expanded from 20 to 22 because Ms Gillard was unable to create more than one vacancy. It is the biggest cabinet since the Whitlam years, when cabinet included all ministers. [114]

Ironically, in the land of a so-called "democracy", the coup against an elected Prime Minister was carried out not only against the will of the Australian voters, but through a series of lies and deceit by a handful of people within a political party itself. A Herald Sun (21 March, 2013) report titled 'Secret pro-Kevin Rudd polling buried by Labor' exposed the following:

> It has emerged that while Labor officials had cancelled a round of scheduled polling the week before the June 24 coup, one had already been commission was in the field. The survey was conducted by UMR research on June 22-23, 2010 in the marginal South Australian seat of Kingston. Results had started to filter back on the night of the coup. They showed Mr. Rudd well in front of Tony Abbott as preferred prime minister – 50 to 39 percent. More critically, the numbers showed the swing against Labor was nowhere near as dire as was suggested to MPs, with only 0.5 percent swing against the Government in that marginal seat. Senior Cabinet sources confirmed no one had been told about the Kingston numbers, claiming they would have been seen as "inconvenient" ... A spokesman for the PM said she had no knowledge of the Kingston numbers. Several Cabinet sources now claim they believe the research shown to ministers and key MPs had been "cooked" up to support the case to dump Mr. Rudd. [115]

In fact, if the coup resulted in an experienced and credible leader leading the country, one would perhaps accept the coup as a rational and justified one. The problem is that Julia Gillard, like Kevin Rudd, is simply another name added to the list of incompetent leaders in the political history of Australia. For example, in an interview with the 7.30 Report on the ABC (6 October, 2010), Prime Minister Gillard admitted that:

> "Foreign policy is not my passion ... So yes, if I had a choice, I'd probably be more comfortable in a school watching kids learn to read in Australia than here in Brussels at International meeting." [116]

To hold on to power, she sacked anybody who dared to support the return of the former Prime Minister, including her cabinet minister, Simon Crean (Australian, 21 March, 2013). [117]

In an interview on 'Q and A' (May 2013), Julia Gillard admitted that she has moments of self-doubt. The following is an excerpt from The Daily Telegraph:

> Ms Gillard says she can't afford to wander around declaring she's anxious and she doesn't know, and in any case that isn't who she really is. But she's declined to reveal just what issues have caused her moments of self-doubt.[118]

Under her leadership, all the public surveys consistently indicated a disaster for the Labor party in the upcoming election. Despite the Nielsen Poll (February, 2012),[119] Galaxy Poll (December 2012)[120] and a number of other polls showing Kevin Rudd as preferred Labor leader by the Australian voters, Julia Gillard was determined to hang onto power. (The Age, 11 June, 2013)[121] Without the backing of those 'faceless men', the Australian voters had no influence over their choice of leader in the upcoming election. (Sydney Morning Herald, 12 June, 2013 – 'Shorten 'believes' Gillard will lead to poll')[122]

Kevin Rudd, as a highly self-centred man, has since challenged Gillard's leadership twice and failed miserably, because many in the Labor Party hated his selfishness and dictatorial leadership style during his time as Prime Minister. His ongoing efforts to smear and challenge the Gillard leadership not only distracted the government from governing, but caused damage to his own party's approval rating. After his second failed leadership challenge to Julia Gillard on 21 March 2013, he promised in front of the camera that he "wishes to make 100% clear to all members of the parliamentary Labor party, including his own supporters, that there are no circumstances under which he will return to the Labor Party leadership in the future." (The Age, 22 March, 2013)[123] How false this is!

As a man without basic ethics and honesty, Rudd tried again on 26 June when the opinion poll showed Gillard's popularity in free-fall, and when many Labor MPs were fearful of losing their job in the upcoming election if Gillard continued to be leader. This time, he succeeded in replacing the current Prime Minister without facing the Australian voters, with the support of Bill Shorten; the most prominent faceless man who knifed him in 2010 in favour of Gillard, and now knifed Gillard in favour of him. (The Telegraph, 27 June, 2013)[124] Immediately after the leadership coup, Rudd promise to be a changed man, but a Galaxy-Daily Telegraph poll reveals that:

> Most Australians believe Kevin Rudd is still the chaotic and dysfunctional leader he was accused of being by dissident colleagues who publicly attacked him before his first leadership challenge in February last year.[125]

The result is that Julia Gillard will retire from politics, and a number of MPs and seven other existing ministers will go as well.[126] Essentially, the cabinet is left with a team of Rudd loyalists who have even less or no experience in governing. None of the members in his original 'kitchen cabinet' during his previous Prime Ministership remain in his new government. At a time of an economic crisis, this is so much for democracy in Australia. Politicians indulge in ongoing power struggle for personal gain, and have no time for policy, and no solution for the country.

The Fairfax group of newspapers, including the Sydney Morning Herald, described his return to the Labor leadership as 'Rudd gets his revenge'.[127] Amanda Vanstone, former Howard government minister in her personal column at The Age raised the following issue:

> Does this look like a bunch of happy campers capable of running the nations? Hardly.[128]

Simon Crean, a veteran Labor parliamentarian and former minister, refused Rudd's offer of a position and decided to exit politics, and warn his Labor colleagues to hold Kevin Rudd to his word to ensure Labor does not again degenerate into a "one-man show". (Sydney Morning Herald, 2 July, 2013)[129]

Sadly, there is a total lack of quality people in Australian politics, so not only are voters frustrated, even people within a political party are facing the same frustration.

Western democracies only look good from the outset, not from the inside. Contrary to the perception of being democratic, there is a common lack of democratic culture among the Western elites. As a result, the authority of these supposedly democratic institutions, such as the Parliament and the Congress, can be compromised at will by a handful of people.

It is now a widely known fact that the illegal invasion of Iraq in 2003 without UN endorsement was a decision made by a handful of people within the Bush regime in America, the Blair regime in Britain and the Howard regime in Australia. Prior to the invasion of Iraq, millions of people across the globe including those in the US, UK and Australia took to the streets protesting against their government's intention to invade Iraq. However, the war still went on as planned.

Ironically, the war was launched under the backdrop of a series of lies about the threat of weapons of mass destruction (WMDs) in Iraq. Not only were no WMDs found after the invasion, but a report from The Guardian (18 March, 2013) revealed that information had been deliberately concealed from the public, the Parliament and the Congress by governments at the time:

> Fresh evidence is revealed today about how MI6 and the CIA were told through secret channels by Saddam Hussein's foreign minister and his head of intelligence that Iraq had no active weapons of mass destruction. Tony Blair told parliament before the war that intelligence showed Iraq's nuclear, chemical, and biological weapons programme was "active", "growing" and "up and running". A special BBC Panorama programme tonight will reveal how British and US intelligence agencies were informed by top sources months before the invasion that Iraq had no active WMD programme, and that the information was not passed to subsequent inquiries.[130]

Earlier on, in an interview with Aljazeera (27 March, 2012), former head of the International Atomic Energy Agency (IAEA) and the then Chief United Nations Weapons Inspector, Han Blix, complained that his assessment that Iraq did not possess WMDs was pushed aside by the Bush administration. He also accused the British government for dramatising the threat of weapons in Iraq in order to strengthen its case for joining the 2003 war against Saddam Hussein.[131]

In fact, there were a number of other UN inspectors at the time also opposed the war, citing the fact that they had already destroyed the WMDs in Iraq during the decade-long UN weapon inspection. Scott Ritter, a former UN Weapons Inspector (UNSCOM) in Iraq, who has served in the US Marines in the Gulf War, attaining the rank of major, and William Rivers Pitt, an expert on the Middle East, jointly wrote a book in 2002 titled 'War on Iraq - What Team Bush Doesn't Want You to Know', telling the story of how the Bush administration lied to the world and the American people in order to invade Iraq.

In March 2003, Andrew Wilkie resigned from Australia's senior intelligence agency, the ONA, in protest over the looming Iraq war. He then wrote a book in 2004 titled 'Axis of Deceit – The Story of the Intelligence Officer Who Risked All to Tell the Truth about WMD and Iraq'. In his book, Wilkie outlines in detail how the Howard government manipulated intelligence agencies into tailoring their reports to support their political objectives. He also provides a detailed account on how the ONA misled the then opposition party (the Labor Party) during intelligence briefings. In addition, Wilkie also complained about the Howard government's censorship of information used by the opposition.

Contrary to the theoretical propaganda of a so-called balance of power among three independent forces within the Western political system - The Executive, The Legislature (Parliament and Congress) and the Judiciary - in practice, those who are in power can, and have manipulated the circumstances their way; they have killed their own citizens by drones without trial, and launched wars without Congressional approval. This was the case for the 2011 war against Libya, which prompted Senator Rand Paul to publicly complain that, "Congress has become 'an irrelevancy' on war powers." (Washington Post, 9 June, 2011)[132] The reality is that Obama is not the only US president to engage in war without Congressional approval. In a recent article on the Foreign Policy (9 May, 2013), Joshua Keating, an associate editor at Foreign Policy and the editor of Passport Blog, points out the fact that, "US Presidents have been going to war without Congress since the beginning." The following is just an excerpt:

> There's a general consensus that the imperial presidency model of war-fighting began with Theodore Roosevelt and expanded dramatically after World War II -- the last time Congress formally declared war. The War Powers Resolution of 1973 was meant to check the president's ability to do this, but several administration's have skirted it. A paper by William D. Adler in *Presidential Studies Quarterly* analyzes the "small wars" of early U.S. history and found that the tradition of the president acting as "generalissimo of the nation" as the pseudonymous "Cato" put it in the *Anti-Federalist Papers*, goes back much further than we think... [133]

One may notice from these incidents that the functionality of the American Congress can sometimes be treated as less significant than a 'rubber stamp' by the American Presidents. In a recent incident, RT's (21 February, 2013) report titled 'Obama moves to keep kill list memos secret forever' revealed that:

> United States President Barack Obama has no plans to show Congress the legal rulings that justify his use of drones to kill US citizens, despite urging from members of his own political party.[134]

A day earlier, the New York Times' (20 February, 2013) report titled 'White House Tactic for C.I.A. Bid Holds Back Drone Memos' came with information on the tactics the White House employs to prevent the Congress from accessing the documents that justify the killing of people across the world, including Americans without trial. [135]

From the above examples, we have once again proven that the concept of democracy cannot necessarily be achieved through having a voting system; it is the values of the individuals within the government that count. Many people outside China are unaware that China has elections at village and county levels. It is just that for people to move to a higher level of government, they have to prove their ability and code of ethics. One should recognise that it is totally practical, reasonable and legitimate to impose such requirements for political leadership; after all, the people who administer public affairs bear the responsibility for the delivering of wellbeing to the entire society. The ongoing political gridlock within a Western political system, with a voting pattern often based on party lines at the expense of the national interest, is just a part of the many systemic problems in the design of the Western political system that require urgent reform. Without an institutionalised process of internal democracy, and a collective, multilayered decision making process by well-educated, rational and quality people within a political party and government, fascists like Adolf Hitler, and know-nothing people like George W. Bush and Arnold Schwarzenegger can rise up again and again under the Western voting system.

Having undergone the process of transforming China from more than 2,000 years of dynastic culture, and a few decades of family dictatorship by the American backed Chiang Kai-shek's nationalist government, no one can deny the fact that the CCP is a reformist political party that has successfully departed from millennia old practices, and has structured its political system from within to achieve internal democracy. The institutionalisation of political succession has successfully ensured quality leadership, continuity in the country's desired direction, political stability, effective government, and careful decision making at the highest level of government.

To prevent an ill thought-out policy, the Chinese government functions through a process of internal consensus and broad-based consultation. In an article on the Foreign Affair (September/October, 2008) titled 'A Strategic Economic Engagement - Strengthening U.S. - Chinese Ties', Henry M. Paulson, Jr., former US Secretary of Treasury serving in the Bush administration, had the following description about the collective nature of decision making in China:

> One of the reasons relationship building is so important is that government decisions in China are often made by consensus and after much consultation. Reform progresses best when an umbrella of support at the top facilitates change at lower levels. Officially, the most important decisions are made by *President Hu* and *Premier Wen Jiabao*, but unofficially, decisions are increasingly made through a consensus-oriented process involving powerful government ministries. The SED/s high level, cross agency approach recognizes this reality and brings key decision-makers to the table to build broad support for reform. [Note: SED refers to the U.S.-China Strategic Economic Dialogue][136]

Please note this statement from the above:

> ...government decisions are often made by consensus and after much consultation.

Contrary to the perception of the Chinese leadership as dictatorial, which is relentlessly promoted by the mainstream media, Christopher R. Hill, former US Assistant Secretary of State for East Asia, points out in an article on the Project Syndicate (24 April, 2013) the following:

> "China" cannot be regarded as a collective noun with a singular view about anything; like any complex modern state, China contains many different views about many different issues ... Xi (Jinping) is no dictator who can impose his will on China. Indeed, for all the characterization of China as a despotic state that one hears from the political right in the United States, its president enjoys fewer powers than his American counterpart. Gaining consensus in China is a glacial process that will not be accomplished in a single speech ... despite a supposed lack of ideology in contemporary China, there is, in fact, a raging debate – often taking place below the radar – about the future of China's political system and its relationship to the economy.[137]

The truth is that there are millions of Chinese citizens living, working and studying outside of China. Unlike most in the West who are monolingual, many of the Chinese intellectuals are multilinguals, open minded and are fully aware of the flaws within the Western political system. Most of them do not believe that the voting system in the West produces real democracy and good governance. In 2009, the then China Parliament chief Wu Bangguo stressed that:

> China would draw on the achievements of all cultures but would not "simply copy" the West.[138]

On many occasions, the Chinese leadership and intellectuals stressed the merits of China's political system as a "multiparty corporation, and consultations under the leadership of the Communist Party, not a Western-style multiparty system." There are well-established theories on why it is defined as multiparty corporation; and that why it has to be under the exclusive leadership of the Communist Party to function smoothly with a high level of unity, efficiency and success. I will get into this later. The only problem is that Western journalists from the mainstream media are often too busy making money by digging dirt against the Communist Party for ideological propaganda, instead of pursuing the truth.

Flaws in the Western system that the Chinese system is designed to avoid

The behaviour of people are shaped by the design of a political system

The Western-style multi-party system is based on the concept of government vs. opposition. As the name 'opposition' suggests, the nature of such politics is to oppose each other. The relationship is about competition, not cooperation. As such, much of the time, resources and energy are spent in fighting each other. It is a political culture based on individualism, where 'winner-takes-all.' The lack of compromise within the Western political system results in ongoing political gridlock in the US Congress, even at a time of a financial crisis, and additional debt being added to the nation's economy at a rate of more than US$1 trillion per year.

An article from the Washington Post (25 October, 2010) titled 'The dysfunction of American politics' had appropriately described such situation in America:

> To its practitioners, politics is about power: getting it, keeping it and using it. But for the nation, the basic purpose of politics is to conciliate ... One reason so many Americans are unhappy with politics today is that it has abdicated its central role. It doesn't narrow our differences; it exaggerates them ... There's a regular cycle of disillusion. Immediately after the election, the victors are euphoric. But it's only a matter of time before they feel betrayed, while defeat had already demoralized the election's losers. Almost everyone is unhappy with political leaders, though often for different reasons ... Politics becomes dysfunctional in that leaders cannot command broad public support and differences of opinion widen. Legislation is often passed with only one party's support.[139]

One should note that the above Washington Post article served only to point out the problems with no proposed solution of any kind. This is a common problem in the West; after decades of media propaganda and censorship by omission of any information relating to the success of other cultures, the West has become intellectually incompetent in understanding the vital role of culture in promoting democracy.

In Australia, the situation is the same; the public hate their political leaders and the major political parties, but have no choice. In fact, public resources have often been abused by the government of the day to dig dirt on their opposition instead of managing public affairs. Kangaroo Court of Australia's (17 June, 2012) report titled 'Australian Prime Minister Julia Gillard sets up Watergate style dirt unit for opposition politicians' came with the following information:

> Alexandra Kirk broke the story this morning on AM (ABC Radio). Labor sources told her the PM's director of strategy, Nick Reece, has coached ministerial staff on how to find background information on Coalition frontbenchers. A document calls on staffers to find details on their opponents' "younger days", articles in student newspapers, and any fundraising, companies or legal cases that they'd been involved in. The Prime Minister says "it's reasonable to scrutinise Opposition frontbenchers." [140]

In fact, many senior public officials are employed by ministers through political appointments based on their personal trust towards the person to do whatever they want them to do; not by the personal credentials of that person as an experienced public servant with a proven performance record. It is not uncommon for ministers to use their know-nothing children or friends as senior advisers with a six-figure taxpayer-funded income. (I will get to this with greater detail in one of the future instalments under a chapter titled 'Princelings') The following excerpt from SBS (21 September, 2012) was just part of the complaint made by the Business Council of Australia about the quality of political advisers:

> Many politicians had lost sight of the role of the public service and the authority of senior officials had been "undermined by political gatekeepers". These ministerial advisers often had "little expertise and no accountability" ... The advisers were not only frustrating the work of senior public servants but their approach was impacting on the Australian economy and policy-making ... "Good policy-making processes are the last line of defence against the whims of short-termism and that is what a high-performing public sector can and must provide." [141]

In reality, the bureaucrats can only be as good as their political masters. The behaviour of people within a political institution is very much dependent upon the design of the political system. When it is structured as competitive, people will behave accordingly. There is no difference whether it is in America, Australia, or elsewhere. People are shaped by the design of political system, regardless of it being a federal, state or local government. For example, a report by the Brisbane Times (13 October, 2011) titled 'Dirt file furore spreads to Brisbane City Council' exposed the story of how the Liberal National Party commissioned a scandalous file on Labor politicians. [142]

The truth is that there are no holy people within the system. A report by the Courier Mail (10 October, 2011) titled 'Justin Bold lashes out at Labor's 'dirt-finding machine''[143] was just a reflection of the reality that both sides of politics were heavily involved in digging dirt against each other. The Brisbane Times (13 October, 2011) was spot-on to publish an article titled 'Dirty talk a turn-off for voters' with the following description:

> The state election will be more about the personalities of Anna Bligh and Campbell Newman than policies ... Political dirt file revelations have been a major switch off for voters as the image of politicians plummets ... While they were a good read, the documents showed Queensland politicians were out of touch with their electorates, ignored policy development and concentrated on marketing ... Three experts contacted by brisbanetimes.com.au all agreed that the demonstration that both the ALP

and the LNP dug dirt on each other's politicians would not surprise anyone.[144]

Therefore, even if voters do not like the politicians' negativity against each other, the sad reality is that when both sides of politics are doing exactly the same thing, what choice do voters have?

In America, the behaviour of politicians is no better than Australia. It is a common feature for presidential candidates to dig dirt from the past and smear each other during an election campaign. Such hostile behaviour occurs not only across political parties, but within a political party. For example, the Washington Post's (23 January, 2012) report titled 'Mitt Romney ad mocks 'historian' Newt Gingrich' tells of how Mitt Romney dug dirt from the past to create a political advertisement to discredit his fellow party comrade and presidential opponent Newt Gingrich. [145]

The infamous 'Watergate scandal' during Nixon's presidency in the 1970s, and the latest revelations about the Internal Revenue Service (IRS) targeting conservative groups in America (Washington Post, 23 May, 2013)[146] are just other examples of power abuse by governments of the day using public resources against their political opponents. Not surprisingly, Wikipedia has a list of tactics American politicians employed to smear each other. Simply search the following terms in Wikipedia to find out how creative, dishonest, and nasty American politicians are against each other in order to win an election. One should note that the examples on Wikipedia include incidents from day one when America introduced a voting system.

- Dirty Trick
- Discrediting tactic
- Dog-whistle politics
- False accusations
- Karl Rove
- Lee Atwater
- Negative campaigning
- Psychological manipulation
- Push poll (Push-polling)
- Wedge issue (Wedge politics)
- Willie Horton

Anybody who browses through the above list of incidents of politicians attacking each other will understand why Western politicians have no time for policy.

There are many more reasons why China would never adopt the current inferior form of a Western political system, and this is rightly so with powerful reasoning and legitimate concerns. The list could be endless; a few more of these follow.

Money-centred politics

Theoretically, a voting system is designed to give the people the ultimate power of choice of government. In practice, election campaigns need money; a lot of money. The issue is: who has the money? Needless to say, it is the wealthy and big corporations. The problem is that these people don't have altruist intentions; they don't give away their money without asking for political favours. The end result is that politicians are very much serving the interests of their donors - the big corporations and the wealthy - instead of the people.

David A. Stockman, former congressman from Michigan, and President Ronald Reagan's budget director from 1981 to 1985, wrote an article in New York Times (30 March, 2013) titled 'State-Wrecked: The Corruption of Capitalism in America', which highlights how eight decades of bipartisan Keynesian spending and Federal Reserve money printing have left America exhausted and bankrupt. In his article, Stockman blamed the American political system for the current situation, and proposed the following as a solution:

> All this would require is drastic deflation of the realm of politics and the abolition of incumbency itself, because the machinery of the state and the machinery of re-election have become conterminous. Prying them apart would entail sweeping constitutional surgery: amendments to give the president and members of Congress a single six-year term, with no re-election; providing 100 percent public financing for candidates; strictly limiting the duration of campaigns (say, to eight weeks); and prohibiting, for life, lobbying by anyone who has been on a legislative or executive payroll. It would also require overturning Citizens United. [147]

The reality is that political corruption in America is a systemic issue directly linked to the design of its political system. The shooting incident at Connecticut Elementary School that killed 26 people, which included 20 children in December 2012,[148] has ignited another round of calls in America to control guns. President Obama was at the forefront of such a campaign with a speech in front of grieving families of Newtown, saying:

> We can't tolerate this anymore; these tragedies must end.

The Guardian (17 December, 2012) regarded Obama's speech as, "the strongest call for change in gun policy by any political leader in a generation."[149] However, even in a country where approximately 100,000 people get shot each year, and about a third (30,000) lose their lives,[150] most lawmakers dare not work against the will of the powerful National Rifle Association (NRA). An article on the New York Times (19 December, 2012) titled 'The N.R.A. Protection Racket' had this description:

> The most blatant protection racket is orchestrated by the National Rifle Association, which is ruthless against candidates who are tempted to stray from its view that all gun regulations are pure evil. Debra Maggart, a Republican leader in the Tennessee House of Representatives, was one of its most recent victims. The N.R.A. spent around $100,000 to defeat her in the primary, because she would not support a bill that would have allowed people to keep guns locked in their cars on private property without the property owner's consent. The message to Republicans is clear: "We will help you get elected and protect your seat from Democrats. We will spend millions on ads that make your opponent look worse than the average holdup man robbing a liquor store ... For decades, Republican politicians have gone along with this racket, some willingly and others because they know that resisting would be pointless. According to the Center for Responsive Politics, the N.R.A. spent almost $19 million in the last federal election cycle. This money is not just spent to beat Democrats but also to beat Republicans who don't toe the line. [151]

As a result of such bully tactics by the NRA, despite the fact that there were another "more than 400 gun deaths in less than three weeks since the Newton Massacre on 14 December" (AlterNet, 3 January 2013),[152] the federal proposal to tighten gun control was stalled in Congress. (Washington Post, 11 April, 2013)[153] The ironic development is that, less than two months after the powerful speech given by President Obama to control guns, the New York Post (2 February, 2013) published a photo released by the White House showing Obama skeet shooting at Camp David, with the following description:

> The release of the photo is a head scratcher to both supporters of gun control and gun rights. The last thing some advocates of gun control want is an image of the president as a gun lover on the shooting range while

> they're trying to get Congress to pass stricter firearm laws in the wake of the Newtown, Conn. shooting massacre. Meanwhile gun owners suspect this is a phony attempt by Obama to show his respect for law-abiding gun enthusiasts and that he's not trying to take away their rights.[154]

A month after the release of Obama's shooting photo by the White House, Fox News (19 March, 2013) report revealed that:

> The leader of the Democrat-controlled Senate dropped a proposed assault weapons ban from chamber's gun-control package – dealing a blow to supporters of the ban, though it could still come up for a vote.[155]

On 18 April 2013, Washington Post's report titled 'Gun-control overhaul is defeated in Senate' had the following information:

> President Obama's ambitious effort to overhaul the nation's gun laws in response to December's school massacre in Connecticut suffered a resounding defeat Wednesday, when every major proposal he championed fell apart on the Senate floor ... But the biggest setback for the White House was the defeat of a measure to expand background checks to most gun sales. The Senate defied polls showing that nine in 10 Americans support the idea, which was designed to keep guns out of the hands of criminals and the mentally ill. [156]

One should note this from the above report: despite "9 in 10 Americans" in favour of gun control, the elected politicians decided to turn down any proposals to tighten gun laws, including a measure to expand background checks to gun sales.

Ironically, soon after the Senate dismissed the gun-control bill, a gun report ordered in by Obama has ended up highlighting the fact that legal guns are actually saving lives and diffusing crime. Infowars.com (27 June, 2013) reported the news with a 'Woops' on the heading: 'Woops! Obama Ordered Gun Report Reveals Guns Actually Save Lives'.[157]

On the 12th September 2013, a report by the Sydney Morning Herald revealed that two American politicians who promoted tighter gun controls after the 2012 Aurora movie theatre massacre have lost their seats in the state of Colorado after a "historically unprecedented recall election, hailed by the pro-gun National Rifle Association (NRA)." According to the report, "the NRA donated some US$360,000 to back the recall ballots in Colorado - the first ever use of a state mechanism allowing for MPs to be kicked out by popular vote."[158]

These incidents demonstrate the reality that Western democracies do not represent the will of the people. It is corporate money that puts politicians into the Senate and Congress; not the people. The voting trend of the people can easily be manipulated by corporate money and the media. Western democracies are fake democracies.

In Australia, it is no different from America: undue corporate influence in government policies has being a common feature as well. For example, at the height of the Rio Tinto bribery case where an Australian executive was arrested in Shanghai, we were told by The Age (15 October, 2009) that the Rudd government's policy on China was "set by BHP". This is the exact wording:

> A former senior Treasury official has accused the Rudd Government of caving in to the wishes of BHP Billiton over Chinese investment in Australia, contributing to a serious deterioration in relations with Beijing. Stephen Joske says BHP bent the ears of senior ministers and exploited the Government's "policy dysfunction" to get its way on China. Mr Joske, who was the Government's top China economist until he left to join the Economist Intelligent Unit in Beijing in July last year, said the Australian bureaucracy abrogated its responsibilities and Treasurer Wayne Swan opened the door for lobbyists to fill the policy vacuum on China. [159]

At a state level, it is the same: a report by Sydney Morning Herald (20 January, 2011) titled 'Coalition lets miners write lands policy' revealed the following:

> A draft Coalition commitment to "improve monitoring and compliance" for any mining project on agricultural land was twice deleted from the "strategic regional land use planning policy" document. The line does not appear in a later policy document given to the farmers association for comment. The manipulation of election policy by miners is bound to call into question Barry O'Farrell's recent conversion to conservation and the environment. Less than a fortnight ago the Opposition Leader said he would create a new national park south of Sydney if he wins office in March... Mistrust between farmers and miners has even descended into industry whispers about why the opposition industry spokesman, Duncan Gay, snubbed the farmers association's Christmas drinks last month but attended the minerals council's soiree... The documents show the miners are desperate to play down tensions, asking for the removal of a reference to growth in the industry as increasing "land use conflict". The council changed that to "seeing expansion of these industries on to high value agriculture land". The council also asked for any reference to "water resources" and the potential impacts of mining on them to be removed, preferring the term "precious environmental assets".[160]

In another case, when the Rudd government tried to introduce a 40% Super Mining Tax in 2010, his policy was countered by the miners' AU$100 million advertising war-chest to discredit his government. The massive daily advertising campaign against his government on the news media, and the coordination of the opposition who cashed in towards the miners' political donations contributed to the eventual sinking of the mining tax and catalysed the removal of Kevin Rudd as Prime Minister. Once in power, the unelected new Prime Minister Julia Gillard immediately offered a truce to the miners by withdrawing the government's AU$38 million counter-miner advertising campaign, and promised to talk to the industry without pre-conditions. (Outcast Journalist, 28 June, 2010)[161] A report by WA Today (1 February, 2011), citing figures released by the Australian Electoral Commission, revealed that the miners actually spent only over AU$20 million on political advertisements to bend the government and sink the mining tax. [162]

On 24 March 2011, The Australian's report revealed that the government accepted 98 recommendations made by the Minerals Resources Rent Tax (MRRT) policy transition group. According to Fortescue Metals' chief executive Andrew Forrest:

> It was a tax designed by BHP. It's amusing the ex-BHP chairman (Don Argus) chaired the independent committee made up of large companies. It's a precedent that should not be supported. Policy should be broad ranging, it should be fair and it should be based on the constitution of being equal among states and equal among companies. That hasn't happened here. BHP has literally written a tax for everyone else to pay. If you attend briefings by BHP, Rio and Xstrata they are not talking about paying a great deal of this MRRT (minerals resources rent tax). They have massive double protection from it which is not available to new companies.[163]

The end result is that the revised mineral resource rent tax "raised [only] A$126m in its first six months of operation, a long way short of the full-year forecast of A$2b contained in the mid-year economic statement." (ABC, 9 February, 2013)[164] One of Australia's leading economists Professor Ross Garnaut reportedly told the Senate Committee (WA Today, 29 April, 2013) that, "the mining tax is highly flawed and may never raise any revenue in its current form." [165]

The strength of China's political system is that they need not compromise with corporate interests like the West, as their political system is based on multiparty corporations under the leadership of the Communist Party. It has layers and layers of structurally workable and theoretically sound internal democracy, supported by a cadre education program and a system of wide-based consultation. I shall explain this in detail later on.

Poll-driven politics, social divides and short-term considerations

The current form of Western democracy not only results in ongoing political infighting among politicians and political parties, but is also divisive in nature and short-term in-focus. The reason for such a phenomenon is simple: to win an election, the most effective marketing technique is to create simple messages so that the average voter can easily be attracted. Instead of working on a complex ten-year reform plan, and trying to sell the policy to the average voter that would either not understand or be interested in it after a tiring day at work, it is a lot easier for politicians to do one of the following things:

(1) Tell voters how much money or what kind of benefits they will give them if elected

(2) Incite hatred and racism to attract the support of certain groups of voters; this can be done without the need for any financial commitments to voters

For example, a Courier Mail (13 February, 2013) report revealed that:

> Redcliffe's five-storey GP super clinic is nothing more than a shell six years after it was pledged as one of four clinics for Queensland during the 2007 election. Six super clinics, including those also pledged for Mount Isa, Townsville and Gladstone, still have not opened while four clinics promised in 2010 do not even have a funding agreement. Delays in the program, which was supposed to bring 64 bulk-billing and late-opening GP clinics to communities around Australia, are exposed in a departmental spreadsheet outlining progress on the $650 million project ahead of today's Senate estimates hearings...[166]

Ironically, merely a week after the above report by the Courier Mail, the Labor government began to offer another GP Super Clinic in Queensland. This is how the Courier Mail (20 February, 2013) put it:

> The Federal Government is to announce yet another GP super clinic for Queensland - which is still waiting for four previously-pledged centres to open ... Queensland is currently waiting on four previously-pledged clinics to open but the Federal Government says three of those should be operational by mid-year - before the September election - and has blamed delays on finding suitable land. Those pledged for Mount Isa, Townsville and Gladstone are yet to begin operations, while one at Redcliffe - first pledged six years ago - is still just a shell.[167]

One should note that during the final term of the Howard government in Australia, in an attempt to save his sliding popularity, his government was heavily involved in irresponsible welfare offers to middle-income Australians. According to the IMF (2013), the Howard government is the most "needless wasteful spending" government in the history of Australia.[168] The consequence, according to Professor Phil Lewis:

> The Coalition's last budget created the ground for the current deficits.[169]

Unfortunately, at a time when the nation is facing a sluggish economy with rising debt and poverty, both the current Gillard government and opposition continue to play politics with their fiscal policies aimed at winning the upcoming election instead of engaging in responsible governance.

Sinclair Davidson, Professor of Institutional Economics, described in an article on The Conversation (16 May, 2013) that the Gillard government's pre-election fiscal policy was "irresponsible" and "a lame effort from a dying government".[170] The Age described the budget as "lies, damn lies",[171] and the Sydney Morning Herald called the budget "Canberra's con job".[172] The problem is that the opposition is doing exactly the same thing. Independent Australia's (19 May, 2013) report pointed out that there were "at least 20 lies" in the opposition leader's budget reply.[173] This is simply another example of a 'no choice election' faced by Western voters, as both sides of politics are equally nasty, morally corrupt and ethically bankrupt.

At a time of an economic crisis with rising debt, the flaws of Western democracies have become even more obvious. In 2009, President Obama promised Americans that he would cut the annual budget deficit by half during the first term of his presidency.[174] However, by the end of his first term, the American economy was still operating at an annual deficit of more than US$1 trillion/year. On 1 March 2013, CBS News highlighted the reality in America with this heading: 'National debt up $6 trillion since Obama took office'.[175] Sadly, due to the lack of quality leaders and choice within the tiny political circles in the US, Obama was re-elected in the 2012 election despite the poor performance in his first term.

Another common problem linked to the current design of the Western voting system is politicians fuelling hate crimes and racial discrimination. A simple search on Google using the term 'democracy and racism' will return more than seven million links to books, articles, reports, surveys, news and videos that tell the stories of how a Western-styled democracy fuels racism. In particular, when the economy is sluggish, and politicians have no solutions to offer, they usually have the tendency to divert attention away from their incompetency by inciting hatred against ethnic groups in their country to win votes. After all, inciting hatred involves no financial commitments to voters.

The moment the USSR endorsed Western democracy, the country erupted into 15 nations; Czechoslovakia broke down into the Czech Republic and Slovakia Republic; and Yugoslavia into Bosnia, Croatia, Kosovo, Macedonia, Montenegro, Serbia and Slovenia.

Scotland, after being with Britain for three centuries, is also working towards independence, as some Scottish politicians have begun to capitalise on the public's hatred towards the English from historical events, and promote the idea that an independent Scotland will no longer need to share gas and oil revenue generated from the North Sea's wells with Britain. The French in Quebec, Canada did the same earlier and is likely to try again sometime in the future.

In fact, the work of a few extremists or racists within a society could eventually ignite separatism amongst ethnic groups. In some cases, the separation of a country has occurred against the public's opinion. For example, the breaking-up of Czechoslovakia in 1993 was the work of some powerful individuals within a major political party: the Slovak National Party. Despite many Czechs and Slovaks desiring the continued existence of a federal Czechoslovakia, their wishes have been overpowered by politicians.[176] My memory of what happened to Czechoslovakia is still fresh to this day because, at the time, I was living in Eastern Europe, based in Hungary between 1991 to late-1994. I have the honour of having my passport stamped under the name of Czechoslovakia, and then the Czech Republic and the Slovakian Republic. I am one of the witnesses to a history of mass poverty, inequality and suffering after a sudden change to a political system.

At a time of economic prosperity, it is a lot easier to hold people together within a nation. However, when there is a prolonged period of hardship, some selfish politicians with no policy, will do and say anything to win votes; even if that means inciting hatred, conflict, violence and separatism with an outcome that will harm the nation's unity and economy. The current form of Western democracy is by no means a solution to social integration, equality, unity, mutual respect and acceptance.

Catalonia of Spain, the engine of Spain's economy, reportedly disregarded Spain's Constitution and the authority of Spain's parliament on the issue of self-determination, and is heading for a referendum for independence in 2014. (Christian Science Monitor, 23 January, 2013)[177]

What follows is an example of how poll-driven politics and racism have caused an Australian Prime Minister to change his long-time beliefs on the issue of immigration in the election year of 2010.

The following is a direct excerpt from one of three examples I wrote in 2010 in an article titled 'Democracy Needs Reform - The Cruelty of Poll Driven Politics'[178]:

> Former Prime Minister Kevin Rudd has always been an enthusiastic supporter of a bigger Australia.
>
> According to a new Immigration Department report on skilled arrivals in 2009, "the Rudd Government has admitted it wants to bring in up to 230,000 migrants annually over the next 40 years." (Herald Sun, 3 September 2009 - 'Federal Government set to maintain record high immigration levels')[179]
>
> A month later, in an interview with the 7.30 report, Kevin Rudd unambiguously spoke of the merits of a bigger population. This is what he said: "I actually believe in a big Australia. I make no apology for that ... I actually think it's good news that our population is growing ... I think it is good for us, it's good for our national security long term, it's good in terms of what we can sustain as a nation." (The Age, 23 Oct 2009)[180]

Another 3 months later, Kevin Rudd, in his speech to mark the 2010 Australia Day Celebration, again spoken about our aging population and the need for Australia to increase its population from 22 million to 36 million by 2050 to maintain our current standard of living. ('Kevin Rudd's speech in full'- The Advertiser, 20 Jan 2010)[181]

However, when the media began to publish a series of anti-immigration articles and speeches by the opposition, activists, and right wingers with strong anti-immigrant sentiment, the public opinion indicated that "two-thirds of respondents - 66 per cent - think the Federal Government should cap immigration rates." (News Limited, 24 Jan 2010)[182] This was when the Rudd government began to reverse its immigration policy in a sudden, brutal, ruthless, unethical, inhumane, and racist manner with immediate effect.

Creating an 'in-demand' skilled migration list to attract overseas students

Before the Rudd government won the last election (2007), the previous Australian governments have been using an 'in-demand' skilled migration list that many migration and education agencies have been actively using that as marketing tools to attract foreign students and their money.

As a result, our education sector has become our 3rd largest export industry with annual revenue of AU$17 billion.[183]

Despite this, there have been many unscrupulous and dodgy colleges over the years collecting a huge amount of tuition fees from overseas students and not offering any proper educational services. As examples:

· ABC Four Corners (27 July 2009) - 'Holy Cash Cows':[184]

"Last year more than 70,000 Indian students came here to buy an education. Egged on by immigration and education agents, many were told if they enrolled in cooking, hairdressing and accounting courses they would not only get a diploma but they could also qualify for permanent residency in Australia."

"Four Corners investigation reveals that foreign students in this country have been targeted by unscrupulous businessmen, who have set up training schools that supply qualifications that sometimes aren't worth the paper they are written on."

“We all know that they have sardine type cooking classes where there's sixteen students to a frypan." (Corruption investigator)

“If a student wants to apply for permanent residency they must pass an English language test. Four Corners has found clear evidence that unscrupulous immigration and education agents are offering English language tests for a price. In some cases the exam paper is worth up to $5,000.

“Another requirement for students in vocational courses, seeking residency in Australia, is a work experience certificate. Each student is required to undertake up to 900 hours of on the job training. Some work for nothing creating a source of cheap labour. Others are offered an alternative. Four Corners reveals an immigration agent was prepared to help procure a fake work experience certificate for students if they were prepared to pay between three and four thousand dollars. This practice clearly makes a joke of the vocational qualification and the integrity of the immigration system."

· The Age (23 July 2009) - ‘College in gross breach of standards’:[185]

“A CONFIDENTIAL report on a Melbourne private college has uncovered big education breaches, painting a picture of shambolic practices that failed to meet the most basic educational standards”

“The audit also found:
* Marketing of education and training services was unprofessional
* Students were not provided with information on emergency and health services
* There were no proper checks on overseas education agents
* Students' course progress was not monitored
* Classes were overcrowded”

· The Australian (29 July 2009) - ‘UNE accused of allowing plagiarists to graduate’:[186]

“More than 100 overseas students graduated from the University of New England with copied masters theses, creating one of Australia's biggest plagiarism scandals after an academic whistleblower tried to raise the alert."

The problem with the Australian government is that, they don't really care as long as the money keeps coming in.

· Times of India (23 Jan 2010) - 'Australian govt ignores advice on Indian students: Report':[187]

"A top body that represents Australia's universities has accused both state and federal governments of ignoring warnings issued by it on problems faced by overseas students, including Indians, in the country."

"Universities Australia, which represents 39 universities, said it had alerted governments to problems relating to student safety, poor-quality colleges, lacks of concessions on public transport and immigration matters for two years ago."

"It (Universities Australia) passed on to Australian authorities warnings from officials in China and India relating to student safety. It also conveyed to governments student disenchantment resulting from a perception they were being treated like cash cows,"

"However; Universities Australia Chief Executive Glenn Withers said that he was disappointed as state and federal governments did not treat the problems as a priority when they were told about them two years ago but acted with urgency only when violent attacks on Indian students attracted intense media attention."

Sudden withdrawal of the favourable skilled migration list

However, when the poll indicated that the government "Big Australia" policy was unpopular in an election year. The reformed policy worked like this:

Only 19 days after Kevin Rudd delivered his Australia Day speech about the merits of increasing our population to 36 million by 2050, his government suddenly decided to have a 'Migration U-turn' (Sydney Morning Herald, 8 Feb 2010),[188] by calling it a 'Crackdown on skilled migrants' (WA Today, 7 February),[189] and immediately 'rejected 20,000 migrants' (Brisbane Time, 8 Feb 2010).[190]

Such a sudden rejection of 20,000 migrants and the withdrawal of the favourable skilled migration list were done without taking into consideration the billions of dollars these students already contributed to the Australian economy. The reality is that these students had already invested years of their time and a huge amount of money in Australia believing in the government's 'in-demand list'. Some had borrowed money as an investment hoping for a better future. Unfortunately, Western democracies do not ensure compassion, basic social ethics and human rights for those who have no voice in the system.

The immediate outcome of such poll-driven politics was a drastic drop in overseas students coming to Australia, so universities began to cut staff. The then new Gillard government was forced to formulate new marketing strategies soon after the election to attract overseas students by lowering the financial requirement for student visas to Australia (Australia Forum, 7 January, 2011).[191] When this didn't work, the government then further lowered the visa requirement "to entice foreign students with quick visa approvals and the right to two years of work after graduation as part of a reform package to stem further losses of overseas student income." (Australian, 23 September, 2011)[192]

Ironically, at the beginning of the 2013 election year, the then Gillard government again used the same technique, like her predecessors, of inciting hate and fear towards migrants as a tool to divert attention away from her government's inability to fix the economy; in the hope that such an anti-migrant posture would attract the support of voters. This time the 457 skilled migrant visa program had been selected as an entry point. The Courier Mail (6 March, 2013) rightly put up a headline to describe the phenomenon in such a circle of poll-driven politics: 'Now it is Julia Gillard's turn to stir fear'.[193] Professor Stephen King of the Department of Economics at Monash University described the behaviour of the government as, "political opportunism, not economics, drives the attack on 457 Visa."[194] Sadly, both sides of politics are doing exactly the same thing. While the Gillard government played the xenophobic card against the 457 Visa, the opposition leader Tony Abbott played it on asylum seekers through the frequent use of the slogan "Stop the Boats". This prompted Michelle Grattan, Professorial Fellow at University of Canberra to put up an article titled 'Gillard and Abbott bet on Australia's xenophobia' with the following description:

> Both sides are demonising their "foreigners" of choice on the low road to September 14.[195]
> [Note: September 14 was the planned election date during the Gillard government's run.]

Perhaps it is due to this kind of poll-driven xenophobic 'US and THEM' political culture that arises from the design of the political system, that the issue of racism against minorities is persistently a serious social problem in many Western societies. There is a pattern of similar behaviour and incidents in many Western societies, from racist rants and assaults against minorities at public places, to a disproportionate number of minority deaths-in-custody, arrests, incarceration and racial discrimination at work, in school, court and other institutions. These are common forms of human rights violations in Western societies that attract little attention in the mainstream media. (Note: an in-depth analysis will be provided in one of the upcoming instalments linking racism to a silent form of authority-endorsed human rights violation in the West.)

As far as my twenty years of observation as a migrant in Australia is concerned, this is an invisible force that has prevented minorities from feeling a sense of belonging in many Western countries. If one has to experience some form of discrimination within a society, being disadvantaged, or being smeared upon by the media, politicians, right-wing supremacists, skin heads, and individuals on the street, work place, school, public transport and social media from time to time due to their skin colour, how can we expect them to develop a sense of belonging? The impression I have as a minority citizen in Australia is that politicians are desperate for money, skills and manpower from non-Western countries to support their aging population and lifestyle while racially rejecting the very people they invited to contribute to their society. This is perhaps the reason why French President Nicolas Sarkozy, UK Prime Minister David Cameron and German Chancellor Angela Markel all declared that multiculturalism has failed in their respective countries (Mail Online, 11 February, 2011).[196]

The truth is that Western democracy in its current form fails to promote social harmony, and the rights of their minorities. It is a 'majority-takes-all' political system and it is not inclusive in nature. The West has yet to learn to genuinely accept and respect other cultures. Deep in the bones of the capitalist elites, their so-called "integration" is always a one-way concept - not a mutual one. Unless there is a hung parliament, or the minority population has increased significantly to proportionately closer to the majority or the mainstream population, a voting system based on the simple formula of 'winner-takes-all' will in reality be almost always a one-way game in favour of the majority.

In 2007, when a black American Barack Obama became a presidential candidate, PEW Research Centre study found that white Americans would become the minority by 2050. This immediately raised alarm across America with provocative headlines: Reuters (12 February, 2008) declaring 'Whites to become minority in U.S. by 2050'.[197] The issue has since become an ongoing concern in US society with the media engaging in a relentless effort to repeatedly remind Americans about this population trend since then. The following are just some examples of interesting news headings on the issue from 2008 to 2013:

* CNN (13 August, 2008): 'Minorities expected to be majority in 2050' [198]
* CBS News (11 February, 2009) 'America's Face Is Changing' [199]
* New York Times (17 December, 2009): 'Projections Put Whites in Minority in U.S. by 2050' [200]
* AlterNet (19 December, 2009): 'Pockets of White America Are in the Throes of an Existential Crisis' [201]
* CBS News (10 March, 2010): 'Whites in U.S. Edge Towards Minority Status' [202]
* USA Today (23 June, 2011): 'Census: Whites make up minority of babies in U.S.' [203]
* PEW (17 May, 2012): 'Explaining Why Minority Births Now Outnumber White Births' [204]
* CBS News (17 May, 2012): 'Census: More minority US births than white now' [205]
* New York Times (17 May, 2012): 'Whites Account for Under Half of Births in US' [206]
* Rolling Stone (27 July, 2012): 'Pat Buchanan: GOP Imperiled by Decline of White Population' [207]
* CNN (7 May, 2013): 'Most U.S. children under 1 are minorities, Census says' [208]
* Think Progress (8 May, 2013): 'When Will Your State Become Majority-Minority?' [209]
* CBS DC (15 May, 2013): 'Census: Immigration Surpassing US Births, White Children a Minority by 2018' [210]

* CBS News (13 June, 2013): 'US whites falling to minority in under-5 age group' [211]
* New York Times (13 June, 2013): 'Census Benchmark for White Americans: More Deaths Than Births' [212]
* NBC News (13 June, 2013): 'Census: White majority in US gone by 2043' [213]
* CNN (22 August, 2013): 'Meet America's emerging minority group – whites' [214]

The worry of some in US society for becoming a minority is understandable when we put in perspectives a political system based on a simple majority rule. In Hawaii, a kingdom where members of the royal family were murdered and overthrown by the US, and then officially annexed as the 50th State of America in 1959, has upset some on the US mainland for persistently not electing as many of their minority whites in elections. An article on the Washington Post (23 April, 2013) reveals unhappiness about the outcome of democracy in Hawaii and mentioned throughout the article the race factor in Hawaiian politics. The following is an excerpt from the article's titled: 'Another race-tinted showdown in Hawaii':

> News broke late Monday that Rep. Colleen Hanabusa (D-Hawaii) would challenge appointed Sen. Brian Schatz (D-Hawaii) in a primary in 2014. It should surprise no one ... The Hawaii Democratic Party has a long history of primaries split along racial lines, with contests often coming down to an Asian-American, Native Hawaiian or Pacific Islander candidate and a white one, referred to as "haole" in Hawaiian. And if it wasn't Hanabusa challenging Schatz, it was likely to be another Asian-American Democrat, because Asian candidates often win in a state that is just 26 percent white ... Of the 10 races mentioned above, Asian-American candidates have won seven of them. Two haole men have been elected mayor of Honolulu, while Gov. Neil Abercrombie is the first white Democrat to hold that job since the 1970s. The state has elected several white members of Congress — including Abercrombie and Case — but its senators and governors have been almost exclusively Asian-American. [215]

If Western democracies delivered equality and fairness for all, there wouldn't have been a 'Tea Party Movement' in 2009 mainly formed by white Americans[216] when Obama become the first black American president in 2008. The same would apply to black Americans; if democracy offered equality and justice, a black presidential candidate wouldn't attract a historic turnout of black voters, with an overwhelming 96%[217] of them voting for Obama. As well, the media, under the control and ownership of the current majority Americans, wouldn't be so worried about their kind becoming a minority in 2050, and repeatedly reminding Americans about the population trend through their media each and every year since 2008.

In reality, the historical election of a black president in America may not have happened without a financial crisis where American voters became desperate and tired of the existing political order. The election of a black president has, on the other hand, sparked the complete rejection of minority lawmakers by the majority voters in future elections. An article at Politico (29 April, 2013) titled 'Black pols stymied in Obama era' has the following observation about a reduction of black lawmakers in America:

> More than five years after Barack Obama won the Iowa caucuses and demolished the notion that white voters wouldn't support a black presidential candidate, progress for other African-American politicians remains elusive. Even as the country elected and re-elected Obama, making it seem increasingly unremarkable to have a black family in the White House, African-Americans are scarce and bordering on extinct in the U.S. Senate and governorships. The president is indeed exceptional — but in the wrong sense of the phrase as it applies to other black politicians.

The article then goes on to outline the following reality in American politics:

> Since Obama broke the presidential color barrier in 2008: There has not been one African-American elected to the Senate — the only blacks in the chamber were appointed to fill vacant seats; the country's sole African-American governor, who was originally elected before Obama captured the presidency, won re-election but may leave the ranks of black governors empty when he leaves after 2013; and a cadre of promising, next-generation black politicians have either lost races (Washington Mayor Adrian Fenty, Reps. Kendrick Meek of Florida and Artur Davis of Alabama) or seen their careers extinguished because of scandal (former Rep. Jesse Jackson Jr.)

Despites speculation by the article that things may improve for blacks in the long-term, the short-term outlook is less optimistic. [218]

In fact, Western-imposed democracies in Iraq, Afghanistan and Libya through violent means have resulted in more chaos, violence and social divides in those societies, with daily sectarian violence and suicide bombings. If Western democracies actually offered equality, justice, mutual respect, the rule of law and human rights, there would be no need to manipulate the voting system through the corrupt process of redistricting.

Vote manipulation, minority rights and human rights

'Redistricting' is a term used to describe the redrawing of electoral boundaries. The process often results in political parties making use of their networking to affect the redistricting process in a way that will disadvantage their opponents. The following were just some news headlines that reflected such a corrupt political process in America:

* 'Mapping out New Jersey's minority representation' (NJ Spotlight, 11 March, 2011) [219]
* 'Perry Accused Of Distorting Redistricting Map To Weaken The Latino Vote In Texas' (AlterNet, 7 September, 2011) [220]
* 'Md. Redistricting's big losers: Minorities' (Washington Post, 14 October, 2011) [221]
* 'Redistricting away Seattle's minority representation' (Crosscut News, 7 November, 2011) [222]
* 'Redistricting GOP Was "Very, Very Clever" in Limiting Minorities' Voting Power, Expert Testifies' (Houston Press, 9 September, 2011) [223]
* 'Albany Redistricting Plan Faulted as Unfair to Minorities' (New York Times, 30 January, 2012) [224]
* 'Voter redistricting disadvantages for minorities' (MSNBC News, 15 February, 2012) [225]
* 'Holder: Texas Electoral Redistricting Maps 'Manipulated' to Minimize 'Minority Electoral Strength'' (CNS News, 30 May, 2012) [226]
* 'New York's Proposed Council Map Is Called Unfair to Minority Groups' (New York Times, 2 October, 2012) [227]
* 'Redistricting in Virginia Hurts Blacks, Democrats Say' (New York Times, 23 January, 2013)[228]
* 'Texas Redistricting Fight Shows Why Voting Rights Act Still Needed' (The Nation, 5 June, 2013) [229]

ProPublica, a reputable independent web media, produced a webpage titled 'Redistricting: How Powerful Interests Are Drawing You Out of a Vote', (http://www.propublica.org/series/redistricting) with dozens of links to stories across America showing how voters' rights were manipulated by powerful people and corporations.

As a country with a big budget in promoting democracy and the rule of law across the globe, there are of course laws in America that make minority vote dilution illegal. However, one should note that the law is administered by people, the personal values or bias of the person who administered the law will directly affect the outcome of the law. Therefore, like the voting system, the so-called 'rule of law' in America is just another illusion. An article on Southern Changes 13 years ago titled 'Minority Vote Dilution Is Still Illegal' with this opening statement:

> The 1990 round of redistricting brought a significant increase in minority representation in Congress, state legislatures, and local offices. The key to this success was the creation of many new districts in which minority citizens comprised a majority of the population. The backlash that followed, culminating with the Supreme Court's creation of a new constitutional claim of reverse discrimination in *Shaw v. Reno*, is well-known. Seven years after *Shaw*, with numerous Supreme Court and lower court decisions interpreting and applying that decision, the message is clear: *it is still legal to draw majority-minority districts*. Opponents of majority-minority districts like to deny that fact.

The author than highlighted the area of laws that minority could focus on to defence their rights in redistricting.[230]

However, as we may observe from the above series of news headings on the issue of redistricting from 2011 to 2013, the prospect for minority rights in American-style democracy is bleak despite the existing of written laws that make minority vote dilution illegal.

Western democracy in its current form has in many ways failed to act in the interests of minorities because it is a 'winner-takes-all' system. Racist governments like Israel's totally ignore the voices of the native Palestinians that comprise 20% of its population. Their immigration policy is based purely on race; people have to prove their Jewish blood link to migrate to Israel. Virtually all the Jewish politicians refuse to deal with elected Palestinian MPs, which results in their presence in the Israeli parliament being nothing more than a 'flower vase': a symbol for propaganda purposes so that the country can claim to be the only "democracy" in the Middle East. There was an incident of a last-minute new law being introduced by the Israeli government to cancel a scheduled election and prevent the native residents from running their own affairs. The National (7 December, 2009) had the following report:

> The vote in Abu Basma was scheduled to take place six years after the council was established under the transitional authority of a panel of mostly Jewish officials appointed by the interior ministry. Critics say the government changed the law specifically to avoid bolstering the position of the Bedouin residents, who are engaged in a legal battle with the state for the return of ancestral lands confiscated decades ago. "The Bedouin have a claim on a large area of the Negev and the government wants someone ruling the council who is on its side until the case is settled to the state's advantage," said Thabet Abu Ras, who was head of an empowerment scheme for Abu Basma's residents until 2007. The residents of Abu Basma are among 90,000 Bedouin in the Negev desert who have been denied any local representation since Israel's founding in 1948. For most of that time the state has refused to recognise any of their villages.[231]

Native Arab Parliamentarians have often been a subject of bullying and prosecution if they are persistent in defending the rights of their people. The following news headings are just some examples:

* 'Arab Politicians Face Tide of 'Persecution' in Israel – Laws set to criminalise dissident' (Global Research, 2 February, 2010) [232]
* 'Watery assault steams Israeli lawmakers' (China Daily, 10 January, 2012) [233]
* 'Israel's Persecution of Haneen Zoabi' (Global Research, 4 January, 2013) [234]

As discussed earlier, the Western voting system brought about Adolf Hitler and Nazism to Germany, which resulted in mass genocide and the destruction of property across Europe, Russia and Germany itself. Western democracies continue to deliver war-mongering governments to this day such as the Bush, Blair and Howard regimes. The work of such "democratic" governments includes manipulating intelligence reports to invade Iraq against public opinion, bombing Libya without Congressional approval, the extra-judicial killing of people by drones without trial, and setting up a network of rendition programs and torture chambers like the Guantanamo and Abu Ghraib prisons.

Most of the wars and proxy wars across the world since World War II are directly or indirectly connected to Western countries, particularly America. In fact, since 1945, America has directly or through proxies attacked more than 40 countries. (Global Research, 11 February 2007)[235] Many of the 54 countries that have co-operated with the CIA for kidnapping and torture tasks through its rendition programmes are democracies. Just to name a few, there's Canada, Sweden, Finland, Germany, Spain, Portugal, Austria, Georgia, UK, Poland, Lithuania and Romania. The comprehensive list of countries that have been involved in such wide-scale illegal CIA human rights violation programmes is compiled in a 213-page report by the New York-based Open Society Justice Initiative (OSJI) titled 'Globalizing Torture - CIA Secret Detention and Extraordinary Rendition'.[236] Unfortunately, the mainstream media are very much totally silent about this kind of documents.

China has, on the other hand, designed its democracy from the inside and extends it to the wider community through a number of mechanisms. Contrary to the perception of being an autocratic regime, as promoted by the mainstream media, the Communist Government is in many ways far more democratic and peaceful than Western governments:

Cultured democracy that is structured from within

After the fall of the Qing Dynasty in 1911, China was still a country occupied and semi-colonised by more than half a dozen foreign powers with no effective government. The country once briefly adopted a Western-style democracy with more than 300 political parties, which created more problems and divisions than solutions. The rise of the Nationalist Party (Kuomintang) under the dictatorship of Chiang Kai-shek with absolute power in 1927 had alienated the Revolutions and the entire society. The Communist Party at the time was still a very small political party with a few dozen members. However, with the right ideologies, strong leadership, and political direction, the CCP had rapidly expanded and successfully united the entire nation through attracting the alliances of other political parties and individuals; that represented a variety of interest groups across the country, including revolutionists within the Kuomintang. These political parties have on their own accord willingly acknowledged the importance of having a powerful centralised authority in China, and accepted the leadership of the Communist Party, whilst serving the system through the roles of consultation and supervision.

On 30th April 1948, the CCP, under the leadership of Chairman Mao, called for a national political consultative meeting to form a democratic alliance, which was immediately supported by Chinese communities. This was the beginning of the evolution of the 'lianghui' system, or in English, the 'two meetings' system: the Chinese People's Political Consultative Congress (CPPCC) and the National People's Congress (NPC).

In recognition that China was a huge country that could only be effectively managed under the leadership of a powerful centralised authority, the Communist Party (CCP) which had successfully led a People Revolution and ousted the dozen of colonial and imperial powers from China, was naturally the government of choice at the time.

Today, China's political system is made up of nine political parties, with the Communist Party as the ruling party, and the other eight parties as participating parties serving the roles of consultation and supervision. The names of these eight participating political parties (参政党) are:

中国国民党革命委员会 （China Kuomintang Revolutionary Committee）

中国民主同盟 （China Democratic League）

中国民主促进会 （China Democracy Promotion Association）

中国民主 建国会 (China Democracy Nation Building Association)

中国农工民主党 (China Peasants and Workers Democratic Party)

中国致公党 (China Zhi Gong Party)

九三学社 (Jiu San Society)

台湾民主自治同盟 (Taiwan Democratic Self-Government League)

[Note: The English name is my personal translation from the Chinese name]

From a simple search on the Internet using any of the Chinese names of the respective political parties, one will be able to access the background information of all the above eight democratic parties in China, including the names of their leaders (past and present), the memberships, party history, objectives and activities. One should note that, as of the end of 2012, the Communist Party had more than 85 million members, while the eight participating parties enjoying an aggregate membership of more than a million. According to the latest figures from the Organization Department of the CPC Central Committee (ECNS, 7 January, 2013),

> The CPC has 85.13 million members at the end of 2012. More than 44 percent of new members are frontline workers, such as industrial employees, farmers, herders and migrant staff. At its birth the Party had only about 50 members and this grew to nearly 4.5 million when the People's Republic of China was founded in 1949. Of the total party members, 20.27 million, or 23.8 percent, are women and 5.80 million, or 6.8 percent, are from ethnic minority groups.
>
> In terms of occupation, farmers, herders and fishers totalling 25.35 million is the largest group, while 7.25 million Party members are industrial workers.
>
> Another 7.16 million members work in Party and state agencies, and 20.20 million are managerial staff and professional technicians working in enterprises and non-profit organizations. Students make up 2.91 million.
>
> More than a quarter of members are 35 years or younger and about 34.09 million have obtained degrees in higher education institutions.
>
> The CPC had 4.20 million grassroots Party organs across the country at the end of 2012. These grassroots organs were set up in 7,245 urban subdistricts, 33,000 towns, 87,000 urban communities and 588,000 villages.
>
> The CPC trained 1.48 million village Party branch secretaries and offered employment and skills training to 15.23 million members during the year. The CPC also set up 11,000 Party organs and 456,000 service centers in order to improve the education and management of floating Party members in 2012. [237]

The evolution of the current political system in China has its historical roots, cultural background and traditions. Like the teachings of Confucius that emphasise heavily the inner qualities of an individual and the code of ethics at each level of social hierarchy, the CCP has not only accepted the consultative and supervisory roles of these democratic parties to this day, but also supported their functions with government resources. These supports include, but are not exclusively, the following:

* Inviting them to recommend competent people to fill government positions across the country from a village to central government level, so that they will not only contribute to the process of government, but also gain first-hand experience in public administration [Note: Many people did not notice that not all the government officials caught and

prosecuted for corruption over the years were members of the Communist Party. According to a Hong Kong media, Ifeng (29 June, 2011), there are 32,000 non-Communist Party personal working above county level across the country.[238]]

* Institutionalising the process of public consultation and creating multiple channels for the participating political parties and individuals to communicate their ideas and thinking at each level of governments
* A rewards system that encourages the submission of quality proposals and suggestions on social, economic and political issues (still experimenting)
* A rewards system to encourage the scrutinising of government officials for reasons such as corruption (still experimenting)
* A funding system to support the activities of participating political parties

However, these democratic parties and individuals must oblige to certain basic principles that include (but not exclusively) the following:

* The acknowledgement of the CCP as the ruling party, and that their own roles are consultative and supervisory
* The objective of socialism as the country's direction, where the end aim of government is to create an inclusive society that extends the benefits of economic prosperity to all

The logic behind such policies is that, when the working relationship between the CCP (ruling party) and the other democratic parties (participating parties) is clearly spelled out, the relationship will become corporative; not confrontational. When the common objective is to do good for the people and the country, it will encourage positive contribution to the policy's direction, instead of the confrontational approach in the case of the Western system.

In fact, in order to encourage wider community participation, the Communist Government also endorsed the emergence of hundreds of thousands of NGOs across the country to identify issues of social, political, environmental, cultural and economic importance. Yu Keping, a Professor and Director of the China Center for Comparative Politics & Economics (CCCPE), wrote an article on the East Asia Forum (9 September, 2011) with the following information:

> The CCP's general principle for social management is 'party leadership, government responsibility, social coordination and public participation'. A larger role for social organisations in social governance is an indispensable element of 'social coordination and public participation'. By 2010, there were over 450,000 registered civil organisations and 250,000

> community organisations, respectively, in China. If we take unregistered civil organisations into account also, the overall number would jump to over three million. The government has taken a cautious attitude towards civil organisations. More recently, however, top leaders have advocated the participation of social organisations in social management innovation. Top Chinese leaders even made it clear that social organisations would receive more support and encouragement from the government. In the recently adopted 12th Five-Year Plan on Social and Economic Development of China, 'pushing the development of social organisations forward' was given an unprecedented level of attention. These changes indicate that although the government has never made reference to the term 'civil society' in official documents, it now recognises its importance. [239]

In 2012, the central government allocated 200 million Chinese yuan to finance non-government organisations (NGOs). According to the China Daily (13 February, 2013), citing a report by Xinhua,

> With this fund, 377 social work projects and more than 120 training programs were carried out, with 17,700 people trained and 1.85 million directly benefited.[240]

From the perspective of some in the West, as many of these NGOs receive support from the government, it will affect the independence of these political parties and NGOs. Their concern may be valid theoretically, but in practice, such policy has to a large extent prevented these organisations from being manipulated by foreign powers and big corporations through political donations and lobbying. This helps China to avoid the existing problems in the West, where political parties and NGOs look after the interests of their donors instead of the people.

In fact, like any political system, the key factor that determines its success is the quality and beliefs of the people within the system. If the sole objective of the parties and NGOs is to better serve the people and the country without the influence of corporate money, the outcome can only be a positive one. As such, the CCP has invested in an ongoing program to educate their officials to be more open to alternative views based on reasoning, and an in-depth understanding of a variety of challenges facing the Party and the country.

Unfortunately, most Western critics of China cannot understand the Chinese language and never watch or read Chinese news. Their impression of China mainly comes from the selective, exaggerated, and in many instances, made-up stories from the mainstream media.

The CCP also institutionalised the requirement for wide-based consultation before a major policy could be up for discussion or submission to the annual CPPCC and NPC for approval. Robert Fogel, director of the Centre for Population Economics at the University of Chicago Booth School of Business, and winner of the 1993 Nobel Memorial Prize in Economics, wrote an article on Foreign Affair (January/February, 2010) titled '$123,000,000,000,000 - China's estimated economy by the year 2040. Be warned' with the following description:

> Most surprising to some, the Chinese political system is likely not what you think. Although outside observers often assume that Beijing is always at the helm, most economic reforms, including the most successful ones, have been locally driven and overseen. And though China most certainly is not an open democracy, there's more criticism and debate in upper echelons of policymaking than many realize. Unchecked mandates can of course lead to disaster, but there's a reason Beijing has avoided any repeats of the Great Leap Forward in recent years. For instance, there is an annual meeting of Chinese economists called the Chinese Economists Society. I have participated in many of them. There are people in attendance who are very critical of the Chinese government -- and very openly so. Of course, they are not going to say "down with Hu Jintao," but they may point out that the latest decision by the finance ministry is flawed or raise concerns about a proposed adjustment to the prices of electricity and coal, or call attention to issues of equity. They might even publish a critical letter in a Beijing newspaper. Then the Chinese finance minister might actually call them up and say: "Will you get some of your people together? We would like to have some of our people meet with you and find out more about what you are thinking." Many people don't realize such back-and-forth occurs in Beijing. [241]

Unlike, the Western system that encourages confrontation (the concept of 'opposition'), China has institutionalised the system into the written Constitution, which positions the Communist Party as the ruling party, and the others are participating parties serving the functions of consultation and supervision. Their right to criticise government policy, air their concerns and make proposals to the government are protected by the Constitution. Multiple channels are being created for people across the country to contribute to social policies and nation building. Such a system has resulted in quality policies being formulated over the years before submission to the CPPCC and NPC for approval into laws. The end result of such a political system is indisputably superior to the Western system due to the following reasons:

* Policies have been well-considered and widely consulted
* Policies have a long-term focus with a sense of continuity
* People who participate in the consultation process are genuinely motivated to do good for the country and without self-interests or an ulterior motive
* No time, resources and energy are wasted in smearing each other
*While different voices are heard and taken seriously within such a system of government, people remain united
* Issues that are discussed are purely targeted at issues and policies; not personal attacks with the intention to demonise the other party
* Policies can be implemented with a high level of efficiency and in good faith without political gridlock
* Mistakes will be picked up at an earlier stage and adjustments will be made in due course
* The Communist Party has become a learnt institution where positive experiences can be passed on, and negative experiences can be taken on-board to prevent repeating old mistakes
* A learnt institution (the CCP) has become the supreme authority of the country instead of a person

There is no dictator and extremism in such a system of government, as the leadership in China is subject to layers and layers of internal scrutiny and consensus in the decision making process by quality people. Low quality and know-nothing characters like George W. Bush and Arnold Schwarzenegger (USA), liars and war-mongers like Tony Blair (UK) and John Howard (Australia), or similar characters such as Sarah Palin and John McCain (USA), and Tony Abbott, Julia Gillard and Kevin Rudd (Australia) would find it hard to not be filtered away through the Chinese political process.

In addition, the policy's set 'age limit' (usually around 68 to 70 year old) to people who can serve in the system has resulted in the smooth transfer of power from older generations of leadership to the young, in a peaceful and orderly manner. [Note: In the US, only the President is subject to a two-term restriction, but no age restriction.]

Thus, the Chinese system is in sharp contrast to the Western political system, where policies are frequently shifting back and forth between ideologies with every rotation of government. In fact, under the influence of political donations and lobbying, there is now hardly any difference in policy between the major political parties. From the outset, parliamentary debates in the West appear to demonstrate "free speech" and "democracy". However, if one ever tunes on to their radio (for example, in the case of Australia, it would be 95.7FM ABC radio in South East Queensland) to listen to the live broadcast of a parliamentary debate, one will easily notice that these highly paid, low quality MPs and Ministers spent more than half the time digging dirt from the past to smear each other, rather than debating on policies. Nobody in Parliament is interested in listening to what the other parties are saying. Not only are these so-called "debates" of low quality, but also the people involved.

Low quality debates by low quality people

As illustrated earlier, the mining industry in Australia has a strong influence over government policies through political donation, advertising and lobbying. What has yet to discuss is the quality of political leadership had on the decision making process. The following is an excerpt from a report by WA Today (22 June, 2011) about the shocked of Andrew Forrest (CEO of Fortescue), in regards to the "complete lack of understanding" among federal politicians about Labor's proposed mining tax during his trip to Canberra to brief members of the government, opposition and independents about the draft laws:

> The current deal "effectively exonerates" Australia's biggest miners BHP Billiton, Rio Tinto and Xstrata from major payments ... For me the lack of understanding of that critical fact has been both a shock to the people I've briefed and a shock to myself ... Far from being a fairer share for all Australians of Australia's resources, it's almost the complete opposite ... The tax totally forgave large multinationals while punishing Australian companies such as Fortescue.[242]

Apparently, Forrest's assessment of the incompetency of Australian politicians was accurate. A report by Sydney Morning Herald (9 August, 2013) revealed the following:

> Rio Tinto has ultimately paid no mining tax to the Australian government during the first year of the controversial tax, after pre-payments made in April were refunded by the tax office. In a blow to the Labor government less than a month before the federal election, review work by Rio and the

> tax office since June 30 has shown the multinational miner was not liable to pay any tax for the 2013 financial year ... The revelation that Rio's pre-payments were refunded has raised the prospect that other companies such as BHP Billiton may have had their pre-payments refunded, too. [243]

Earlier on, we have already produced examples of low-quality political leadership in the US, this is just another example: In March 2012, former House speaker and the then presidential candidate Newt Gingrich in a speech at a GOP dinner in Chicago blasted the American political system as a 'stupid political system'. The following excerpts from Washington Post are some of the statements made by Gingrich:

> We're at the edge of extraordinary opportunities. We can provide for the American people such a dramatically better future that it's almost unimaginable ... And our political system is so methodically and deliberately stupid – and I use that word deliberately, the willful avoidance of knowledge -- that it's astonishing ... The thing I find most disheartening about this campaign is the difficulty of talking about positive ideas on a large scale because the news media can't cover it, and the other candidates, my opponents, can't comprehend it ... We have a real series of challenges. We have a deeper challenge, which you know in Springfield, which we know in Sacramento, we know in Albany, and that is that the systems of governance that we've inherited are decaying -- that we now have interest groups so powerful that democracy is simply a shadow of them floating on top of the power of the interest groups. [244]

The same situation has occurred in Britain; David Hayes, Deputy Editor of Open Democracy, analysed in an article titled 'Britain's Economic Tunnel' on the Inside Story (3 December, 2012) about politics in Britain with this observation:

> An endless recession has changed politics and livelihoods. But in a many-sided national argument there is no consensus about its lessons. [245]

An editorial on The Independent (18 September, 2012) titled 'Editorial: Our governance has yet to enter the 21st century - too often, ministers feel the need for an outsider alibi before they take decisions' rightly points out the incompetence of British politicians to make their own decisions on policy issues and having to rely heavily on outsiders to do the job for them. This raises a legitimate question about the purpose of having these politicians. This is how The Independent put it:

> One concerns democracy and how far the "tsars", like the quangos before them, really do bring a fresh perspective to policy. And the answer provided by the King's College study is that – in their profile at least – they

> represent all too often more of the same. Fewer than one in five is a "tsarina", for instance, and the vast majority are over 50. There is more than a whiff here of nice jobs for (the older) boys. Should the net not be cast much wider? Whatever the qualifications of those chosen, however, such appointments raise another question – one that goes to the heart of how Britain is governed today. If so many additional individuals and organisations are deemed necessary to policy-making, not just by the last Labour government, but by a Conservative-led Coalition, what are ministers and the country's thousands of civil servants actually for? [246]

All these problems arise from having a Western political system that is similar from country to country. In a 2011 report by the Institute of Government in the UK, one of the proposals by this British think tank was to place ministers on "regular performance review in the same way employees do in every other profession".[247] The issue here is that, without an internal party and cultured democracy like China, would Western "democracies" ever be able to hop out of the current cycle of mutual hostility, an individualistic culture, internal dictatorships, internal sectarianism, and corruption driven not solely by human greed, but the systemic problem of a political system being centred around corporate money?

The perception of Western democracies and the welfare system

The truth is that, besides the propaganda power of the Western media, the false perception of Western governments as civilised and caring is in many ways the result of the welfare system. Such welfare systems are the foundation of social stability in the West, made possible by the resources and wealth they control across the world. With careful analysis, it is not hard to realise that the foundation of many Western economies relies on four factors: advanced technologies, an educated workforce, modern management techniques, and most importantly, the cumulative advantages derived from centuries of exploitation of weaker nations' land, labour and resources. The fourth is undertaken through ongoing military aggression, proxy wars, assassination plots, covert operations, blackmail, and bullying, through the freezing of the targeted nation's assets, trade embargoes, commercial isolation and diplomatic isolation.

Not only is there a history of genocide of indigenous populations in America, Australia, Canada and New Zealand before declaring those territories and resources Western, there is also the fact that Africa has almost been exclusively under the control and looting of the West for a number of centuries until recent years. One should note that after centuries of Western slave trading and colonialism, hardly any infrastructure was built in most parts of the African continent beyond those necessary to transport resources out of the respective countries. Consequently, despite being rich in natural resources, Africa was condemned by the front cover of The Economist in the year 2000 as 'The Hopeless Continent'.[248] However, after merely a decade of intensive Chinese investment since then, the welfare of the continent enjoyed a 180-degree U-turn, with The Economist changing its assessment with an article in 2011 titled 'The Hopeful Continent - Africa Rising'.[249] Not surprisingly, one can hardly find any praise from the mainstream media about China's positive contribution to Africa besides portraying China as 'neo-colonialist'. I will have a chapter on Africa in one of the upcoming instalments.

Since August 1945, America has directly or indirectly, through NATO and proxies; attacked more than 40 countries. There are more than 1,100 American military bases across the globe,[250] and drone operations in 76 countries.[251] A report by an award-winning investigative reporter Dave Lindorff on the Global Research (2010) revealed that America spent "more than 53% of tax bill on military".[252] If wars weren't profitable, it is hard to imagine how a country could sustain its economy by injecting 53% of its tax bill on warfare.

However, the world has changed in the 21st century. Modern management, an educated workforce and technological advancements no longer provide an absolute advantage for the West on the world stage. Military aggression has increasingly become too expensive to be profitable. In the cases of Iraq and Afghanistan, a locally-made improvised road-side bomb, and bombs strapped around human bodies have proven to be an effective measure against the powerful and barbaric invasion forces. Without the ability to continue making money through wars and looting, the West has apparently lost its ability to revive their economy through the free market system under the conditions of non-violence and fair competition. As a result, we observe an emerging pattern of trade protectionism in US and Europe, from telecommunication products to solar panels; which will do nothing to revive the economy, but will instead be harmful to free trade and the world economy.

The flaws of the Western political system have increasingly shown up when national debt, unemployment, the cost of living, suicide, bankruptcy, homelessness and poverty are all on the rise; while developing countries under the leadership of China continue to grow. A 2011 IMF report noted that since 2007, China has contributed more - much more to world growth than any country.[253] Sjamsu Rahardja, a senior economist for the World Bank country office in Indonesia pointed out in an article on the East Asia Forum (9 August, 2012) that "China contributes up to 80 percent of GDP in developing East Asia." [254]

The false perception of Western political systems as being civilised, humane, democratic, and superior is quickly diminishing when street protests are increasingly met with mass arrests, tear gas, tasers, and police brutalities. In a way, this may be a good thing for the world, as it is time for the Western public to realise that their political system in its current form does not ensure good governance, human rights, freedom and a strong economy. Such a realisation will hopefully help to liberate the world's nations from decades of Western oppression in selectively dictating what kind of political system nations should adopt.

The world's nations have been deprived for far too long their freedom to explore and experiment with political systems that best suit their unique cultures, customs, ethnic mixes, and economic conditions. A recent report on East Asia Forum (5 October, 2013) revealed that "PNG (Papua New Guinea) has persisted with a Westminster system since before its independence in 1975." However, "no one party has ever won enough seats to rule outright in the single-chamber parliament, resulting in a high degree of political instability, seemingly endless cabinet reshuffles and a series of votes of no confidence." As a result of such ongoing political instability and gridlock, the "PNG Constitutional Law Reform Commission is currently scrutinising the viability of PNG's Westminster system of government."[255]

Several years ago, troubled with the ongoing instability with its Westminster system of government, the Bainimarama government of Fiji decided to reform its political system and was met with hostility from Australia. However, the rise of China has provided the Fijian government with alternative source of trading relation. A report by New Zealand based Scoop news (1 August, 2012) titled 'Australia's humiliating backdown over failed foreign policy on Fiji' with the following description:

> So it has finally come. Oceania's greatest power – Australia – has finally bowed to the inevitable. That five-and-a-half-years of trying to destroy the Bainimarama government in Fiji has failed. That one of its island satellites has thumbed its nose at its big neighbour and determined its own course in the world. [256]

'One-size-fits-all' political system?

It is important to note that there are no two identical political systems between countries due to disparities in histories, cultures, ethnic mixes, traditions and economic conditions. Even among Western countries, there are different administrative systems; the most common one includes the presidential system, parliamentary system, and constitutional Monarchy, whereby the taxpayers are made to pay for the lifestyle of a special group of people, who by birth or marriage are linked to a special class of families in the society. Even among those with a presidential system, there are differences between the American system and the French one. The voting system is also different from country to country. For example, there is the 'first-past-the-post', where the majority within an election constituency call the shots, and the 'proportionate representation' system, where the number of seats in parliament is decided by the total percentage of votes received nationwide or within a state. There is also the uniquely Australian 'preferential voting system', where voters mark their ballot paper with numbers right next to the names of the candidates in order of preference so that when no candidate wins an outright majority on their primary (1) votes, the secondary (2) and third (3) preferences will do the job.

The Switzerland democracy was created after a civil war in 1847, so the political system was designed to accommodate various tribal regions in the country. There is no full-time president in Switzerland; the representational functions of a president are taken over by one (or all) of the government members. Every year, another member of the government team is elected as federal president so that every government member assumes this role once in seven years. The president is 'primus inter pares' (first among equals) with very limited special powers.[257]

Each of these Western political and voting systems has its merits and shortcomings and is derived from a long history of conflict and bloodshed. The important lesson here is for nations to learn to respect each other's rights to create their own political system that best suits their unique national conditions.

We were told that Saddam Hussein was an evil man; but under his leadership, Iraqis - particularly Shia, Sunni and Christians - at least managed to coexist peacefully without the daily sectarian violence and bloodshed that we now witness. There may have been incidents of the use of chemical weapons against the Kurdish people in Iraq under Hussein, but the complex background of these incidents was not properly explained by the mainstream media. One thing's for sure, however: Saddam Hussein was once an ally of the West, and the chemical weapons and loans he received to attack Iran and the Kurds were mainly from the US government.[258] In addition, the number of Kurds killed because of Saddam is by no means comparable to the number of Iraqi deaths as a result of Western economic sanctions and invasions. A Global Research report (6 December, 2012) cited a statement made by Professor Francis Boyle of the Kuala Lumpur War Crimes Tribunal with the following death statistics:

> Approximately 3.3 million Iraqis, including 750,000 children, were "exterminated" by economic sanctions and/or illegal wars conducted by the U.S. and Great Britain between 1990 and 2012.[259]

The trial of Western politicians in a Malaysian court for war crimes did not attract the attention of the mainstream media, so the Western public is largely ignorant about the level of atrocities their government has committed in Iraq. The same situation applies to many other countries such as Afghanistan, Libya and Syria. Western governments provide no solid justification to bomb and destroy much of a nation's infrastructure and cause millions of deaths, injuries and refugees to promote "human rights" and "democracy". Such an act of state terrorism and state-sponsored proxy terrorism is itself undemocratic and inhumane. The issue here is that, by directly or indirectly causing the deaths of millions of people in the name of promoting democracy and human rights, the behaviour of 21st century Western governments are no different from the Crusaders in the Roman Empire, who slaughtered their way to force people to accept Christianity. This is one of the reasons why I passionately believe that there is a general lack of democratic culture among Western elites, whom unfortunately have always been a powerful force behind Western politics and the mainstream media, which is unfortunate for many genuine rights defenders in the West such as Edward Snowden, Bradley Manning and Julian Assange.

A case for regime change in the West using Western logic

In retrospect, most Western democracies only began allowing their minorities the right to vote in elections a few decades ago. For example, in Australia, the state only regarded the native Aborigines as human beings, and automatically included them in the national population census after the 1967 referendum.[260] Prior to 1962, there was still a restriction on Aboriginal rights to vote in elections; Queensland was the last state to remove such a restriction in 1965.[261] The White Australia Policy only ended in the 1970s.[262] However, despite most Australians being good people, modern Australia is still very much a racist country. The reasons are simple:

To this day (2013), the racially biased Australian Constitution has yet to recognise the indigenous people in a positive way.[263] Despite the Royal Commission Inquiry into Aboriginal Deaths in Custody (1998) having 339 recommendations for reform, much of this has not been implemented. Today, among those behind bars in Australia, indigenous Australians, that only comprise 2 percent of the general population, account for 26 percent of the prison population. [264]

The number of Aboriginal deaths in custody has risen sharply over the last five years, and is in line with an almost doubling of the number of Aboriginal Australians being locked up. (ABC, 24 May, 2013)[265] A recent high court ruling found that, "from the late 1990s, prison sentences had lengthened disproportionately for indigenous offenders," and suggested that "Judges will need to consider the Aboriginal background of an offender when sentencing them." (The Age, 3 October, 2013)[266]

There are numerous incidents of police brutality against indigenous Australians, just a few examples below for people to have an idea on the level of brutality:

There was an incident of an Aboriginal person (Mr. Ward) being arrested for drink-driving, and later found cooked to death in a prison van at a temperature of 50 degrees Celsius (122 degrees Fahrenheit) due to faulty air conditioning. Despite a coroner inquiry found that the state's Department of Corrective Services, the security officers, and their employer had all contributed to the man death, no charges were laid against any of the parties. (The Telegraph, 28 June, 2010)[267] Another incident had an indigenous person arrested for public drunkenness, and found dead soon after with four broken ribs, a cleaved liver, a ruptured portal vein and face injuries (Townsville Bulletin, 9 March, 2010).[268] Despite court hearing, and the fact that the man died less than an hour after a struggle with the police officer, the officer involved in the case was acquitted at a manslaughter trial, and an inquest held in 2010 was unable to determine whether the fatal injuries were inflicted deliberately or by accident. (Brisbane Times, 24 May, 2011)[269] There was also an incident of an Aboriginal woman, who had been pregnant for eight months, tasered up to 8 times by police. She ended up with a lot of bruises on her "from where she was handcuffed, and burn marks from the tasering." (WA Today, 15 October, 2010)[270] Yet another incident involved an Aboriginal Australian sitting quietly in a police station being suddenly attacked by a group of police officers with tasers. This case only came to light after a video was posted on social media and went viral on the internet (WA Today, 24 February, 2011).[271] Later investigations found that the Aboriginal man was tasered 40 times in a week by the police officers (WA Today, 11 April, 2013). [272]

Ironically, in the land with a mouthful of "human rights", none of these police officers were actually punished besides a court hearing in some cases and a fine of between AU$750 to AU$1,200. Some of the police officers involved in these cases of violence against Aboriginal Australians have even been promoted. In fact, the legal bills of these police officers were paid by the Police Union, and the state government reimbursed the Police Union up to 75 cents for every dollar. (Brisbane Times, 21 May 2011) [273]

In 2011, I contacted some of the "free-Tibet" Australian politicians such as Hanson Young and Bob Brown with the submission of a 248-page book I wrote that linked racism to massive human rights violations in Australia. I requested these 'free-Tibet' politicians to address the issue of racism in Australia, and the more than 2,200 deaths in institutional custody (both Aboriginal and non-Aboriginal), with 22 deaths without any classification on the causes of their deaths due to "missing data". I also highlighted the fact that there were a high percentage of indigenous deaths in custody being classified as dying of natural causes; yet, up to 44 percent of the indigenous deaths in prison custody were Aborigines younger than 25 years. However, I was met with total silence from these "human rights" politicians. Hypocrisy and double standards towards human rights are increasingly a source of world resentment against the West.

Even now, Aboriginal people in Australia are still subjected to enormous levels of racial discrimination, and have a life expectancy up to 20 years shorter than the nation's average (UN report, 14 January, 2010).[274] A report by Joel Orenstein at NACLC Conference Perth (18 September, 2009) titled 'Being Nobody' revealed that up to 13% of Aboriginal Australians in Koori, Victoria do not have a birth certificate, and are deprived of their basic human rights to exercise the basic rights of citizenship such as:

- Obtaining drivers license
- Enrolling to vote
- Opening bank account
- Enrolling in School
- Obtaining tax file number
- Receiving social security benefits
- Obtain passport
- Visit prison
- Prove ID to police [275]

In other region of Australia, Aboriginal health and living conditions are regarded as equal to or below third-world standards. Yet, there was been an incident of a local government in Adelaide (South Australia) threatening to order police and dogs to chase away Aboriginal Australians if they dared to migrate to their community. In fact, there is strong evidence that many announcements made by the Australian government over the years to improve the well-being of native Australians are nothing more than lip-service for the consumption of the media and international community. Opinion polls over the years have consistently indicated around 70 to 80% of the Australian population having either witnessed or experienced some form of racism, or believe that Australia is a racist country. I will get into all these in greater detail with proper documentation in one of the upcoming instalments.

One should note that the indigenous culture and languages in Australia had been virtually totally extinguished since Captain Cook set foot on this continent. Today, we can hardly find any indigenous Australians living in major cities, or indigenous Australians who can speak their own language. The first and only so-called indigenous free-to-air TV channel (NITV on SBS) was launched on 12 December, 2012. The fascinating thing is that they sing in the morning and late night in English, while the Tibetan Chinese in China still speak their own language, not subject to China's 'one-child policy' and have their life-expectancy doubled since the Communist Government took over China in 1949. However, Western politicians and the media continue to relentlessly demonise China for cultural genocide in Tibet. We will get into this in a later instalment.

Given the human rights record of Australia against minorities, should the US-led Western coalition impose economic sanctions against Australia in the name of a "humanitarian intervention"? Should they cause widespread poverty across the country by crippling the currency, banking system, social services, and international supply chains for medicine, machineries and raw materials through a series of trade embargoes and economic sanctions? Should they secretly finance, train and arm the Aboriginal rebels and force the Australian government to respond with military means, and then use that as an excuse to declare a 'no-fly zone' in Australia, then "target-bomb" military facilities, government buildings, power plants, political leaders residential compounds, communication networks and water litigation systems? If that fails to topple the brutal Australian regime, universities, hospitals, factories, TV stations, warehouses and residential areas would then be identified as 'suspicious sites' for further bombing. Eventually, direct invasion would be used to install a new Aboriginal government. Should we have a well funded 'Free Aborigines' campaign at international level?

The reality is if we want to make a case for regime change in any country using small stories like what I have just done to Australia, it isn't very hard at all. In fact, this is specifically the kind of technique utilised by America and NATO prior to every military action. The important question is that, will this enhance human rights and good governance? Is there justification to destroy the lives and livelihood of millions in a country to promote "human rights"?

The truth is that if a regime has lost the support of the majority in a country, the people of that country will remove the regime without foreign intervention. There are thousands of such examples in the world's history of people revolutions, including the 1986 People Power Revolution in the Philippines that removed the US government-backed Marcos regime,[276] the 1979 Iranian Revolution that overthrew the US and UK-backed Pahlavi Dynasty,[277] the 2011 Egyptian Revolution that ended the Western-backed Mubarak regime,[278] and the dissolution of the USSR in 1991[279] are just a fraction of the examples. These cases demonstrate the people's will do the job themselves when the time comes. When the decision to remove a regime is made by the masses without foreign intervention and military aggression, the transition is usually more peaceful and smooth. However, when it is done through foreign aggression like with Afghanistan, Iraq, and Libya, there will be decades of chaos and bloodshed that follow. Therefore, the most humane thing the West can do for the rest of the world is to mind their own business. The West should try to improve their own human rights records, and perfect their own 'worst form of political system' before trying to claim superiority and force the world to accept a specific line of thinking and political model.

The Truth

Western voting system

As illustrated throughout the book, so-called Western democracies in their current form are nothing more than a voting system. It is by no means democratic, or a representation of a legitimate government or an assurance for good governance, social fairness, justice, inclusion and harmony. To this day, there is absolutely no supporting evidence to suggest that the current form of Western political system has a well established theoretical framework that will uphold the objectives of good governance, human rights, and fairness to all. The merits of the Western political system in its current form are unable to sustain scrutiny in terms of its internal design, structure, process, and performance. The assertion by Winston Churchill that, "Democracy is the worst form of government except for all those others that have been tried," may have been somewhat an accurate perception in his time when the entire world had been colonised and obliterated into poverty, but is no more in the 21st century when the absolute advantage, wealth and power derived from centuries of looting and exploitation of others' land, resources and labours are rapidly diminishing.

Without the backing of a strong economy, people will eventually realise that their admiration of the West has all along been an illusion created by their material lifestyles and welfare programmes made possible through centuries of bullying and exploitation of others. Beyond the media rhetoric and propaganda power of the mainstream media, there is increasing awareness among the world's people that there is no such thing as Western values in the way their political system works. There is nothing that the West has alleged others – whether it being income inequality, dictatorship, corruption, human rights violations or media censorship - that the West did not themselves commit the same crimes at some point in the past, and continues to commit the same crimes to this day. The only difference is that the West do not have the basic moral value - 'the sense of shame' – while committing human rights violations at least as deplorable as those it was criticising; the West seek to distract attention from their own human rights problems by criticising others.

In fact, in many instances, the West is the master of all these crimes. Through the good work of some genuine Western freedom fighters and human rights campaigners like Bradley Manning, Julian Assange, Edward Snowdon and many other righteous former Western whistleblowers who had been murdered or likely to have been murdered by Western authorities such as Dr. David Kelly,[280] we now know that what the American military and NATO did in Iraq and Afghanistan constituted a war crime; we also realise how notorious the level of privacy intrusions against the world's citizens and Western citizens by Western governments; and the level of collusion between Western governments and corporations (including Google, Facebook, Apple and Microsoft, etc) in spying on their own citizens on an unprecedented scale in the history of governance. [281]

As the flaws of the current form of Western voting system have already been outlined earlier, I will not repeat them here. However, I would like to use a few more examples to reinforce the fact that there is no such thing as a perfect political system, and that all civilisations should make an effort for ongoing self-improvement instead of smearing others.

In countries where voting is voluntary like the US and Japan, the number of voters that turn out for voting is usually around 50% - sometimes higher and sometimes lower. Therefore, in a numerical sense, President Obama narrowly defeated Mitt Romney (50% to 48%) in the 2012 election[282] can only be regarded as having around 30% (or below) of the total eligible votes; his election win does not reflect the actual will of most voters in the entire pool of eligible voters. A report by PEW (26 December, 2012) titled 'The Growing Electoral Clout of Blacks Is Driven by Turnout, Not Demographics' pointed out the following:

> Blacks voted at a higher rate this year than other minority groups and for the first time in history may also have voted at a higher rate than whites ... Unlike other minority groups whose increasing electoral muscle has been driven mainly by population growth, blacks' rising share of the vote in the past four presidential elections has been the result of rising turnout rates.[283]

An article on the Washington post (25 October, 2012) titled '2012 voters: The biggest racial split since' 88' highlighted the racial components in the voting pattern:

> The 2012 election is shaping up to be more polarized along racial lines than any presidential contest since 1988, with President Obama lagging behind Republican Mitt Romney among white voters by 21 percentage points, a steep drop in support from four years ago. As he did in 2008, Obama gets overwhelming support from non-whites, who made up a record high proportion of the overall electorate four years ago. In that contest, 80 percent of all non-whites supported Obama, including 95 percent of black voters, according to the exit poll. In the Washington Post-ABC News national tracking poll released Wednesday, Obama wins 79 percent of non-whites, and support for his reelection is nearly universal among African Americans.[284]

Therefore, the election of Obama as president is by no means a representation of the people's will. The American political system is not as inclusive as people are made to believe. Like the case in Hawaii, the voting pattern on the American mainland is very much based on racial lines as well. This is specifically the reason behind an effort by some in America to restrict the voting rights of minorities through a series of corrupt and manipulative redistricting processes as mentioned earlier. In addition, we also notice from earlier information that since the election of Obama as president in 2008, there was a wholesales rejection of black politicians in America in the past five years. In short, the Western voting system only allows people to feel good when they are the absolute majority in the country. As a result, we also notice that the American media is so worried about the population trend soon after the election of their first black president in 2008, that they have repeatedly since 2008 (year-on-year) reminded Americans about the possibility that the majority will become minority.

We also noticed the recent decision by the American Supreme Court to change a five-decade law that protected the voting rights of minorities. This prompted AlterNet (25 June, 2013) to raise alarm with an article that highlighted the issue with a powerful heading: 'Supreme Court's Right-Wing Clique Guts the Voting Rights Act -- After Five Decades of Protecting Minorities, Suddenly, It's 'Unconstitutional''. [285]

Of course, there are merits with the current form of Western voting system as well. One of the most significant merits is its function in releasing "steam" from a "pressure cooker": the frequent rotations of power between the two equally self-centred, corrupt and incompetent major political parties create the false perception of choice and freedom. Such an illusion has the effect of releasing the "steam" (tension and frustration) amongst voters from their dissatisfaction for the government of the day. At a time of economic prosperity, such voter frustration against the government can also be stabilised by a well-funded welfare programme. However, with a prolonged period of budget austerity, high unemployment, rising cost of living, homelessness and poverty, the magical effect of such an illusion will diminish. Like the case of violence crackdowns on protestors in Germany (The Independent, 31 May 2013 with an image),[286] Spain (The Guardian, 15 November,

2012 with images),[287] Slovenia (Before its News, 30 November, 2012 with images),[288] UK (The Guardian, 12 June, 2013 with images),[289] Sweden (MWC News, 22 May, 2013),[290] USA (RT, 14 March, 2013 with images)[291] and many other parts of Europe, the stability of Western societies is clearly an issue directly linked to the economy, rather than the "superiority" of their voting system. [Note: To view more images of police brutality in the West, simply search on YouTube using terms such as 'Australia police brutality', 'US police brutality', or 'UK Police brutality', and one will be shocked by images not seen on their TV screens. One thing is for sure: if those images were from China, it would be broadcasted internationally to every TV screen with the narration: "the brutal Communist regime".]

The truth is that the economy is the foundation of social stability, relative freedom and human rights. These are the very reasons why Western countries systematically and relentlessly use their military and economic power to unfairly impose all kinds of trade and financial restrictions against countries who dare to persuade an independent policy, such as Iran, North Korea and Cuba. Such trade and financial restrictions are designed to keep these countries poor and unstable. China is so far the only country with an independent national policy that has managed to make use of the Cold War, international relations, its hardworking population, its size, innovation and commercial skills to move out of the Western shadow. The rapid rise of China helps liberate the world from the exclusive manipulation of the West. A multi-polar world with fairer international relations is in the making. This is also the very reason why the developing world has managed to weather the 2008 global financial crisis while most Western countries are in trouble with rising debt, poverty and social unrest. It is also the very reason why many Latin American nations dare to openly defy the will of the imperialistic American regime after centuries of being oppressed.

Without the backing of a strong economy, governments produced under Western democracies not only enjoy a very low level of citizen satisfaction, but their legitimacy is also increasingly questionable.

In an interview with the New York Times (27 July, 2013), Obama warned that, "racial tensions in America are likely to deteriorate if greater efforts are not made to narrow the rich-poor divide and create jobs for hard-pressed ordinary Americans ... The lingering effects of the financial crisis had frayed the country's social fabric and undermined American's belief in opportunity." [292]

George Friedman, founder and chairman of Stratfor, put up an article (5 March, 2013) with a title appropriately pointing out the relationship between the economy and social stability in Europe: 'Europe, Unemployment and Instability'. [293]

The truth is that it is the state of an economy that ensures social stability and human rights; not the Western voting system. The chaos in Egypt prompted Christian Science Monitor (2 August, 2013) to point out the reality that, "struggling Egyptians are more concerned with putting food on the table than democracy."[294] Just search the Internet using the term 'failure democracy', and one will be presented with millions of links to examples of why democracies failed in many countries; particularly developing countries. The notion that Western democracies are the solution to many problems is simply disinformation created by the powerful Western propaganda media machine through the techniques of smearing against others, and the censorship of other success stories. The reality is that, without a powerful economy, even the process of integration within European Union, an award winning organisation (2012 Noble Peace Prize) is in trouble. According to Stratfor (6 March, 2013), the integration process has being on a stand-still. The exact wording used by Stratfor is "Europe stalling integration'.[295]

More accurately, Europe is now haunted by separatism, and is no longer as stable and harmonious as in recent memory. The reason I use the term 'in recent memory' to describe European harmony is because the entire European history is filled with violence and sectarianism, far worse than many other civilisations. After the two World Wars (started in Europe), Europe has divided into two camps: Eastern and Western Europe. Setting aside the Balkan War and the bombing of Serbia in the 1990s, Europe has only enjoyed two decades of relative peace. Gordon N. Bardos, a Balkan politics and security expert based in New York has this observation on The National Interest (17 January, 2013) about the rising separatism in Europe:

> The spectre of separatism seems to be hovering over Europe these days. From Belgium, Britain and the Balkans to Catalonia and the Caucasus, regional independence or autonomy movements are gaining strength

> everywhere. And unless the European Union comes to grips with its current existential crisis, history suggests they could become...[296]

The latest is the dispute between Britain and Spain over the territory of Gibraltar where the British immediately dispatched their warships as response. (Scrape TV, 12 August, 2013)[297] However, as this is a dispute between two Western democracies, the mainstream media did not pay a lot of attention, or portray the move by Britain to dispatch warships as an act of aggression.

A well-researched webpage on Global Issue (25 September, 2005) titled 'Military expansion serving economic objectives' has a collection of links to a number of great articles and research that explains the relationship between the never ending Western aggression across the globe and the economic incentives of those military actions. Here is the link to that webpage:

> http://www.globalissues.org/article/449/military-expansion-serving-economic-objectives

As mentioned earlier, when military aggression no longer profitable, the flaws of the Western voting system have increasingly become unbearable. An article by David Hayes, Deputy Editor of Open Democracy (2003 to 2012) on Insight (25 July, 2013) titled 'A politics out of time' had this opening statement about the inability of the British political system to cope with mounting problems:

> The scale of Britain's problems leaves its party and electoral systems struggling to catch up.

From the information produced by the article, we notice that the problems that arise from the British voting system are similar to Australia; namely the influence of corporate money, the lack of quality political leadership, out of touch politicians, declining party membership, internal party dictatorship, and corruption in the leadership succession process. The following is just an excerpt:

> The inability of parties and governments to deliver on their promises, the subordination of parliament to private interests, the gap between a cloistered Westminster and a restless society, the sense of a privileged elite gorging on the illicit benefits of power while millions of playing-by-the-book citizens struggle – it's a picture that leads many observers to the conclusion that, beneath the surface drama and noise, the deep structures of British politics are eroding.

As for the decline in party membership, the following information from the article is exactly identical to the trend in Australia:

> Conservatives' biggest problem is much more than cyclical. The party is depleting: it has fewer than 130,000 members compared with three million in the early 1950s ... Their average age is sixty-eight. Labour's membership, too, is shrinking: it has 193,000 members, against over a million in the early 1950s [298]

Given the current trend of dramatic economic decline in the West that threatens social stability and basic human rights for food, housing, employment, health and basic social services, it is unavoidable that Western societies will need to face up to their currently outdated and inferior form of political model. The Independent UK (9 August, 2013) has fired a shot with this heading: 'British politics at a crossroads: Disenchantment with Westminster sees party membership plummet'. [299]

This is a good sign: we need more of this in the Western media. When Western countries begin to humble themselves, acknowledge the flaws in their current form of inferior political system, and stop promoting democracy as justification for international aggression, the world will then be able to enjoy the freedom to explore political models that best suit their unique local conditions. The Western public will then be able to enjoy the freedom to receive information on the success of other cultures, and benefit from the positive experience of other civilisations.

As discussed earlier, the problem arises from having a Western voting system that is similar from country to country, regardless of if it is in the West or elsewhere. The behaviour of people within a political institution is very much dictated by the design of the political system. In Japan, with a prolonged period of economic stagnation, we have witnessed a frequent change of political leadership with no solution to the nation's problems. There are 17 Prime Ministers in Japan between the periods 1989 to 2013; [300] that is, 17 Prime Ministers within 14 years - an average survival rate of political leadership in Japan is around 10 months. Like its Western counterparts, the quality of the political leadership in Japan is also highly questionable. A couple of the latest examples follow:

(1) In January 2013, Taro Aso, the current deputy prime minister, and former prime minister (24 September, 2008 – 16 September, 2009) urged old people in Japan to "hurry up and die" so as to alleviate the government's financial burden. This is an excerpt from

Sydney Morning Herald (23 January, 2013) titled 'Hurry up and die, Japan deputy PM tells old folk':

> Japan's deputy prime minister has been forced to apologise after suggesting that old people should "hurry up and die" to save the state the cost of providing them with medical care. Taro Aso, 72, who was speaking at a meeting of the National Council on Social Security Reforms, described patients with serious illnesses as "tube persons" and said they should be "allowed to die quickly" if they wanted to. "Heaven forbid I should be kept alive if I want to die," he said. "You cannot sleep well when you think it's all paid by the government. This won't be solved unless you let them hurry up and die."[301]

This incident reflects the lack of ideas on the part of Japanese politicians to come out with a viable solution to the problems relating to the aging population and the two decades of economic stagnation. On another occasion, Taro Aso raised alarm in Asia by suggesting that Japan can learn from Nazi tactics by quietly removing article 9 from the peace constitution that bans Japan from military aggression abroad. Such a ban was imposed upon Japan by the US soon after WWII. The following is an excerpt from The Wall Street Journal (31 July, 2013):

> Japan's finance minister expressed regret Thursday over the furor caused by his recent remarks about Nazi Germany, saying he wants to retract the remarks ... During a speech Monday, Mr. Aso--who also serves as deputy prime minister and was once prime minister--said Japan should learn how Germany's constitution under the Weimar Republic was transformed by the Nazis before anybody realized what was happening. "Germany's Weimar Constitution was changed before anyone noticed. It was changed before anyone was aware. Why don't we learn from that technique."[302]

(2) The above depict the personal qualities of current Japan Deputy Prime Minister; how about the Prime Minister himself? An analysis in EX-SKF (24 April, 2013) about TPP (Trans-Pacific Partnership) pointed out the fact that, while the Abe administration campaigned for Japan to join the TPP proposed by the US, he admitted that he did not know much about what was involved. The following is an excerpt:

> As far as Japan goes, the media and the Abe administration have been breathlessly touting the numerous benefits of joining the trade block, while the prime minister himself has admitted he doesn't clearly know what's involved. But not to worry, TPP will help pull Japan from 2 decades in the economic and societal doldrums! No one clearly explains how. [303]

Like the West, not only did Japan's voting system fail to produce quality leadership, but also the entire political system in Japan was designed for politicians to oppose each other for personal gain at the expense of the national interest as well. Political gridlock in Japan's parliament is no less severe than the American Congress. Michael Cucek, a Research Associate at the MIT Center for International Studies posted an article on East Asia Forum (16 December, 2012) titled 'Japan's nothing election' with the following observation:

> There was no ideological clash behind either act of self-sacrifice: the opposition was simply saying 'no' to everything the DPJ-led government proposed. Opposition intransigence reached an absurd zenith in August, with the LDP voting to condemn a bill it had voted for only two months earlier and refusing to approve a bill it itself had authored.[304]

In Taiwan, while the US government-funded career dissident Chen Guangcheng claimed in his June trip to Taiwan that "Taiwan can be a political model for China" (VOA, 24 June, 2013),[305] a Taiwanese media, Focus Taiwan News Channel (30 June, 2013) thinks otherwise with an article titled 'Taiwan struggling with democracy'. The following is an excerpt from the report:

> Taiwan has gained international media attention lately for the repeated chaos that has erupted in legislative sessions, with lawmakers falling over each other. President Ma Ying-jeou's approval rating has repeatedly hit new lows, and it has almost become conventional wisdom that Ma's administration is incompetent, lacks direction and is inconsistent in making policy. Taiwan's overall situation is deteriorating, and its industrial, financial, education and media policies are riddled with problems, even when everybody agrees immediate steps are needed to tackle the country's brain drain, high unemployment, soaring housing prices and the volunteer military system. The media, which has failed to fulfil its obligation by providing reports that are neither objective nor balanced, has made things worse by fostering judgmental audiences who lack international vision, are full of negative emotions, and like to criticize government policies without any attempt at rational analysis ... Taiwan's political parties are exaggerating the shortcomings of the pact for their own interests at the expense of the country's long-term development, and we want to ask if this approach reflects loving Taiwan or selling it out.[306]

The above short description of Taiwanese politics by a Taiwanese media already tells us that by having a Western-style voting system, Taiwan is having the same problems that any Western democracy experiences. An article on The Economist (17 November, 2012) revealed that the popularity of President Ma has plummeted to a record low of 13 percent. And that "Ordinary people do not find their livelihoods improving. Salaries have stagnated for a decade." [307] On a 15 September 2013 poll, Ma's approval rating traced a new low of 9.2 percent.[308]

It is hard to image that when a political system fails so miserably from country to country in fostering competent leadership, it should be promoted worldwide as the only form of legitimate government.

Soon after the 1986 People Power Revolution in the Philippines that removed the US government-backed Marcos regime, Philippines was once held by the West as the model for democracy in Asia. However, beyond the media rhetoric, what democracy actually brought to the Philippines was the so-called 3G: Gun, Goons and Gold. The following news headings over a period of 21 years tell us that the so-called democracy in the Philippines had led to nothing more than corruption, violence, cheating and chaos:

- Los Angeles Times (10 February, 1992) titled "Guns, Goons, Gold' Time in Philippines: Election: Authorities brace for traditional violence and cheating as campaigns get underway' [309]
- BBC (30 January, 1998) titled 'Democracy Philippines-style' with this statement: "There's a saying among Filipinos that what decides elections here are guns, goons and gold: gold being the money to bribe the voters, guns being the alternative method of persuading those voters who you can't bribe, and goons being the thugs who wield their guns." [310]
- Jakarta Post (1 December, 2009) titled 'The Philippines politics: guns, goons, god and the war on terror' [311]
- The Inquirer (5 November, 2010) titled 'The 4th G to Guns, Goons, Gold: Glitches' [312]
- Balita (15 February, 2013) titled 'Guns, Goons and Gold are back' [313]

It is not hard to observe from these news headings for the periods 1992 to 2013 that democracy in the Philippines fails to change a thing about violence and corruption in the society. Many unnamed civilians including children, women, journalists and election candidates peril in the course of each election campaign. However, because it is a Western-style democracy, no mainstream media or Western politician will question the legitimacy of the respective Filipino governments produced under the supposedly "superior" Western voting system.

Chinese Socialist Consultative Democracy

Besides what has already been discussed, including the annual surveys by PEW and Professor Tony Saich that shown the Communist Government in China consistently enjoying a very high level of people satisfaction; a Tokyo-based international current affair magazine, The Diplomat (14 June, 2013) titled 'Government for the people in China?' [314] by Wenfang Tang, Michael S. Lewis-Beck, and Nicholas F. Martin also disputed the political commentaries in the media that frequently portray a "growing level of dissatisfaction" towards "the ruling of the Communist Party." In a major national face-to-face survey conducted by the authors (Wenfang Tang, Michael S. Lewis-Beck, and Nicholas F. Martin) with results published in the Political Research Quarterly titled 'A Chinese Popularity Function: Sources of Government Support', [315] the authors also uncovered an "extremely high level of public satisfaction" towards the Beijing government. Based on the responses from a national random sample of 3,763 Chinese, the authors found that "the average person's support for the government in Beijing was about 8.0 on a 10-point scale." According to the authors, "this result is consistent with calculations from other recent surveys. For example, according to the 6th Wave World Values Survey (http://www.worldvaluessurvey.org/), conducted at the end of 2012 and beginning of 2013, the average level of support among Chinese respondents was 7.50 on a 0-10 scale." The authors then explained that:

> This level of support compares favourably with many democratically elected governments across the world. From these numbers, then, the Chinese government hardly appears on the verge of collapse, as some commentators would have it. Instead, our research shows that, with respect to the political psychology of the Chinese people, political trust – a belief in the legitimacy of the government – appears as the dominant reason for their broad support of the political system.

The authors then examine the number of theories that have been advanced to explain the Chinese people's high level of public trust in government, and that the public opinion polls in China are simply not accurate. These theories include:

- In a repressive society like China, people are too afraid to tell researchers what they really believe
- Media censorship

- Economic performance
- Confucianism

The authors then dismissed each and every of the above theories point by point and highlighted the fact that the Chinese government is more open to free speech, street protests and public activism than what have been portrayed by political commentators. The authors then insist that it is the responsiveness of the Communist Government to address issues of people dissatisfaction that enables the government to enjoy such an extremely high level of people satisfaction. This is the link to the well-researched article:

> http://thediplomat.com/2013/06/17/government-for-the-people-in-china/2/?all=true

It is extremely difficult to find any mainstream journalists writing anything positive about the Chinese government. I can only find a handful of positive reports about China on some very rare occasions - once or twice a year or perhaps longer - and only in certain publications such as The Times, The UK Telegraph and The Guardian. I should say that such positive or semi-positive reports about China would only occur once in every hundreds, perhaps thousands of negative reports. We could perhaps regard such a phenomenon as a Western-style "balanced" reporting. However, there is a common characteristic when a positive remark is made about China; that is, in most cases, these journalists or writers are unlikely to compare the positive performance of the Chinese government to Western governments. For example:

Austin Ramzy's article (Time, 19 January, 2010) titled 'Haiti and China - A Tale of Two Earthquakes' comparing the speedy response of the Chinese government towards the 2008 earthquake in Sichuan to the snail pace of the Haitian government towards their 2010 earthquake. This is how Ramzy described what he witnessed six months after the Sichuan earthquake:

> I went back to Sichuan six months after the catastrophe and was amazed at the speed of physical and economic recovery. In Dujiangyan, the largest city in the quake zone, the rubble and tent cities had disappeared. The jumble of debris was replaced by piles of new bricks, lumber and other construction materials. There was a building boom across the region, and dozens of temporary villages were erected to house the 5 million people who were rendered homeless by the quake. The prefab housing was made out of blue aluminium siding lined with Styrofoam insulation. It had concrete floors and was arranged in neat rows in flat spots at the

> bases of the mountains. Conditions weren't luxurious, but the camps were clean and the housing dry and fairly warm. I found no evidence of homelessness ...[316]

The reality is Ramzy could have compared the Chinese government's response to the 2008 Sichuan earthquake with the 2005 Hurricane Katrina in New Orleans, USA, if he was allowed to do that in the mainstream media. He has instead using an impoverished developing country like Haiti as a comparison.

Peter Foster is currently the Telegraph's US editor based in Washington DC. Before his promotion to Washington as an editor, he was a China Correspondent based in Beijing after being in India for several years. In an article on his personal blog on The Telegraph (15 April, 2009) titled 'China v India: Two kinds of people power', Foster expressed his amazement by the responsiveness of the Chinese government towards the corrective voices of the Chinese citizens. The following is an excerpt:

> China might not be run by a democratically elected government, but I suspect that many Westerners would be surprised at how sensitive the country's autocratic leadership is to public opinion ... But on any level, the Party is evidently deeply concerned about – and more importantly, reactive to – public opinion in a way not understood by Western audiences reading about dissidents being locked up and protests being cracked down upon.

Foster then describes his conversation with an "extremely senior figure from China's sovereign wealth fund," and a "very senior international health official" who has been intimately involved with the evolution of the $125bn national healthcare plan, and came to realise "just how closely the Party watches and reacts to public opinion." According to Foster, based on the account of the "very senior international health official," the initial blue print for the national healthcare plan was:

> Actively consulted not only with international agencies ... but also the public who had put in thousands of submissions ... And the exercise was not purely cosmetic. Substantial changes were made to the policy to reflect many people's concerns, including ...

However, one should note that, as a mainstream journalist, Foster apparently has to uphold the superiority of Western democracy and use the word "autocratic" to describe the Chinese government in his opening statement. The following is another statement made by Foster implying the superiority of Western democracies:

> It is less obvious, accountable and direct than in a democracy, but the people of China do have a collective power to influence government. It happens all the time. As a former correspondent in New Delhi, I also must confess to finding myself constantly amazed by the responsiveness of China's rulers when compared to India's who, in my experience, were spectacularly unconcerned about the well-being of ordinary people.[317]

Again, like Ramzy (Time), Foster could have compared the responsiveness of the Communist Government towards public opinion in China with the governments in Britain and USA, but he instead chose to use another developing country like India for direct comparison.

I have great respect for The Telegraph (UK) compared to many mainstream media. The Telegraph (UK) is more open to facts with less self-censorship. We are able to find reports in the UK's Telegraph relating to the US government funding the Dalai Lama, and the statement made by the then British foreign secretary David Miliband in 2008, which acknowledged China's sovereignty over Tibet and admitted that what Britain did in Tibet a century ago for its geopolitical interest was a historical mistake - an "anachronism" as Miliband puts it. I will evaluate these in greater detail with proper documentation in a coming instalment when I address the issue of Tibet.

Through the integrity and honesty of Peter Foster, I see hope that, one day, there will be more and more people working for the mainstream media willing to use their wisdom to tell the truth about China in their own skilful ways when the flaws in the Western political system become so unbearable that a consensus for urgent reform becomes an unavoidable issue to prevent a people revolution.

The West has a very long history of an indoctrination culture. It took the Catholic Church an entire century to quietly accept the observation of Galileo that it is the Sun and not the Earth that is at the centre of universe. The Catholic Church then took another three centuries to officially acknowledge on 31 October, 1992 by Pope John Paul II about the mistreatment of Galileo in the 1600s over his observation.[318] Though it may have taken the West 400 years to say sorry for their brutal treatment of a scientist in the 1600s, I am still hopeful that the rapid decline of the West in the 21st century will help to put forward the day when they will acknowledge that the Communist Party of China has found a political model proven to be more democratic, caring and responsive to the corrective voices of the average people. Let the world prosper together with shared experience and wisdom; not media disinformation to brainwash the world and justify international bullying and military aggression.

Even though the Chinese leadership has over the years repeatedly made it very clear that China's political system is based on "multiparty corporation under the leadership of the Communist Party, not a Western style-multiparty system," no one in the mainstream media will explain to us how it actually works besides portraying the Communist Government as an autocratic regime. There is a tendency in the Western media to suggest that China is moving towards Western political model despite the contrary. An interesting article on The Guardian (20 January, 2011) titled: 'China's tentative steps towards democracy' has the following opening statement:

> During the state visit for Chinese President Hu Jintao, President Barrack Obama should not only press President Hu on human rights, but should push a message about the importance of spreading democracy in China. If he does that, he may be surprised at what he will hear.

This kind of statement simply gives people an impression that the debt ridden American political system is superior to the Chinese, and that it is the Chinese system that needs reform not the American. It also provides readers an impression that a country like America who uses drones to kill its own citizens without trial is a human rights country. As illustrated earlier, the Chinese political system and their concept of democracy is very different from the West, however, many Western writers still like to suggest that China is moving towards Western-style democracy. Steven Hill, a political writer and columnist, then went on with a series of descriptions in his Guardian's article linking elections to democracy. And suggest that "if Chinese democracy continues to develop, it is likely to be an exact copy of the Western model." The overall impression I had with Hill's article is that, election is the only form of democracy. Just when I feel sick about reading another piece of simplistic, far from reality article to promote the superiority of Western democracy, Hill surprised me with the following statement:

> Many are intrigued by the vision promoted by Confucian-inspired intellectuals like Jiang Qing, who have put forward an innovative proposal for a tricameral legislature. Legislators in one chamber would be selected based on merit and competency, and in the other based on elections of some kind. One elected chambered may be reserved only for Communist party members, the other for representatives elected by everyday Chinese. Such a tricameral legislature, its proponents believe, will better ensure that political decisions are made by more educated and enlightened representatives, instead of the rank populism of western-style elected factions.

Hill then quoted a statement made by Daniel Bell, a Canadian-born professor of political theory at Tsinghua University in Beijing saying China may be groping towards a "political model that works better than a Western-styled democracy." [319]

This kind of 'softy-softy' approach towards explaining the Chinese political model appears to be the only way to occasionally get the message out through the indoctrinated Western media. Despite the lack of details and the shallowness of Hill's article about the actual Chinese political model, I am still hopeful that we will one day be able to read more factual description about the superiority of the Chinese political system in the Western media beyond The Guardian, The Time and The UK Telegraph.

A report in The Atlantic (18 July, 2013) titled 'Young Chinese People May Just Not Be That Into Western-Style Democracy' found that among the 18-21 age group in China, only 44.1% think that democracy is a good thing, and 48.3 percent in the 22-31 age group. When asked about whether China or America is better, 38.1% of Chinese respondents from all age groups (including those 32 and above) believe that China is better, 8% think America is better, 51.5% chose "they have different national conditions, can't be simply compared", and 2.5% don't know. [320]

Therefore, the assumption by Western commentators over the years that Chinese people want a Western-styled democracy is totally unfounded and baseless.

While the mainstream media promoted the idea that China was having a Jasmine Revolution in 2011, a PEW centre report (31 March, 2011) titled 'Upbeat Chinese Public May Not Be Primed for a Jasmine Revolution' pointed out that "91% of Chinese characterised their country's economic situation as good." [321]

One should note that the design of the Chinese political system is based on releasing positive energy through multiparty co-operations than the Western concept of opposition. The Chinese consultation process is highly inclusive and widely based base on reasoning rather than the Western concept of 'majority-takes-all'. All 56 ethnic groups in China have their representatives in the Chinese parliament and inside the Communist Party, and are given the channels and opportunities to air their views, concerns and contribute to policies. The Communist Party membership is rising at a rate many times faster than the rate of population growth in China - this is in sharp contrast to the negative trend in Australia and Britain. In fact, through the unique function of the CPPCC (Chinese People's Political Consultative Conference), ordinary Chinese citizens from all walks of life are given a voice as well. For example, during the recent 'two sessions' (lianghui), a migrant woman worker whose career is to wash people's feet in the service industry has been selected as a representative. In a press conference, she told journalists her personal story and how she was chosen to be a member of the CPPCC, and the kinds of qualities needed on her part to be selected. She also raised issues relating to difficulties migrant workers faced in China including their sex lives. (Ifeng, 10 March, 2013)[322] Another new member of the CPPCC is a young girl born in the 1990s. She works as a cashier at a toll road. She was reportedly diving into a river to save the lives of four workers while on holiday with her father in 2010. Her story was circulated by social media and she was named for the 2011 National Ethics Award. She was very surprised by her selection to the CPPCC, but committed to do her best with her new responsibility. She told journalists the issue that concerned her most is the education and welfare of children in villages where parents seeking work elsewhere. (Takung Pao, 28 February, 2013)[323]

Unlike the indoctrinated mainstream media in the West, the Chinese media is rather open in discussing the strengths and witnesses of such a system of people representation. They also mentioned the fact that there are some chosen representatives who have failed in their duty since their appointments. Some enjoy the status as a member of the CPPCC but didn't do much with their new responsibility; people like Liu Xiang turned up for the meetings only twice since being chosen for the job partly due to his injuries during his training for the two Olympics. But one thing is for sure: both the Chinese media and communist officials are committed to exploring the issues and ways to improve the quality and processes of such diverse representation of people in the Chinese parliament. Generating positive energy and making ongoing improvement to the socialist consultative democracy are among the core objectives the Chinese political system is designed to achieve.

Voting in the Chinese parliament is free with no name written on the ballet papers. More than 50% of the parliamentary seats are set aside for the Communist Party to ensure political decisions are made by more educated and enlightened representatives, instead of the rank populism of Western-style elected factions. People who are interested in politics are encouraged to join any of the existing nine political parties, and prove their ability and commitment from there. Only those who have the passion, patience, commitment, works ethic, skills, knowledge, and leadership talent will be able to get to the very top position of the Chinese leadership team; like what the current Chairman Xi Jinping had done over a period of 40 years. The Chinese political system exercises a high level of professionalism and responsibility in delivering experience and quality people to the top job. After all, quality political leadership is the foundation for good governance. The competency of political leadership will in turn directly link to the ability of a government to regulate the economy, ensure social stability, and the management of basic human rights for a decent lifestyle in terms of employment, affordable housing, food and the cost of raising a family.

It must be stressed once again that an important element of the Chinese political system is that it ensures voices from every corner of the society be heard. Can any Westerner image their President or Prime Minister travelled hundreds of kilometres by car to an impoverished remote region of their country to personally visit the local residents, engage in personal dialogue asking questions about their income and livelihood, and eat with them the same type of food? However, to the Communist Party of China, it is their basic belief and ideology to care for the disadvantaged. The following screenshot from a Hong Kong media (Ifeng.com, 30 December 2012) shows Chinese leaders including Chairman Xi Jinping accepting food handovers by a villager during one such trip. I couldn't image an American president or a British Prime Minister that would dare to accept food offered in such a way. Unfortunately, Western journalists in China show no interest in reporting this kind of people oriented leadership culture in China.

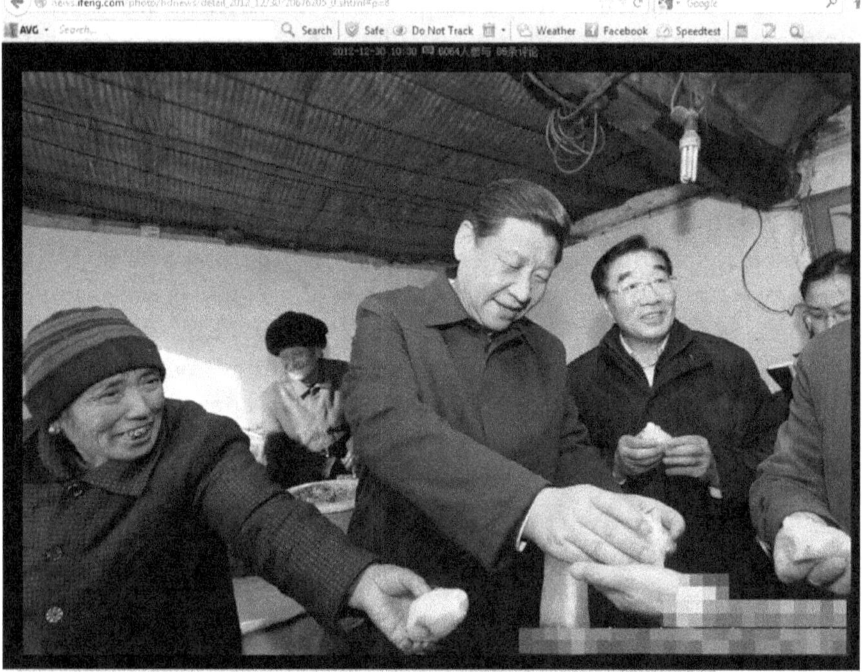

In fact, it is not uncommon for the Communist Party to dispatch their cadres to live with villagers in remote areas for a period of one to two years, in order to find out firsthand their living conditions, the difficulties they face on a daily basis and the reasons it is so hard to build a viable local economy in the region. The cadres who are involved in such projects are often offered incentives for promotion should they be able to come out with solutions through their firsthand personal experience living amongst the villagers, listening to their experiences and suggestions, and exploring the physical, social and economic environment of the region. For example, a report from people.com.cn (4 May, 2012) revealed an initiative in Guangdong that required cadres to live with villagers in their home at various points during the year to gain an in-depth understanding of the local community for reform direction and policy setting. [324]

Political meritocracy, consultative democracy and the institutionalisation of leadership succession in China is a form of responsible governance not found in many countries. Imagine if the managers and CEOs of Microsoft, Apple and Huawei are selected through a Western-style voting system instead of their personal credentials such as their skills, knowledge, profession, work experience, and proven performance record, what would these companies become? Imagine a well-spoken know nothing former priest who promises to give everybody a 20% pay rise with shorter working hours being elected CEO of Microsoft; and a well spoken know nothing English teacher an elected finance manager of Apple; and an assembly line worker become an elected new product design manager of Huawei. Will these companies do well under this kind of 'democratic leadership'? If Western-styled democracies don't do any good for corporations like Microsoft, Apple and Huawei, what makes people think that it is a good thing for a country?

History – The Judge

The truth is that the Western-style voting system is not suitable for every country. If the study of history is of any value, one should learn that there are far too many examples of countries falling apart with decades of sectarian violence and civil unrests after adopting a Western-style political system. Just a simple search on the modern history of Afghanistan, Algeria, Congo, Iraq, Mali, Haiti, Libya, Yugoslavia and many other Asian, African, South American and Middle Eastern countries will reveal that; by forcing countries into adopting a Western-style voting system often creates more harm than good to social unity and stability. Human rights can only be achieved through first having a stable and workable government to develop the economy, maintain social stability, generate employment, manage inflation and provide basic social services - not a Western-style voting system.

Human history is full of conflicts and violence regardless of if it is in the West or elsewhere. The very reason countries like Afghanistan, Iraq, Libya and Syria could hold on as a nation with little or no sectarian violence under the Taliban, Saddam Hussein, Muammar Gaddafi and the Assad government before the so-called Western "humanitarian" intervention is the balancing acts these governments performed that were acceptable to the majority ethnic groups in their respective countries. By upsetting such a balance with economic sanctions, military aggression and Western funded/armed radicalism resulting in the violent removal of a sovereign government, most Western-backed puppet regimes are not only incapable of maintaining order in the respective country, but their ability to hang on to power are usually highly questionable should their puppet master decided to handoff their country at some point in time. For example, after twelve years of brutal Western occupation of Afghanistan, this is how Bloomberg News (29 June, 2013) titled its report a year before the scheduled 2014 military withdrawal by Britain: 'Afghan Army May Need NATO Support Until 2020, U.K. Official Says'.[325] The truth is that the election in Afghanistan has being manipulated. Of the elections in Afghanistan, Sima Samar, former Afghan Minister for Women's Affairs, claimed, "This is not a democracy, it is a rubber stamp. Everything has already been decided by the powerful ones."[326]

The same situation has happened in Iraq: at the 10th anniversary of the invasion, The Nation's article (7 March, 2013) titled 'Why the Invasion of Iraq was the Single Worst Foreign Policy Decision in American History' had this highlight: "Ignore the jingoism, from politicians and the press – the tenth anniversary marks a tenth year from hell."[327] A recent report by the United Nations Assistance Mission for Iraq (UNAMI) reveals that July 2013 was the deadliest month in Iraq since 2008, with a total of 928 Iraqis civilians including civilian police killed, while 2,109 injured. A further 129 members of Iraqi Security Forces were killed and 217 wounded. (Aljazeera, 1 August, 2013)[328]

The fact that The Nation claimed in its report that the invasion of Iraq was the single worst foreign policy decision in American history, is itself a reflection of just how easily history can be forgotten. One needs just to search the net using the terms 'Vietnam war was a mistake' and 'the history of Vietnam war' to know that the number of deaths and injuries in that US-led brutal war were around three million and five million respectively, including the death of more than 56,000 American soldiers. The Vietnam War was a senseless war that led to decades of American military contraction in Asia until the Obama regime decided to return to Asia with his Pacific Pivot. Today, the chemical (Agent Orange) that was sprayed on Vietnam at the time continues to contaminate large area of the Vietnamese soil, rivers, underground water systems, plants and animals. As a result, generations of Vietnamese people living in those areas continue to suffer from birth defects and cancer without compensation from the "humanitarian" West. However, the mainstream media has done nothing to campaign for the human rights of these Vietnamese victims to claim compensation against Western governments who committed those crimes only 40 years ago. As a result, the Vietnam War was just another forgotten part of history in the short-memory of the Western public. A simple search on the internet using the terms 'Agent Orange and Vietnam War' will allow us to find out the details of such massive Western crimes against humanity.

It is therefore a must for people to study history to know who the world's worst human rights violators, so that the people can pressure their government to prevent the repetition of past mistakes.

America has a notorious history of intervention in the internal affairs of governments across the world. There is no lack of examples of democratically elected government being overthrown by the US government for their selfish geopolitical and economic interests. In a long analysis by John A. Tures, titled 'Operation Exporting Freedom: The Quest for Democratization via United States Military Operations' (http://blogs.shu.edu/diplomacy/files/archives/09_tures.pdf), Tures highlighted the outcome of 228 cases of American intervention from 1973 to 2005. The summary can be found on Wikipedia as follows:

> Most studies of American intervention have been pessimistic about the history of the United States exporting democracy. John A. Tures examined 228 cases of American intervention from 1973 to 2005, using Freedom House data. A plurality of interventions, 96 caused no change in the country's democracy. In 69 instances the country became less democratic after the intervention. In the remaining 63 cases, a country became more democratic. [329]

The truth is that the West does not believe in democracy and human rights despite the frequent use of the two terms to demonise others. The cruel reality is that the terms 'democracy' and 'human rights' are nothing more than a modern propaganda tool used by the capitalist West-ruling elites to justify military aggression and covert operations to topple governments not tolling their line of interests regardless of their political system. Without such justification and the propaganda power of the mainstream media, I suspect many Western citizens would allow their governments to repeatedly commit such humanitarian crimes across the world time and again. The following are the latest examples illustrated that the West does not care for democracy and human rights:

In the case of economic sanctions against the Palestinians soon after the election win of an Islamic party (Hamas) in January 2006, the West basically allowed the brutal repression of the Palestinians by Israel to go on that includes (but not exclusively) these: (1) withholding tax revenue collected in the Palestinian territories by Israel, (2) cutting off international aid to the Palestinian National Authority from the Quartet countries, (3) restrictions by Israel of movement within the Palestinian territories and of goods moving in and out, and (4) US banking restrictions. [330]

The same thing took place in Egypt: after the 2011 Egyptian Revolution that ended the Western-backed Mubarak dictatorial regime, the election win of an Islamic party (Muslim Brotherhood) had agitated the United States. When a democratically elected government was forcibly removed by the Egyptian military a year later, with ongoing mass arrests and killing of protesters by the thousands on the street of Cairo, Fox News (9 July, 2013) published an article titled 'A nation can be a democracy and still be a mortal enemy of the US' - expressing support for the military coup, and the US government's continued support of such a military regime. This is the opening statement of the article:

> America need not be ambivalent about our continuing support for the Egyptian military after their overthrow of Mohammed Morsi and the Muslim Brotherhood. The democratic election of Morsi should never have guaranteed U.S. cooperation. Even the violence that has followed the removal of Mohammed Morsi should not end our support, though we should do the most we possibly can to argue against that violence and for humane treatment of all Egyptians.[331]

Below is the screenshot from the Fox's article demonstrating the double standard and hypocrisy of the US government and mainstream media on the issues of democracy and human rights:

www.foxnews.com/opinion/2013/07/09/nation-can-be-democrac democracy for tl

A nation can be a democracy and still be a mortal enemy of the US

By Dr Keith Ablow / Published July 09, 2013 / FoxNews.com

America need not be ambivalent about our continuing support for the Egyptian military after their overthrow of Mohammed Morsi and the Muslim Brotherhood. The democratic election of Morsi should never have guaranteed U.S. cooperation.

Even the violence that has followed the removal of Mohammed Morsi should not end our support, though we should do the most we possibly

On 19 August 2013, US defence secretary Chuck Hagel told journalists "Our ability to influence the outcome in Egypt is limited ... It's up to the Egyptian people. And they are a large, sovereign nation. And it will be their responsibility ... to sort this out. All nations are limited in their influence in another nation's internal issues." Three days later, The Washington Post published an article titled 'U.S. intervention in Egypt is not the solution' in support of the double standard approach of the American government on the issue of democracy and human rights. [332]

Many people may not notice this, but if one observes the tone of the US government policy on a specific international event, and compares the subsequent media reports and articles over a period of time, one will slowly come to realise that the mainstream American media is actually a mouth piece of the American government. When the government undergoes military aggression against certain country, the mainstream media will create all kind of stories including fake ones in support of the wars. They even go to the extent to expel journalists and columnists who dare said otherwise. I will get to this in a coming instalment when I explain in detail how the West controlled the media.

As for other Western governments, besides making some noises against the mass arrests and killings of protesters by the US-backed Egyptian military, they have obviously silently endorsed the overthrowing of the democratically-elected Muslim government in Egypt. There was no action on the part of the West to at least impose economic, financial and banking sanctions against the Egyptian military dictatorship, nor there a call for the military regime to release the elected Egyptian President.

Robert D. Kaplan, a chief geopolitical analyst for Stratfor points out in an article on The National Interest (1 August, 2013) titled 'The Tragedy of U.S. Foreign Policy' that "sometimes American interests and values don't align perfectly. Accepting that is painful but necessary." The following is how Kaplan described the outcome of Western military intervention in Libya:

> Syria is not unique. Before Syria, humanitarians in 2011 demanded military intervention in Libya, even though the regime of Muammar Qaddafi had given up its nuclear program and had been cooperating for years with western intelligence agencies. In fact, the United States and France did lead an intervention, and Libya today is barely a state, with Tripoli less a capital than weak point of imperial-like arbitration for far-flung militias, tribes, and clans, while nearby Saharan entitles are in greater disarray because of weapons flooding out of Libya.[333]

It is important to study history to have an objective view on world events. The entire history of the Roman Empire is more about slavery and exploitation of others than a civilised state. The brutal repression of religious freedom with three centuries of Crusader movements, who killed to force conversion to Christianity, was a kind of relentlessly indoctrinated and repressive culture unparalleled in the history of mankind. The subsequent slave trades in Africa, America and Asia in recent centuries were only an extension of such bullying and exploitative tradition at the top end of the Western capitalist culture. Contrary to the perception of Western democracies as a form of political system that promote freedom, equality and human rights - propagated by the mainstream media, the concept of a Western democracy didn't start out as a product to build a civilised state with equality for all; it was a system to maintain peace and order among the wealthiest and the ruling class at the time. There is no need to take my words for granted; one needs only to do a bit of simple research on the history of democracy in US, UK and other European countries; will realise that Western democracies started out by excluding women, minorities and the poor. The right to vote was determined by the amount of wealth (properties) one owned. One should note that African Americans were only given the right to vote in America 50 years ago; and it is the same situation for the native Aboriginal people in Australia.

The truth is that Western democracies were designed by the rich and the ruling class at the time; the so-called freedom and equality were never meant for everyone. We have being brainwashed into believing that the Civil War in the US is a noble course to liberate Blacks from slavery; but history tells us that the causes of the War were a complex one relating to the issue of taxation, federal and States rights, economic and social differences between the North and the South, and a variety of other issues. The reality at the time was that slavery was still allowed in some States years after the war.

We have also been deceived into believing that the Declaration of Independence is a noble document that promotes equality and freedom for all. The reality is that women and minorities did not have the right to vote until a few decades and a century ago. By searching for the terms 'suffrage' and 'Women suffrage' on Wikipedia, one will be able to know the forms of exclusion from suffrage each Western country had on women, minorities and the poor. The following are the web addresses:

http://en.wikipedia.org/wiki/Suffrage
http://en.wikipedia.org/wiki/Women%27s_suffrage

The truth is, the American Founders such as Thomas Jefferson, who wrote "all men are created equal" in the Declaration of Independence owned slaves himself.[334]

Today, through legalising the corrupt practice of political donations, advertisements and lobbying, it is still this special class of people (the 1%) in the society who dictate government policies - not the average citizens.

In a 2002 book titled 'Wealth and Democracy: A Political History of the America Rich', Kevin Phillips traced the phases of wealth concentration and the politics of the affluent from John Jacob Astor to Bill Gates, to demonstrate how the rich have profited at the expense of the lower and middle classes through dubious government practices such as bank bailouts and suspect tax and tariff policies in the past two centuries. (Foreign Affair, January/February, 2013)[335]

In a speech in Bonn, Germany, at a DW Global Media Forum, Professor Noam Chomsky lays out how the majority of US policies are opposed to what wide swaths of the public want. According to Chomsky, the political system in America is a capitalist democracy whereby:

> Roughly 70% of the population – the lower 70% on the wealth/income scale – they have no influence on policy whatsoever. They're effectively disenfranchised. As you move up the wealth/income ladder, you get a little more influence on policy. When you get to the top, which maybe a tenth of one percent, people essentially get what they want, i.e. they determine the policy. So the proper term for that is not democracy; it's plutocracy. (Salon, 13 August, 2013)[336]

Therefore, the current form of Western political system is still a class political system. The nature of politics in the West is still very much about how to serve the interests of the richest and the ruling class. From the way:

* How an election campaign is structured
* How political donations, advertisements and lobbying are legalised
* How the expensive justice system is designed
* How the property and stock markets can be manipulated
* How there are taxation loopholes that allow the rich to pay proportionally much lesser tax then the average working citizens
* How there is a high concentration of media, banking and major resource ownership; and
* How there is an ongoing privatisation process from healthcare to prisons

We will then come to realise that everything in a Western society is designed to favour the super-rich with greater and greater monopoly power. In short, the voting system in the so-called "democratic" West is just an illusion of choice. The maintenance of the status quo to ensure the rich get richer, while the poor suffers from wage stagnation and rising cost of living, will simply get worse when the ability of the West to continue exploiting other nations is rapidly diminishing; as the war on Iraq and Afghanistan has demonstrated.

Without the ability to exploit others, the welfare system will eventually collapse. Western societies will experience what many developing nations have experienced when adopting a Western-style voting system. The recent ongoing brutal crackdown on protesters in Greece, Spain and Portugal is just the beginning of what can be expected of Western societies when unemployment, homelessness, the rising cost of living, poverty and the diminishing government-funded social safety net become causes of social frustration and anger. EU President Jose Manuel warned in 2010 that democracy could 'collapse' in Greece, Spain and Portugal unless urgent action is taken to tackle the debt crisis. The following is an excerpt from a report by Daily Mail (15 June, 2010):

> Mr Monks, now head of the European TUC, said: 'I had a discussion with Barroso last Friday about what can be done for Greece, Spain, Portugal and the rest and his message was blunt: "Look, if they do not carry out these austerity packages, these countries could virtually disappear in the way that we know as democracies. They've got no choice, this is it." 'He's very, very worried. He shocked us with an apocalyptic vision of democracies in Europe collapsing because of the state of indebtedness.'[337]

The level of exploitation within the Western society itself was so serious just a century ago that it had ignited a communist movement. With a simple search on the internet using the terms 'Australia sedition law and communism', 'US sedition law and communism', or 'UK sedition law and communism', one will be able to explore the issue of how Western capitalist governments introduced laws to brutally crackdown on the communist and labour movements at the time. The introduction of the 1940 Smith Act in America is just an example. It was due to the pressure from the communist movement that actually forced the capitalist West to look into the welfare of its workers to ensure social stability and to maintain their grip on power. However, as mentioned earlier, such welfare systems and economic prosperity in the West, and in particular America, UK and France, were made possible through endless military actions, bullying and exploitations of weaker nations to this day. Virtually most of the wars and conflicts across the world in recent decades directly or indirectly had a US and NATO elements.

In a book first published in 1968 titled 'Industry and Empire' on the economic history of Britain, Professor Eric J. Hobsbawn (pg 14) pointed out the intention of Britain in keeping developing countries undeveloped. The following is an excerpt:

> And because Britain began with the immense advantages of being indispensable to underdeveloped regions (either because they needed us or because they were not allowed to do without us), and indispensable also to the systems of trade and payments of the developed world, Britain always had a line of retreat open when the challenge of other economies became too pressing. We could retreat further into both Empire and Free trade – into our monopoly of as yet undeveloped regions, which in itself helped to keep them unindustrialized, and into our functions as the hub of the world's trading, shipping and financial transactions.

This is specifically the kind of tactic used by the West as a whole to keep many developing countries poor. Any country that attempted to break away from such a Western monopoly faced the risk of Western-engineered covert operations, economic sanctions, proxy wars, and so-called "humanitarian" military interventions when all other options failed to produce a desirable outcome. One must acknowledge that not all Western countries are involved in US military operations across the world, but NATO and EU countries have on many occasions supported the military actions and economic sanctions initiated by US, UK or France. Australia and Canada appear to follow every such US and UK-led foreign aggression.

In a Council on Foreign Relations book (1999) titled 'China Joins the World - Progress and Prospects' (pg. 11-12), a series of strategies on how to dictate and control the Chinese government were presented as a different line of thought in America. However, when we put into perspective the actual action taken by the US government over the years, these are actually the kind of techniques the American regime used to control developing countries. One of these thoughts is from the Economic Nationalists, who believed that the US government could use its economic power to compel other countries to comply with its demands. The following is the exact wording:

> They are not in favour of economic self-sufficiency, but they believe that the terms of trade must be carefully set by the U.S. government and that

> American economic strength is sufficiently great that, through confrontation, tough minded negotiations, and use of sanctions, the United States can compel other countries to comply with its demands.

Another is the Neoliberals line of thinking, who wants to use the US military as insurance to enforce the will of the US government. The following is the exact wording:

> ...the effort to integrate China into the world community on mutually acceptable terms may fail. Therefore, while they welcome China's desire to participate, they stress that the terms of entry must protect the purposes of the systems they seek to join. And the United States must retain an insurance policy in case the effort fails, especially through maintenance of robust bilateral alliances with its partners in the region and a credible, forward-deployed military presence in the region.

I will get into the details of such barbaric and undemocratic tactics the West have frequently used to enforce their will across the world for their selfish geopolitical and economic interests when I address the issue of Africa in a coming instalment.

The reality is that China's rise offers the world an alternative to Western monopoly. China is in the process of liberating the world from centuries of Western systematic exploitation and oppression. In the past decade, the Chinese leadership has being actively promoting the concept of an inclusive world based on the universal values of mutual respect and prosperity. This is in sharp contrast to the Western 'zero-sum-game' on the barbaric assumption that 'you-win-I-lose' or 'I-win-you-lose'. The speeches given by Chinese leaders often receive overwhelming and enthusiastic responses from their audiences in Asia, Latin America, the Middle East, Africa and Russia. However, the Western media will not show us the content of their speeches and the footage of such a Chinese soft-power. The long accumulated feeling of resentment against centuries of Western oppression in many developing countries is a global phenomenon that the mainstream media is doing a good job in keeping from the Western public. The capitalist West is living in a self-indulgent wonderland based on media censorship and disinformation. How long can the capitalist elites in the West bury their heads in the sand?

There is a saying that 'knowledge is power'. However, as I may observe, one of the main contributors to Western decline is the general lack of knowledge about the achievements of other cultures in recent decades, and ignorance about their own human rights record. The level of Western ignorance about the world and historical events is so serious that even the American President makes a fool of himself at times. An article on the National Interest (4 August, 2013) titled 'Obama's Sloppy History Problem' by James Jay Carafano, vice president of defence and foreign policy studies at The Heritage Foundation, pointed out that the US led Vietnam War was a "great mass murderers of history"; and yet Obama was so naive as to tell a visiting Vietnamese leader that their former anti-American war leader was an admirer of "one of America's founding fathers and authors of American liberty". [338]

It is therefore very important for people to revisit history to understand the nature of Western democracies, and the invisible hands behind the Whitehouse and Parliament that dictate government policies. It is a well known fact that political donations, advertising and lobbying is a form of corporate bribery that directly influences government policies, however, over the years, no one has had the power to outlaw such a corrupt practice. The following news headings in Australia, Britain and America are not a coincidence, but a reality within the corrupt Western political system:

* Australia: Inside Story (8 August, 2013) 'Political donations: the real-time disclosure option – Labor failed to take the opportunity to make historic changes to campaign finance disclosure' [339]
* UK: The Independent (19 August, 2013) 'Exclusive: David Cameron condemned over 'ridiculous' reforms to lobbying – New scrutiny for legislation regarded as a joke within £2bn industry' [340]
* USA: New York Times (21 January, 2010) 'Justices, 5-4, Reject Corporate Spending Limit' [341]
* USA: Christian Science Monitor (17 July, 2013) 'Jimmy Carter: Unchecked Political Contributions Are 'Legal Bribery'' with this statement: "It's accepted fact, 'Carter said during a speech in Atlanta. 'It's legal bribery of candidates, and that repayment may be in the form of an ambassadorship…'" [342]

The reality is that Western corporations are almost virtually behind every major government policy. The so-called "elected" politicians are just a window dressing. As examples, the engineers behind the concept of the latest Trans-Pacific Partnership (TPP), an oppressive US-led "free" trade agreement, are 600 corporate advisers. (AlterNet, 20 August 2013,[343] and Global Research, 2 April 2013[344]) The Australia Reserve Bank board was formed with a number of current and former corporate executives as broad members such as Woolworths, Bluescope Steel and Brambles, Fairfax and US retailer Walmart. (The Australian, 20 October, 2010)[345] In the US, the Federal Reserve is controlled by a cartel that consists of eight families (Global Research, 1 June, 2011)[346] In the UK, a report by the Guardian (8 November, 2011) revealed that one in five staff-pass holders in the House of Lords is linked to lobbying. [347] In fact, many current and former Western politicians and public servants are working as lobbyists for the big corporations.

Pragmatism: Communism and Democracy

There is no lack of former and current Western politicians who are frustrated by the way their political system works, and express their opinion publicly. However, their views often fail to receive widespread reports in the mainstream media. I should say that the shallow statements made by Chen Guangcheng, Ai Weiwei and Liu Xiaobo against the Communist Government in China enjoyed far greater attention and high profile coverage then many high profile Western politicians who complained about their own political system. The inability of anyone in Australia, UK and US to do anything to reform their political system against political donations is an indication of just how powerful the invisible hand is on the Western political institutions.

As illustrated earlier, the many flaws in the current form of Western political system is a systemic problem caused by the design of the political system. The origin of democracy is about maintaining peace and order among the wealthiest and the ruling class. The so-called freedom, equality and justice are never meant to be an inclusive one. It is an absolutely inferior form of political system when compared to the socialist model in China. The question here is: should people simply discard the concept of democracy because of that? The same question could be asked about communism: should we reject the ideology of communism because of the failure of the USSR in 1991?

China is obviously more democratic than the West given their political culture, structure and process based on the ideology of socialism, multi-party corporations and a system of wide-based consultation centred on reasoning rather than the Western-style 'winner-takes-all'. For example, in the latest incident, voters in the Italian speaking Swiss canton of Ticino voted to be the first district in the country to back a ban on face-covering veils. (Euronews, 23 September, 2013)[348] The moral question is: can this be regarded as democratic when the Christian majority in the district used the voting system to openly oppress minority Muslims of their freedom to wear veils? Does this so-called "democracy" represent freedom, equality and human rights for all?

Despite the democratic and inclusive nature of the Chinese political model, the Chinese government has often been labelled as autocratic by the agenda-based mainstream media. The false perception of China by the Western public is very much due to ignorance. Many people who criticise communism actually haven't read a thing about communism from the works of Karl Marx and the subsequent thoughts of the Chinese leaders. They are totally ignorant about the actual theory and concept of communism. It is just like many Western intellectuals, writers, journalists, NGOs and politicians who criticise the Communist Government in China, but have never read a thing about China from the perspective of the Communist Party, the Chinese media, and the powerful arguments made by many Chinese intellectuals. They simply recycle the information they read and hear from the agenda-based mainstream media and the US government-funded NGOs and career "dissidents", and regard the information from these sources as facts without verification. Like Chen Guangcheng and Liu Xiaobo, the Dalai Lama is another US government-funded puppet, and I will get into the detail of this in a coming instalment.

Despite the mounting debts and austerity measures, the American government has invested tens of billions of dollars each year across the world for regime change in the name of promoting democracy. A eleven-paged policy brief by Freedom House (15 May, 2012) titled 'Exercising US Leadership: Democracy Funding in a Time of Global Change' urged the US Congress to fully fund the Administration's request for US$56 billion to support international affairs for Fiscal Year (FY) 2013, a 2% increase over FY2012. According to Freedom House:

> This budget is one of the primary tools the United States uses to maintain leadership abroad, pursue its international priorities and promote American values. As Americans display growing fatigue over military

> interventions abroad, the Obama Administration has appropriately placed greater emphasis on diplomacy and development to advance U.S. foreign policy and national security objectives. In order to do so effectively, a robust foreign assistance budget is needed, along with carefully targeted use of available funds. [349]

There is a common tendency from those who receive funding from the US government; that is, part of their job is to smear against the Communist Party on the issue of democracy. This news heading from the Zakat Foundation of India (17 September, 2013) is just a latest example: 'China must follow world trend of democracy: Dalai Lama'.[350]

A 2013 PEW survey found that only 1-in-4 Germans have a positive view of China. However, a report by Deutsche Welle (20 July, 2013) titled 'German anxieties over China rise' pointed out that "only 7% of Germans actually know something about China." The following is an excerpt from the report:

> Ignorance is the biggest problem, Carsten Senz thinks. In Germany, he works for the Chinese company Huawei. A few months ago, he co-curated a study by the company looking into the picture Germans have of China. The study showed that only seven percent of Germans actually know something about China. "The fear of China can't really be pinned down to exact details," Senz says. "The fear is difficult to grasp." What is perhaps most easily put into words is the fear of Beijing's economic power. But that, in turn, has benefited the German economy a lot.[351]

Kishore Mahbubani, Dean of the Lee Kuan Yew School of Public Policy at the National University of Singapore, wrote an article on the Project Syndicate (24 May, 2013) titled 'America's Blinders' rightly point out the following:

> Many Americans remain shockingly unaware of how much the rest of the world, especially Asia, has progressed ... But the belief that America is the only virtuous country, the sole beacon of light in a dark and unstable world, continues to shape many Americans' worldview. American intellectuals' failure to challenge these ideas – and to help the US population shed complacent attitudes based on ignorance – perpetuates a culture of coddling the public ... China, which remains a closed society in many ways, has an open mind, whereas the US is an open society with a closed mind.[352]

While the annual PEW Surveys, Professor Tony Saich Survey, Wenfang Tang, Michael S. Lewis-Beck, and Nicholas F. Martin Survey, and the 6th Wave World Values Survey all point to an extremely high level of public satisfaction towards the Communist

Government in China, the New York Times, one of the most notorious anti-Communist newspapers in America continues to put up articles that suggest otherwise. For example, an article on the New York Times (9 September, 2012) titled 'What Keeps the Chinese Up at Night' by visiting professor Gerard Lemos at Chongqing Technology and Business University from 2006 to 2010, blatantly described the lives of Chinese people as desperate and anxious. [353]

While China has emerged from the 2008 Global Financial Crisis stronger with a 7.5 to 10% growth rate, and a national reserve of over three trillion US dollars (up from US$1.9 trillion in 2008), and the US is running at a debt level of more than US$1 trillion/year to a staggering total of US$16.4 trillion of cumulative debt by the end of 2012, Professor Lemos authored a book "The End of the Chinese Dream: Why Chinese People Fear the Future" (30 July, 2012) suggesting a bleak future facing the Chinese people instead of a bleak future for the American people.

Zhang Yanshuang, a Chinese Ph.D student at the University of Queensland, had this remark after visiting my personal blog: outcastjournalist.com:

> I really admire your anti-media disinformation project as well as your great efforts in bringing the world to a better understanding of China and other developing countries. Most of the time the biases in western media come from the ideological divergence rather than people's ignorance of undeniable facts/truth. That's also the hardest to change.

Unfortunately, we are not living in a perfect world where nations learn to respect each other as equal. This is just like how we are not living in a perfect society where we can comfortably assume that all people are well-educated, well-informed, rational, objective, caring and selfless. Therefore, many great ideologies such as communism and democracy cannot function as they ideally should without factoring these human elements into the design, structure, process and culture of a political system.

As illustrated throughout the book, Democracy cannot be achieved through a Western-style voting system and a political system based on the concept of 'opposition' and 'winner-takes-all'. In any human society, it is the personal qualities and beliefs of the individuals working in the system that dictate the behaviour of the institution. The design, process, and structure of a political system will also in turn influence the behaviour of the individuals within the system. Nazism is a part of Western history produced by a voting system; and racism is still very much a part of the politics in any Western-style election campaign. Corruption is a human problem driven by greed and can only be reduced but not totally eliminated. In the West, the corrupt nature of political donations, advertising and lobbying has being legalised largely due to the way the political system is designed. In China, a developing country with 20% of the world's population, with a GDP expanding at a rate of more than 40 times within the last 30 years, also has its own problems with corruption. However, unlike the capitalist West in legalising corruption, the Chinese leadership has been very open about the issue, and has severely punished many corrupt officials each and every year with the introduction of new laws and regulations to bridge any detected gaps and loopholes within the system. As I may confidently predict, their determination to crackdown on corruption will see China becoming one of the least corrupt countries in the foreseeable future.

In the West, all incidents of political corruption are reported as individual behaviour, while the cases in China are reported as the work of the "corrupt Communist regime." The difference in tone is the trick that makes a difference in the perception of Western democracies and Chinese socialism.

The quality of a political leadership and its beliefs is the foundation of any great society. Without the basic belief in a political leadership in creating an equitable and inclusive society, the Western voting system is nothing more than a system for the exchange of favours between politicians and the voters. The process of promising some benefits in exchange for votes is itself a kind of corrupt behaviour. Therefore, the intention of Western leaders to look after their people is never a genuine one. The culture of caring is not a part of the capitalist ideology, which is reflected in the way these Western-style governments handled a major natural disaster in their respective countries, namely the 2005 Hurricane Katrina in New Orleans, the 2009 bushfires in Victoria, the 2011 earthquake in Christchurch, and the 2011 tsunami in Japan.

At a time of economic downturn with no spare money to spray around, all sides of politics resorted to lies to win votes. That left voters with no choice, as all sides of politics were equally corrupt with no moral authority. Such lying political culture has itself created a moral issue for society; the lack of trust, satisfaction, and choice by voters towards their political leadership will eventually develop into an issue of legitimacy when income inequalities and social pains become unbearable. In an interview on the issue of Anarchism and the problems with Libertarians, Professor Noam Chomsky pointed out that:

> Authority is not self-justifying. They have to give a reason for it, a justification. And if they can't justify that authority and power and control, which is the usual case, then the authority ought to be dismantled and replaced by something more free and just.[354]

At the beginning of the 2008 financial crisis, a report by infowars.com (20 November, 2008) revealed that the then Finance Secretary, Henry Paulson, was behind the threat of martial law and a new great depression prior to the passage of the bailout bill.[355] US politician, Newt Gingrich in an article on The Washington Post (22 May, 2009) urging Americans to look "carefully" at "the anti-politician, anti-government mood exhibited in California." [356] We then witnessed an anti-Wall Street movement spread across America with a relentless crackdown by authorities (nearly 8,000 arrested[357]), and a series of new laws and judicial techniques to suppress the ability of protesters to sustain their movement. America is not a society as free and stable as people think. The mainstream media has done a great job by not reporting many of these government crackdowns. In fact, there is an undercurrent of massive social unrest and a series of preparations by the US government for a brutal crackdown in the foreseeable future. The revelation by Edward Snowden is an indication of just how notorious the US and other Western governments are spying on their own citizens on an unprecedented scale. A recent Public Mind Poll by Fairleigh Dickinson University (1 May, 2013) revealed that 29% of registered voters in America think that an armed revolution might be necessary in the next few years in order to protect liberties.[358]

While the indoctrinated West has continued to indulge in their inferior form of capitalist democracy using Winston Churchill's age-old statement as unquestionable truth, the Communist Party in China has been pragmatic and is actively improving its political process, institutions and culture based on practice and ongoing self-reflections. They continue to draw on the achievements of other societies. In an article on Qiushi (1 January, 2013) titled 'The development of Socialist Consultative Democracy in China', Jia Qinglin, Chairman of the National Committee of the Chinese People's Political Consultative Conference, asserted that:

> We also need to give full play to the strength of the socialist political system whilst drawing on the political achievements of other societies. However, under no circumstances will we ever copy the Western political system. Through our efforts, we will make people's democracy wider in scope, fuller in form, and sounder in practice.

According to Jia, the belief in socialism is the foundation of China's politics. Based on the principles of socialism, people are positioned as the master of the country. Therefore, the Chinese form of democracy is designed to "fully embody the authenticity, broadness, and inclusiveness" of public consultation. The strengths of such wide-based consultative democracy are that:

> Given that its participants come from all sectors of society and all walks of life, consultative democracy is able to reflect the general wishes of the majority whilst taking the rational claims of the minority into account. This allows for the democratic rights of the overwhelming majority of the people to be realised to the maximum extent.[359]

As mentioned earlier, the amount of investment, resources and manpower the Communist Government injected into helping the victims of the 2008 earthquake in Sichuan is in sharp contrast to the behaviour of the so-called "elected governments" in Australia, Japan, New Zealand and USA. There is absolutely no exchange of interests in the process between the Communist Government and the victims – it is a simple culture of caring: 'Serving the people' (为人民服务). This kind of caring leadership is fostered through the ideology of communism, the philosophies of Karl Marx, Mao Zedong, Deng Xiaoping, Jiang Jemin and Hu Jintao, and the traditional Chinese culture where the rulers regard their subjects (citizens) as children (子民), and the citizens regard their local governors as "father-mother officials" (父母官). One should also note that, the Chinese people call their army "people's son and brother soldiers" (人民子弟兵). This kind of family culture between the leaders and the people is an old tradition developed over many centuries; it is not something that can easily be understood by the war mongering capitalist elites in the West who regard the people in their respective countries as 'citizens' or 'residents'.

One of the greatest contributions Chairman Mao had on the Chinese political culture is the culture of ongoing self-reflection through self-criticism (自我批评). After 30 years of experimenting with the principle of a market economy, Chinese leaders saw the benefits of the 'invisible hand' in unleashing the inner motivation of individuals to work hard and be creative. However, they also came to understand the downside of uncontrolled capitalism, where the rich would eventually corrupt the entire system, and monopolise everything at the expense of the masses.

As somebody living in the West for over 20 years, I have noticed that the cost of living and the cost of running a small business are getting higher and higher. The entire economy is gearing towards consumption and speculative activities. The price of everything (shares, property values, currencies, precious metals, raw materials, energies and others) can be manipulated by wealthy cartels. Profit is the only GOD the capitalists know. The only objective CEOs have is to increase profits annually by any means. More and more shopping centres are built at a rate faster than the rate of population growth; while business is getting harder with the per capital ratio between the number of retailers and the population contracting each year. Shop rental is allowed to rise virtually at will by a handful of wealthy owners with a system to observe how well each shop is doing to decide on the next round of rent rises - making a lot of small business owners working just to pay rent. The 2008 financial crisis saw Western politicians printing money and borrowing big to bailout those 'too-big-to-fail' corporations, while cutting all kinds of social safety net spending to struggling families, the homeless, and the unemployed.

While wages are largely frozen, the lucky one or two may enjoy a 2 to 3% increment after a long hard fight; big corporations (banks, energy, insurance, drugs, food, and multinational companies) are allowed to upwardly adjust their profit margins annually at a rate many times greater than official inflation rate. While corporations are bailed out by taxpayer's money, struggling families are not allowed to default the big banks and financial institutions without the risk of losing their home. While big corporations use their monopoly power to impose all kinds of fees and premiums to achieve record profits year-on-year, they continue to cut services through downsizing or simply move their operations to another country with cheaper wages so that they can enjoy even greater profits in the coming years. Western economies have virtually moved toward a speculative economy with no factories to produce anything. Their economies are supported by ongoing quantitative easing and military aggression across the globe so as to continue exploiting others. Five years into the 2008 financial crisis, income inequality in the West has sharply widened.

The Western capitalist economy is not a real economy, it is a speculative economy. It is designed for the super-rich to make easy money through the manipulation of shares, commodities, properties and currency markets. It is not a people's economy. The latest Forbes report (16 September, 2013) titled 'Inside the 2013 Forbes 400: Facts And Figures on America's Richest' revealed that "Buoyed by public markets, the average net worth of America's 400 richest rose $800 million a year to a record $5 billion." According to the report, the net worth of Bill Gates climbs to US$72 billion, the wealth of Warren Buffett has increased by another US$12.5 billion, and the stock of Facebook has pumped up Mark Zuckerberg's fortune by US$9.6 billion. [360]

While the 400 richest Americans made USD$320 billion in just one year, a report by AlterNet (28 February, 2012) suggested that "1 in 7 Americans [are] pursued by debt collectors."[361] The Los Angeles Times (30 January, 2013) report revealed that "nearly 44% of American households do not have enough savings to cover basic living expenses for three months if something unforeseen happens such as losing a job or falling sick." And that "almost a third of Americans have no savings account at all."[362]

The structure and design of the capitalist economy is not a people's economy. I read a report last year but was unable to trace back the web link: approximately 52% of the profit in America is based on share and property speculation. A report by MWC News (18 September, 2013) titled 'Poverty soars in US despite economic recovery' revealed that "the number of US residents living in poverty edged up to 46.5 million in 2012, the latest sign that an economic recovery marked by a stock market boom has not trickled down to ordinary Americans." [363]

A report by the Census Bureau revealed that "even as the recession has ended, the (New York) city's poverty rate continues to inch up and the gap between the rich and poor remains stubbornly large." According to David R. Jones, president of the Community Service Society, "We're three years into a recovery and the poverty rate is creeping upward." (New York Times, 19 September, 2013) Of course, Jones denied that the US is a class society. [364]

The reality in today's "democratic" USA is that many people are struggling with low-wage jobs - working hard but remaining homeless. A recent report on the New York Times (17 September, 2013) had a title that reflected such a reality: 'In New York, having a job, or 2, doesn't mean having a home'.[365] An editorial article on the New York Times (14 September, 2013) titled 'Tips and Poverty', revealed that employers in the restaurant industry are allowed to pay sub-minimum tipped wages of US$2.13/hour to tipped-workers (waiters and waitresses); and the outcome is that many of these hardworking Americans are living in poverty. According to the New York Times, the sub-minimum "tipped" wage was first instituted in 1996, when it was set at 50 percent of the minimum wage. However,

> The restaurant industry had successfully lobbied Congress to deny tipped workers any minimum-wage protection, leaving them to live on tips alone. Over the next 30 years, the tipped wage sometimes rose as high as 60 percent of the minimum wage, but it never fell below 50%, reaching its current level of US$2.13 an hour in 1991. Then, in 1996, the republican-led Congress agreed to raise the minimum wage, but on the condition that the tipped wage remain frozen. It has not budged since, and today it is 29 percent of the minimum wage. [366]

In a country with a mouthful of human rights against others, the New York Times reported the above news without condemning the American Congress as a corrupt and brutal regime serving only the 1%. If people think that the mistreatment of tipped workers in America is an isolated event, this only reflects just how ignorant people are towards the human rights reality of a capitalist democracy like America. While Western NGOs such as Amnesty International and Human Rights Watch relentlessly demonising developing countries over the issue of child and prison labour, they have failed miserably in addressing the issue of slave labour in America. A report by ProPublica (28 June, 2013) titled 'To Cope with Sequester, Justice Department Staffs Unpaid Attorneys' revealed the following:

> The Department of Justice has an opening for what could be a dream job for many newly minted lawyers: serving as a special attorney in the Office

> of Enforcement Operations. Among other responsibilities, the new hire could be helping the Electronic Surveillance Unit review applications for wiretaps in major federal criminal investigations. But they'll have to forego a salary for experience: the one-year position is completely unpaid. [367]

Ironically, in a land that portrays the 'Declaration of Independent' as a noble document that champions the universal values of equality, freedom and justice, not only is the American Justice Department involved in the slavery of its own citizens with "unpaid jobs for experience", but many of the human rights NGOs and other government institutions also use the same tactic on desperate graduate students seeking employment. ProPublica has a webpage under the title 'Internships' with dozens of examples of how these organisations have offered "unpaid jobs for experience":

> http://www.propublica.org/series/internships

A report by the National Poverty Center (May 2013) titled 'Rising Extreme Poverty in the United States and the Response of Federal means-Test Transfer Programs' revealed for the first time the following:

> In mid/2011 and based on cash income, about 1.65 million American households, with 3.5 million children, lived in extreme poverty: around US$2 or less per person per day.

The report also explains the history of how social safety nets in America shrink to allow such a dire situation. [368]

A PEW report (23 April, 2013) titled 'A Rise in Wealth for the Wealthy; Declines for the lower 93% - An Uneven Recovery, 2009 - 2011' revealed the following:

> During the first two years of the nation's economic recovery, the mean net worth of households in the upper 7% of the wealth distribution rose by an estimated 28%, while the mean net worth of the households in the lower 93% dropped by 4%.[369]

Interestingly, while the US government billing out the 'too-big-to-fail' corporations and borrowing money at a debt level of an additional over $1 trillion a year, 93% of Americans are worse off, with many people struggling to put food on the table, or having to work for nothing to gain work experience. Despite this, the American media and politicians continue to declare that the US economy has enjoyed "three years of recovery". This means that, so long as the upper 7% or the 400 super-rich continue to make big money from the share and property markets, America will be regarded as a great democracy, and a symbol of the civilised world that enhances the universal values of justice, equality and freedom.

People may think that this is exclusively an issue for the Americans, but it is not. In capitalist democracies, the class problem between the super-rich and the average population is similar from country to country; if not, identical. For example, an analysis on the Inside Story (15 September, 2013) titled 'Poverty in a time of prosperity', told of how social safety nets in Australia shrank to allow poverty at a time of prosperity. [370]

At a time of rising unemployment, bankruptcy, suicides, homelessness, and a rising number of Australians needing assistance from the government, a report by The Age (18 September, 2013) revealed that up to a quarter (1,100 to 1,200) of the nation's Centrelink call centre workers are set to "lose their jobs before the end of the year."[371] [Note: Centrelink is a government agency administering social welfare]

Earlier on, a report by the Courier Mail (4 November, 2012) titled 'Millions of Aussies missing out on financial help' revealed that more than one million Australians are missing out on government benefits and payments because they don't know they are entitled to the money. This is because of the government's policy not to tell people about their entitlements if they don't ask. The main problems with such a policy are as follows:

> The benefits payment system is too complex with 76% of respondents of an online poll finding it confusing.
>
> The most common access barrier identified by parents was that they did not know what (assistance) was available or how to find out what was available.
>
> When make inquiries to the Department of Human Service for help, the response is: if you don't know the specific benefits or assistance to ask about, no one can help.
>
> Difficult forms and procedures create barriers to claim benefits.
>
> The perceived "stigma" of receiving assistance is reinforced by the language used by Centrelink.[372]

Apparently, once the ability of the capitalist West to exploit other nations through wars and economic sanctions has declined, their ability to offer welfare seems to go with it. The once highly promoted welfare system - a symbol of Western superiority, humanity, freedom, equality and universal values - is fast becoming a burden to the economy. With no solution to reverse the trend of rising unemployment and debt through military aggression, Western politicians begin to blame the poor in their own society. For example, in Australia, a report by Sydney Morning Herald (17 April, 2013) titled 'Kill poor to fix budget, writes lobbyist with Liberal links' revealed the content of an article published by a Liberal Party-aligned think tank that advocates killing off the poorest 20 percent of Australians as a way to get the budget back on track. The following is an excerpt from the article:

> In contrast to the fabulous rich, the enormous poor make little useful contribution to society ... They consume more than they contribute, putting tremendous strain on the national budget. A modest cull would strike at the root of our fiscal dilemma. If the least productive 20 percent of citizens were decommissioned it would directly release a recurrent $25 billion, which would almost cover overspending by the Gillard government between now and September 14th, assuming Mr. Swan maintains his long-term average rate of profligacy.[373]

Earlier on, a report by The Age (6 July, 2012) titled 'Coalition targets welfare 'bludgers'', blatantly described people on welfare as "idle with habits of apathy", and blamed workers and unions who fought for a decent wage to compensate for the rising cost of living (a tiny fraction over the over 30% increment the politicians received in a single increment in 2011) as "militancy, lack of flexibility and inadequate productivity trade-offs." [374]

Given the current economic climate, and the nature of capitalist democracy, it is not hard to imagine that the basic human rights of the average Western citizens for decent housing, food, electricity, income protection will continue to be ignored by the corrupt and incompetent political institutions. The following news headings will give us an indication of what is already happening in the capitalist democracy in Australia:

* 'Food relief: 65,000 Australians a month ask for help but get nothing' (Guardian, 16 October, 2013) with this information: "End Hunger survey of 900 welfare agencies finds situation has worsened this year, with a 9% increase in people seeking help. More than 65,000 vulnerable Australians are being turned away by food relief charities every month

because there is not enough to go around, with the majority being low-income families rather then unemployed or homeless people."[375]

* 'WorkCover review could strip workers of right to compensation (Courier Mail, 23 September, 2013) [376]
* 'Retirees' home ownership set to plummet to 2 percent' (Brisbane Times, 22 August, 2013) [377]
* 'Struggling consumers can't pay soaring power bills with some pensioners being left in the dark' (Courier Mall, 25 March, 2013) with this information: "1,071 Queensland's pensioners and concession cardholders had their power cut off due to non-payment in the December quarter, a 36 percent increase over the 787 in the previous three months." [378]
* 'Power struggle: homes cut off' (The Age, 10 December, 2012) with this information: "Victorian households struggling to pay soaring energy bills are having their electricity and gas disconnected at increasing rates, with gas disconnections up to 50 percent." [379]
* 'Children's well-being report captures Australia's growing inequality' (The Conversation, 15 March, 2013) with this information: "Around one in six Australian children live below the poverty line ... Even though we're doing very well on our gross national product, the nationals wealth it just not evenly distributed and the level of inequality could be growing rather than diminishing ... Indigenous Australians faced some of the worst social, educational and health outcomes ... So how come we, as a very wealthy and competent nation, we can't effectively deliver services that are closing the gap here?" [380]
* 'Human Rights Alliance media release: WA mining boom and record poverty and homeless rates' (Independent Media Australia, 23 July, 2012) [381]
* 'Almost 3 million adult Aussies lack basic financial services' (The Conversation, 29 May, 2012) [382]
* '1 in 100 homeless in past year' (ABC, 30 April, 2010) [383]
* 'The average Australian waste 200kg of food a year – yet two million of us also go hungry. Why? (The Conversation, 14 February, 2012) [384]

Instead of tackling the root of the economic problems within the system, Western politicians seem to focus their attention solely on either continuing borrowing more money to stimulate the economy, or balancing the budget through austerity measures, such as lowering the social safety net, extending the retirement age, extending the regulatory age for workers to withdraw their pension funds, removing unions from enterprise bargaining, government downsizing, and tax cuts for the rich (such as Bill Gates and the 7%) under the assumption that these super-rich can then expand their businesses and employ more people. Should there be a tax increment; the focus is more likely aiming at taxing everybody with a generalised tax system such as the GST or VAT, or any generalised new tax with a noble name such as the Carbon Tax. A handful of countries like France, that are doing the reverse by taxing the rich, bear the risk of being defeated in the next round of election due to corporate influences through political donations, advertising and lobbying.

The rising cost of basic services, and income inequality, are actually among the main causes of the economic problems in the capitalist system; much of this can be linked back to the ongoing privatisation process. When everything in the economy, including basics items, are in the hands of privately owned businesses whose sole objective is to generate more profit for owners and shareholders, how can the entire population not be exploited? When each and every big corporation, including the major banks and financial institutions, are enjoying record profits at an annual incremental rate of extra billions year-on-year, how can the 93% of the population not getting poorer and poorer? For example:

* 'Melbourne Airport fee hikes to cripple small bus and parking businesses' (Herald Sun, 8 October, 2013) [385]
* 'Double-digit shock as electricity bills set to surge by 21.4 percent' (Courier Mail, 22 February, 2013) [386]
* 'Huge profit for CTP insurers in NSW as premium prices skyrocket' (The Daily Telegraph, 24 June, 2013) [387]
* 'Census reveals extent of soaring mortgages, rent' (WA Today, 22 June, 2012) with this information: "WA's median mortgage repayment has soared 58 percent in five years to nearly $2000 per month, while renters are paying almost double what they did in 2006, the latest Census shows ... Adding to the rental pressure is the fact there are 109,328 unoccupied private dwellings ..." [388]
* 'Ian Narev defends CBA record profit' (Sydney Morning Herald, 14 August, 2013) with this information: Commonwealth bank "cash earnings jumped 10 percent to $7.8 billion in the year to June." [389]
* 'NAB (National Australia Bank) on track to hit $6bn profits' (Courier Mail, 7 February, 2013) [390]
* 'Australians slapped $4 billion in bank fees, RateCity finds' (Daily Telegraph, 21 June, 2011) [391]
* 'Virgin's call rates increase by up to 1289%' (Sydney Morning Herald, 19 February, 2013) [392]

* 'Airport car park prices go sky high' (Sydney Morning Herald, 24 August, 2012) [393]
* 'Australia Post faces backlash over increased delivery charges' (WA Today, 8 April, 2013) with this statement: "Price increases by Australia Post for delivery services will make it impossible for Australian websites to complete online with their foreign counterparts." [394]
* 'Unit owners fight huge increases in body corporate charges' (Courier Mail, 3 April, 2012) [395]
* 'Caltex Australia profit up 33pc' (The Australian, 22 April, 2010) [396]
* 'Westfield Group posts lift in FY profit' (Business Spectator, 27 February, 2013) with this information: "In the 12 months to December 31, Westfield Group posted a net profit of $1.718 billion, an 18.3 percent lift on the previous corresponding period." [397]
* 'Supermarket duopoly blamed for soaring food prices' (WA Today, 9 November, 2009) [398]

When many of the 93% of the consumers having no money to buy anything else due to rapidly rising costs of unavoidable expenses (basic human rights) such as electricity, council rate, fuel and gas, insurance, rent, mortgage repayment, public transport, and food, how could the rest of the economy not suffer? The nature of a market economy is based on consumption; so when 93% of consumers are in trouble, how can the economy be productive? As a result, we witness factories closing down and workers being laid off; we then see a series of supporting industries such as parts and accessories, retail and wholesale either gone into bankruptcy or downsizing, with more workers being laid off. Then, tourism, hospitality, restaurants, gifts, homeware, arts and a series of other industries begin to experience the domino effect.

Just imagine: many hardworking mums and dads have worked, and contributed to society and promptly paid their taxes for decades, and now, suddenly found themselves unemployed and unemployable because of the state of the nation economy; their age and skill. At a time of social distress, what they get in return from society is a reduction of their social safety net through a series of austerity measures, and a system of 'don't ask don't tell' that prevents them from claiming social benefits, and being shamed through descriptions such as "idle with habits of apathy". Imagine if Bill Gates was born in one of these distressed families struggling to pay rent, having their electricity cut off, having problems putting food on the table, and being abandoned by the corrupt capitalist political institution - would Bill Gates still have been able to become the Bill Gates we know today?

As a result of decades of relentless privatisation; taxation has become the main source of government revenue; all kinds of taxes in all forms are jacking up the cost of living for everybody and reducing the people's buying power. People are taxed from the day they are born to their deaths. Western citizens are the slaves and not the masters within capitalist democracies. More than a year ago, there was an email circulating on the Internet about taxation in Australia. I have no idea who the author is, but I received three such emails from three different sources. The content is very powerful:

> At first I thought this was funny. Then I realised the awful truth of it. Be sure to read all the way to the end!
>
> Tax his land,
> Tax his bed,
> Tax the table at which he's fed.
>
> Tax his work,
> Tax his pay, he works for peanuts anyway!
>
> Tax his cow,
> Tax his goat,
> Tax his pants,
> Tax his coat.
>
> Tax his tobacco,
> Tax his drink,
> Tax him if he tries to think...
>
> Tax his car,
> Tax his gas,
> Find other ways to tax his ass.
>
> Tax all he has
> Then let him know that you won't be done till he has no dough.
>
> When he screams and hollers'
> Then tax him some more,
> Tax him till he's good and sore.

Then tax his coffin,
Tax his grave,
Tax the sod in which he's laid.

When he's gone,
Do not relax; it's time to apply the inheritance tax.

Accounts Receivable Tax
Airline Surcharge Tax
Airline Fuel Tax
Airport Maintenance Tax
Building Permit Tax
Cigarette Tax
Corporate Income Tax
Goods and Services Tax
Death Tax
Driving Permit Tax
Environmental Tax (Fee)
Excise Taxes
Federal Income Tax
Fishing License Tax
Petrol Tax (too much per litre)
Health Tax
Hunting License Tax
Interest Tax
Luxury Tax
Liquor Tax
Marriage License Tax
Medicare Tax
Mortgage Tax
Personal Income Tax
Property Tax
Poverty Tax
Prescription Drug Tax
Real Estate Tax
Vehicle Tax
Retail Sales Tax
Service Charge Tax
School Tax
Vehicle License Registration Tax
Vehicle sales Tax
Water Tax

Watercraft Registration Tax
Well Permit Tax
Workers Compensation tax
And now a Flood Tax and then a Carbon Tax!

Still think this is funny?
Not one of these taxes existed 100 years ago.
What in the "Hell" happened?
It's called 'politicians'
I hope this goes around Australia at least 100 times!!!

The fundamental issue here is that it is alright for governments to tax the society if the revenue is properly reinvested for the greater good of the community such as infrastructure and disaster relief. But, in a capitalist democracy, a lot of these expenses go into the coffers of big corporations who lobby through political donations in the form of industry subsidies. If these subsidised industries were publicly owned, the profit could be redistributed for public use. However, the subsidies usually go to privately owned industries, so the profit goes only to a handful of owners and shareholders.

When businesses are closing down in the masses and there's rising unemployment, the ability of governments to raise revenue through taxation is rapidly diminishing. We can then expect another round of privatisation by the low quality, know-nothing Western politicians for easy cash flow. The cost of living will get higher and higher as more and more of the economy will be monopolised by a handful of super-rich individuals and corporations. The economic bubble will get bigger and bigger, and will have a bigger burst in the foreseeable future. After all, in a capitalist democracy, there is limited ability for government to tax the super-rich due to the fact that the taxation system is designed in favour of them. As examples:

* 'Mining tax embarrassment as Rio funds returned' (Sydney Morning Herald, 9 August, 2013) with this information: "The revelation that Rios' pre-payment were refunded has raised the prospect that other companies such as BHP Billiton may have had their pre-payment refunded, too, and comes just a week after the Rudd government downgraded its revenue estimate for the tax over the next four years." [399]
* 'Magnate's company paid no tax' (WA Today, 12 April, 2012). This news is referring to Australian billionaire Clive Palmer's company. [400]
* 'Tax system at risk: Treasury' (Brisbane Times, 24 July, 2013) with this information: "The Treasury has admitted it is virtually powerless to stop multinational companies such as Apple and Google dodging tax." [401]

* 'BHP has a victory in its $2.2bn tax case' (Australian, 18 March, 2010) [402]

The reality is that in a capitalist democracy, the Western public is educated and trained to obey the law on absolute term. Police brutality can often be forgiven and let go of lightly, but if you are rude to the police by expressing your frustration through swearing, you may be punished with a fine of up to A$750[403] in Australia depending on which state you are in. If you swear at a judge, you may be fined or even jailed for contempt of the court. The basic freedom to swear – an expression of a basic human emotion - has been deprived in the name of the law; and yet nobody thinks that this is a violation of basic human rights and freedom. The ability of the capitalist West in brainwashing people into accepting their exploitation and oppression as an acceptable norm can never be underestimated. The wealthy and big corporations are allowed to increase their prices at will on expenses that you cannot avoid, and yet you have no right to refuse payment when you are broke. The rich may be bailed out by the government with your tax money, but your inability to pay your mortgage will find you homeless. You are born to a system that makes you pay and pay. The average people are the target of government taxation - not the rich. A report on The Age (7 May, 2013) titled 'Millionaires snub taxman' revealed the following:

> The annual tax statistics released last week show that the 70 earned $194 million in income between them, but by the time their accountants had finished, that had been reduced to less than $20,000 in taxable income between them: $1 of taxable income for every $99999 that went untaxed. Only 30 of them claimed deductions for advice, but between them they paid their accountants and lawyers $33 million, or more than $1 million each. [404]

It is the same situation in America - the following news headings will provide us some ideas of what's going on:

* 'Unfair Share: How Oil and Gas Drillers Avoid Paying Royalties' (ProPublica, 13 August, 2013) [405]
* 'US blocks crackdown on tax avoidance by net firms like Google and Amazon' (Guardian, 15 July 2013) [406]
* 'Noble Prize-Winner Joe Stiglitz Blasts America's 1 Percent-Coddling Tax System' (AlterNet, 15 April, 2013) [407]
* 'Inside the End of the U.S. Bid to punish Lehman Executives' (New York Times, 8 September, 2013) told the story of how executives who

> presided over the biggest bankruptcy in United States history could escape without a single civil charge. [408]

However, if you are not one of the super-rich, you will be treated very differently in the capitalist world. This report was made by Washington Post (8 September, 2013) without emotive language to condemn the human rights violations of the capitalist government in America. The following is an excerpt from the report:

> On the day Bennie Coleman lost his house, the day armed U.S. marshals came to his door and ordered him off the property; he slumped in a folding chair across the street and watched the vestiges of his 76 years hauled to the curb. Movers carted out his easy chair, his clothes, his television. Next came the things that were closest to his heart: his Marine Corps medals and photographs of his dead wife, Martha. The duplex in North Washington that Coleman bought with cash two decades earlier was emptied and shuttered. By sundown, he had nowhere to go. All because he didn't pay a $134 property tax bill.

One should note that in between this Washington Post report, under the subheading 'Should D.C. offer protections for people who can't pay their taxes, including elderly, disabled or low-income residents? Explain', the following information is about the costs of justice for struggling families in America:

> With no caps on fees, families have paid a steep price, facing bills for legal fees and court costs often more than triple their original tax debts, The Post found. Rates for the attorneys hired by the tax lien companies have reached $450 an hour. Even the smallest expenses have been passed on – including the paper that ordered property owners to court at 25 cents per page. One attorney billed for preparing the bill itself - $25. Time and again, the bills came without receipts or breakdowns justifying the costs. [409]

This is just an example of the true nature of the so-called rule of law in the West. It is still a capitalist justice system, not for the average person. Ironically, whenever this kind of human rights issue takes place in the West, they are either not widely reported by the mainstream media, or, when reported, there is a total lack of emotive terms such as "the brutal capitalist regime" or "a brutal violation of basic human rights". The reality is that there are a lot more human rights problems in the West than many people notice due to the way the mainstream media structures their wording, and also the frequency of such human rights incidents being reported.

Unlike the capitalist democracy in the West who blamed the poor and unions for the country debt, the communist government in China has long noticed such downsides in an uncontrolled market economy. The CCP understands that growth in GDP does not automatically translate into happiness to everybody in the society. Long before the then Chairman Hu Jintao officially announced the concept of a harmonised society and transferred the responsibility to Xi Jinping to carry out reforms to slow down the economy, and to restructure the economic system towards a policy of sustainable and inclusive growth, the theoretical framework for such a new policy had already taken shape with consensus within the Communist Party.

In 2007, the Communist Party published a 478-page, 430,000-word book titled 'Analysing the Strategic Difficulties in Constructing a Harmonised Socialist Society'. The following is a scanned image of the book:

Unlike Western politicians who generate ad hoc policies over the course of an election campaign to cheat votes, many of the policies announced by the Chinese leadership are well researched and thoroughly thought out over a number of years before turning them into official policies with a clear sense of direction. As a long time observer of Chinese politics, it is my heart-felt acknowledgement that I have never seen any political party as diligent as the Communist Party of China, who care so much for the wellbeing of their nation and people, that, they are so actively and regularly monitored, reviewed and assessed the outcomes of their present and past policies in order to overcome any flaws, loopholes and insufficiencies within the system. Many of the issues raised by the

2013 new leadership team were discussed in this 2007 book. I will get back to some of the issues raised in the book when I address the issues of income inequality and minority policies in China in a coming instalment.

Unlike the indoctrinated West that promotes democracy as if it was a religion through unquestionable authority and superiority to justify military aggressions across the world; the communist government in China is a lot more pragmatic. They have studied and practiced communism from the works of Karl Marx and adapted it to suit the local environment and international conditions with Mao's thought, Deng's theory, Jiang's three represents, Hu's scientific development and harmonised society, and now Xi's China dream aiming at inclusive growth and the reemphasis on the need to create a sustainable society based on the ideology of communism.

Through the practices of a market economy, the communist party has decided to keep the element that rewards those who derive their wealth from hard work and creativity, but will not allow the rich to make use of their market position to hijack the price of basic products and services such as housing, food, electricity, water, and public transport. In an article titled 'Democracy Needs Reform: Human Rights – Housing policies – Australia and China compared', I listed a series of investments and policies the communist government introduced to ensure affordable housing in China. Their attitude is in sharp contrast to the capitalist Australian government. This article can be found via: OutcastJournalist.com: click on 'Care for Australia' then look for the article title. [Note: As English is my second language, articles on my personal blog come with grammar and spelling mistakes as I did not send them in for editing. Please forgive me for the imperfection.]

China may be a developing country with 20% of the world population, but home ownership in China is a lot higher than in the West. Affordable housing is regarded as basic human rights in China. An article on the Japanese magazine, The Diplomat (17 August, 2012), titled 'Cooking the books'? China's Data Dilemma' mentioned that many have disputed the data published by the China Household Finance Survey, which suggested that the average urban household in China has assets worth 2.47 million yuan, and that 89.68% of Chinese households owned their own homes, but the author believes that the data might be correct.[410]

I have spoken to a Chinese friend in his 70s, and was told that during the first 20 years of economic reform, many of the properties including the one he lived in were offered at a very low price for them to own. The price is determined by the number of years one works for a state agency (单位）.

In the beginning of 2009, few months into the 2008 Global Financial Crisis, the New York Times (2 February, 2009) report titled 'China's Unemployment Swells as Exports Falter' revealed that due to massive factory closures, there were about 20 million unemployed migrant workers, and suggested China was in dire conditions with possible unrest.[411] Such a line of assumption may be accurate for any other country, but not for China as these workers were able to return to their original homes in their respective villages where they basically pay no rent, and that their cost of living is very low. The exciting thing was that many of these migrant workers found that there were jobs in their villages due to the decade of government investment to speed up development in rural regions. As a result, the coastal region in China actually experienced a shortage of labour with rising labour cost at a time of Western recession.

It is very easy to demonise a country using partial information. Like the West, China has its problems with income inequality, which has often been used by the mainstream media as a human rights issue against the Communist Party. However, in contrast to capitalist democracies, the Chinese government is working on the issue, and is making great progress. While the situation in the West is getting worse, a report by the Australian-based Financial Standard (2 November, 2012) titled 'Wealth gap narrows in China' revealed that "Farmers in China have seen their incomes grow rapidly this year, helping to close a wealth gap between rural and urban areas. It was the third year in a row that the gap has narrowed."[412] A report by China Daily (4 April February, 2012) titled ''Lost' Staff prompt a headache' revealed that tens of thousands of migrant workers returning to their villages during the Chinese new year did not return to Guangzhou due to job opportunities closer to home.[413] A report by CNTV (19 February, 2013) titled 'Migrant workers in shortage after Spring Festival holiday' revealed that the trend has continued.[414] A report by Al Jazeera (14 August, 2009) titled 'China puts people before banks' had this highlight: "Al Jazeera economist Samah el-Shahat says the west can learn from Beijing."[415]

The collapsed of communism in the USSR and Eastern Europe in the 1990s has effectively given people the impression that Western capitalist democracy is the best form of government. The 2008 Global Financial Crisis has proven otherwise. As mentioned earlier, in 2008, Chinese leader Jia Qinglin claimed that "China will not simply copy the West". Now, the statement made by the same Chinese leader has become a definitive one:

> Under no circumstances will we ever copy the Western political system. Through our efforts, we will make people's democracy wider in scope, fuller in form, and sounder in practice

Through scientific evaluation, practice and ongoing self-criticism, Chinese leadership now know for sure that Western democracy is a fake democracy. And that an economic model based on capitalist exploitation is unsustainable for the long-term survival of mankind. In a recent grassroots visit, Chairman Xi Jinping reiterated the need for the country to hold dear the policy of Mass Line, and to defend the redness of the country. (Ifeng, 12 July, 2013)[416] The core objective of Premier Li Keqiang's economic policy is about the livelihood of the masses. (people.com, 19 July, 2013)[417] One of the objectives of the new leadership team is to double the income of the nation by 2020 based on the level in 2012. Through practice and pragmatism, the Communist Party is working towards the ultimate ideology of communism with genuine social equality, fairness and justice. They have incorporated the spirit of democracy through a system of wide-based consultation and internal consensus through reasoning. They also appropriately using of the invisible hand of market economy to reward personal hard work and creativity without allowing the rich to corrupt the entire system, and dictate the price of products and services regard by the Communist party as basic human rights.

China's rise is not a miracle; their ability to defy Keynesian theory and the many predictions of a blast and collapse by Western intellectuals and economists over the last 60 years is because of their ability to foster a pragmatic and competent leadership team that is able to stand firm with their vision, and work in difficult times despite pressure within and from the outside world. There is no such thing as left or right, hardline or reformist at the top of the Chinese leadership circle - those who are able to make it to the top are all reformists. The less competent ones, once identified, will be removed through the process of internal democracy based on reasoning and not sectarianism.

The reasons behind the 2008 financial crisis was accurately predicted by Karl Marx, and I believe that the West should put aside its indoctrinated attitude towards the ideology of communism, and invest some time to study the works of Karl Marx for the benefit of the Western public. Let the world be pragmatic and open-minded to all sorts of political ideologies. Civilisations should respect each other's rights and freedom to select their own development model. It would be more beneficial for civilisations to learn from each other's merits then to demonise each other.

Please bear in mind the following:

> **Do not criticise the ideology of Communism until you read the works of Karl Marx.**
>
> **Do not criticise the Chinese government until you read or listen to the speeches and thoughts of the Chinese political leaders and their intellectuals.**
>
> **Do not fall into the propaganda of the mainstream media and simply dismiss any reports in the Chinese media as propaganda or "mouth pieces" until you verify the information and examine their reasoning.**
>
> **Do not trust reports from the mainstream media without factual verification.**
>
> **History is the most objective reflection of a culture. Learn from one's own history to avoid making the same mistakes again and again.**
>
> **Values are principles that should be used for disciplining oneself, and not as a political tool to belittle others.**
>
> **There is no need to spend US$56 billion per year to promote a political system if it is a "superior" one. The American capitalist regime should use this money for the human rights of its citizens to enjoy basic housing, food, employment and health care.**

If anybody feels uncomfortable with the way I describe Western governments using the terms such as "regime", "brutal", "indoctrinated", and "warmongering", they should ask themselves the following:

- **Are the examples cited in the book accurate?**
- **If one feels offended by the presentation of truth, what will others feel when their culture is demonised by the West through a series of lies, selective information and fabricated evidence?**

This is a universal value:

Confucius: "Don't do to others if you do not want them to do to you!"

Coming Soon:

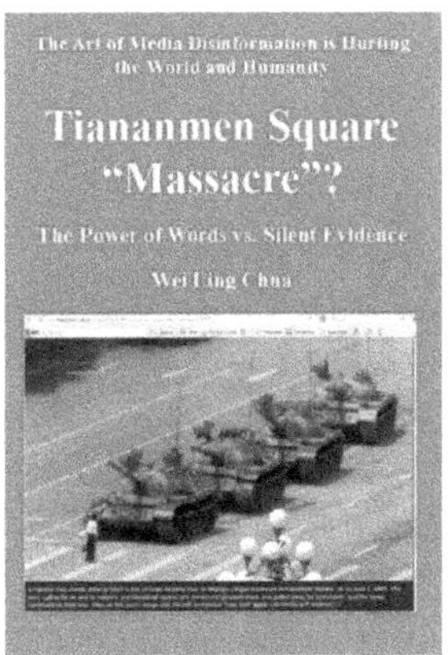

Tiananmen Square "Massacre"? - The Power of Words vs. Silent Evidence: The so-called Tiananmen Square "Massacre" is one of the most misleading events the US government and the Western media have used to demonise the Chinese government each and every year since 1989. There was ample silent evidence in the images produced by the Western media that told the story of a highly restrained and caring Chinese government facing a protest similar to those in the West at various stages in their economic development. However, the West and anti-communist forces had capitalised on the situation in 1989 to fuel the public's anger, intending to overthrow a good government. How the Western media lied about a massacre given the silent evidence that suggests otherwise, and the moral implications of Western powers making ongoing use of common pain and dissatisfaction within an economic cycle of a society to justify the overthrowing of governments across the globe are issues that this book is structured to explore.

About the author

Wei Ling Chua is a freelance journalist accredited by the Australia News and Feature Services (ANFS) and the International News Syndicate (INS). However, since 2009 he has been banned from accessing any of the benefits derived from his accredited membership due to an assignment he submitted to the Morris Journalism Academy questioning the honesty and ethics of the Western media. Wei Ling specialises in media disinformation.

Bibliography and References

[1] PEW Research, "Satisfaction with Country's Direction". China page, search for other countries at the dialog box on the left. http://www.pewglobal.org/database/indicator/3/country/45/

[2] Tony Saich, "Chinese governance seen through the people's eyes". East Asia Forum, 24 July, 2011. http://www.eastasiaforum.org/2011/07/24/chinese-governance-seen-through-the-people-s-eyes/

[3] "'Reforms or Violence,' Chen Tells Xi" Radio Free Asia, 3 December, 2012 http://www.rfa.org/english/news/china/blind-12032012131356.html

[4] Matthew Pennington, *"China's system is doomed: Blind Dissident".* The Australian*, 29 January, 2013* http://www.theaustralian.com.au/news/latest-news/chinas-system-is-doomed-blind-dissident/story-fn3dxix6-1226564506199

[5] "Chinese Dissident Chen Guangcheng Appears on VOA" BBG, 4 February, 2013 http://www.bbg.gov/blog/2013/02/04/chinese-dissident-chen-guangcheng-appears-on-voa/

[6] NBC News/Wall Street Journal Survey, March 11, 13-14, 2010 http://online.wsj.com/public/resources/documents/wsjnbcpoll03162010.pdf

[7] PEW Research, "Frustration with Congress Could Hurt Republican Incumbents GOP Base Critical of Party's Washington Leadership", Center for the People & the Press, 15 December, 2011 http://www.people-press.org/2011/12/15/section-1-congress-the-parties-and-the-anti-incumbent-mood/?src=prc-number

[8] "Washington Post-ABC News Poll" Washington Post, January 12 to 15, 2012 http://www.washingtonpost.com/wp-srv/politics/polls/postabcpoll_011512.html

[9] Frank Newport, "Congress's Job Approval at New Low of 10%", Gallup Politics, 8 February, 2012 http://www.gallup.com/poll/152528/Congress-Job-Approval-New-Low.aspx

[10] Frank Newport, "Congress begins 2013 with 14% approval." Gallup Politics, 11 January, 2013

http://www.gallup.com/poll/159812/congress-begins-2013-approval.aspx

[11] 中国共产党新闻网,"中纪委官员：习近平在中纪委全会上总结苏共亡党教训" 凤凰网, 27 February, 2013 http://news.ifeng.com/mainland/special/fanfu/content-3/detail_2013_02/27/22545677_0.shtml

[12] "Xi reiterates adherence to socialism with Chinese characteristics" CNTV, 5 January, 2013 http://english.cntv.cn/20130105/106636.shtml

[13] "Unequal treaty" Wikipedia: http://en.wikipedia.org/wiki/Unequal_treaty

[14] "Second Sino-Japanese War – Chinese casualties" Wikipedia http://en.wikipedia.org/wiki/Second_Sino-Japanese_War#Casualties_assessment

[15] History and documentary, "黄金密档：国库黄金运台揭秘" 凤凰网, May 2011 http://v.ifeng.com/documentary/history/201105/906fa1b1-a9bc-45eb-afd7-2672eb4bc5af.shtml

[16] "Statistics Show China's 50-year Economic Development" Chinese Embassy in Iceland, 12 May, 2004 http://is.china-embassy.org/eng/zgjm/GeneralEconomicSituation/t98253.htm

[17] Noah Shachtman, "Pentagon Paying China – Yes, China – To Carry Data" Wired, 29 April, 2013 http://www.wired.com/dangerroom/2013/04/china-pentagon-satellite/

[18] Xinhua, "China launches French-made satellite" China Daily, 31 March, 2012 http://www.chinadaily.com.cn/china/2012-03/31/content_14962557.htm

[19] "China launches Nigerian satellite" BBC, 14 May, 2007 http://news.bbc.co.uk/2/hi/6653067.stm

[20] Jeffrey Hill, "China Wins First European Satellite Construction, Launch Contract" Via Satellite Magazine, 21 September, 2011 http://www.satellitetoday.com/telecom/2011/09/21/china-wins-first-european-satellite-construction-launch-contract/

[21] Corina Pons, "Chavez Says China to Launch Second Venezuelan Satellite in 2012" Bloomberg, 11 February, 2012

http://www.bloomberg.com/news/2012-02-10/chavez-says-china-to-launch-second-venezuelan-satellite-in-2012.html

[22] PTI, "China's own GPS makes inroads into neighbouring countries" The Hindu Business Line, 30 April, 2013 http://www.thehindubusinessline.com/news/international/chinas-own-gps-makes-inroads-into-neighbouring-countries/article4670533.ece

[23] Andrew Shen, "Unbelievable Facts About How China is Winning The School Race" Business Insider Australia, 22 October, 2011 http://www.businessinsider.com.au/china-education-2011-10?op=1#the-youth-literacy-rate-is-994-percent-1

[24] Katherine Morton, "China's positive stance on global food policy" East Asia Forum, 12 February, 2013 http://www.eastasiaforum.org/2013/02/12/chinas-positive-stance-on-global-food-policy/

[25] "China university knocks US off its perch with supercomputer" The Australian, 19 June, 2013 http://www.theaustralian.com.au/higher-education/china-university-knocks-us-off-its-perch-with-supercomputer/story-e6frgcjx-1226665896597#

[26] John Dotson, "The Chinese Communist Party and Its Emerging Next-Generation Leaders" US-China Economic and Security Review Commission, 23 March, 2012 http://www.uscc.gov/Research/chinese-communist-party-and-its-emerging-next-generation-leaders

[27] Walter Pincus, "Kissinger offers wise words on China" Washington Post, 9 October, 2012 http://www.washingtonpost.com/world/national-security/kissinger-offers-wise-words-on-china/2012/10/08/9d27c27c-1210-11e2-855a-c9ee6c045478_story.html

[28] "Xi Jinping" Wikipedia: http://en.wikipedia.org/wiki/Xi_Jinping

[29] Simon Elegant, "China's Nelson Mandela" Times, 19 November, 2007 http://world.time.com/2007/11/19/chinas_nelson_mandela/

[30] Rowan Callick, "Malcolm Fraser praises China's 'stability and sense of purpose'" The Australian, 26 September, 2012 http://www.theaustralian.com.au/national-affairs/policy/malcolm-fraser-praises-chinas-stability-and-sense-of-purpose/story-fn59nm2j-1226481377406#

[31] Bonnie Malkin, "Australian PM Kevin Rudd under pressure over George

W Bush 'leaked phonecall'" The Telegraph, 3 November, 2008 http://www.telegraph.co.uk/news/worldnews/australiaandthepacific/australia/3375598/Australian-PM-Kevin-Rudd-under-pressure-over-George-W-Bush-leaked-phonecall.html

[32] Chris McGreal, "George Bush accused of borrowing from other books in his memoirs" The Guardian, 15 November, 2010 http://www.theguardian.com/world/2010/nov/14/george-bush-accused-borrowing-memoirs

[33] John Crace, "Digested read: Decision Points by George Bush" The Guardian, 16 November, 2010 http://www.theguardian.com/books/2010/nov/15/decision-points-by-george-bush

[34] "Test: Obama claims Romney is not tough on China" First Coast News, 5 October, 2012 http://www.firstcoastnews.com/news/politics/article/276973/23/Truth-Test-Obama-claims-Romney-is-not-tough-on-China

[35] "China urges US politicians to be responsible" China Daily, 27 February, 2012 http://www.chinadaily.com.cn/china/2012-02/27/content_14705807.htm

[36] Kate Andersen Brower, "China-Bashing as Campaign Rhetoric Binds Obama to Romney" Bloomberg, 14 June, 2012 http://www.bloomberg.com/news/2012-06-04/china-bashing-binds-obama-to-romney-with-trade-imbalance-as-foil.html

[37] Robert G. Kaiser, "Act of Congress – How America's Essential Institution Works and How It Doesn't" Knopf, first edition 7 May, 2013 http://www.amazon.com/Act-Congress-Americas-Essential-Institution/dp/030770016X

[38] Oliver Duggan, "Politicians 'should face performance reviews'" The Independent, 24 May, 2011 http://www.independent.co.uk/news/uk/politics/politicians-should-face-performance-reviews-2288236.html

[39] "Our governance has yet to enter the 21st century" The Independent, 18 September, 2012 http://www.independent.co.uk/voices/editorials/editorial-our-governance-has-yet-to-enter-the-21st-century-8145118.html

[40] "Political Career of Arnold Schwarzenegger" Wikipedia http://en.wikipedia.org/wiki/Political_career_of_Arnold_Schwarzenegger

41 Matthew Kaminski, "How California Became France' The Wall Street Journal, 21 February, 2009 http://online.wsj.com/article/SB123517419077037281.html

42 Daniel A. Bell, "What America's flawed democracy could learn from China's one party rule" The Christian Science Monitor, 24 July, 2012 http://www.csmonitor.com/Commentary/Global-Viewpoint/2012/0724/What-America-s-flawed-democracy-could-learn-from-China-s-one-party-rule

43 Francis Fukuyama, "What is Governance?" The American interest, 31 January, 2012 http://blogs.the-american-interest.com/fukuyama/2012/01/31/what-is-governance/

44 "New leadership of Communist Party of China – Members of Standing Committee of Political Bureau of CPC Central Committee" China Daily, 17 March, 2013 http://www.chinadaily.com.cn/china/2013npc/2013-03/17/content_16314798.htm

45 David Rood, "Ailing Liberals need young members, says president" The Age, 31 March, 2008 http://www.theage.com.au/news/national/ailing-liberals-need-young-members-says-president/2008/03/30/1206850707180.html

46 Paul Austin, "Faction-hit ALP 'face extinction' The Age, 26 January, 2009 http://www.theage.com.au/national/factionhit-alp-faces-extinction-20090125-7pgl.html?page=-1

47 Phillip Coorey, "Colleagues see red over Rudd's plans" Brisbane Times, 28 November, 2011 http://www.brisbanetimes.com.au/national/colleagues-see-red-over-rudds-plans-20111127-1o1io.html

48 Michael Mckenna, "Unions urged to intervene as members abandon ALP" The Australian, 28 March, 2013 http://www.theaustralian.com.au/national-affairs/policy/unions-urged-to-intervene-as-members-abandon-alp/story-fn59noo3-1226608001630#

49 Same reference as 45

50 Katharine Murphy, "It ain't easy being Brown" The Age, 12 March, 2012 http://www.theage.com.au/federal-politics/it-aint-easy-being-brown-20120311-1usbv.html

51 Barry Jones, "The decay of the political process" The Conversation, 27 March, 2012

http://theconversation.com/the-decay-of-the-political-process-6079

[52] Grey Giroux, "Voters Throw Bums In While Holding Congress in Disdain" Bloomberg, 13 December, 2012 http://www.bloomberg.com/news/2012-12-13/voters-throw-bums-in-while-disdaining-congress-bgov-barometer.html

[53] Dennis Atkins, "Queensland voters facing a bruising time as fertile election ground" Courier Mail, 18 July, 2010 http://www.couriermail.com.au/archive/news/queensland-voters-facing-a-bruising-time-as-fertile-election-ground/story-fn5z3z83-1225893494373

[54] Malcolm Farr, "Labor or Liberal? We don't want either latest polling shows" News, 27 April, 2011 http://www.news.com.au/national-news/labor-or-liberal-we-dont-want-either-latest-polling-shows/story-e6frfkw9-1226045725700

[55] Gay Alcorn, "Voters tune out in droves with 4 months to go" The Age, 6 May, 2013 http://www.theage.com.au/federal-politics/political-news/voters-tune-out-in-droves-with-4-months-to-go-20130505-2j1fd.html

[56] Steven Scott, "Labor making ground in Queensland but Gillard, Abbott don't understand Queensland issues, voters say" Courier Mail, 26 November, 2012 http://www.couriermail.com.au/news/queensland/labor-making-ground-in-queensland-but-gillard-abbott-dont-understand-queensland-issues-voters-say/story-e6freoof-1226523746795

[57] Michelle Grattan, "Turnbull twice as popular" Sydney Morning Herald, 17 September, 2012 http://www.smh.com.au/federal-politics/political-news/turnbull-twice-as-popular-20120916-260mu.html

[58] Patricia Zengerie, "US vote in 2012 will be record, $6 billion election" Reuters, 30 August, 2011 http://www.reuters.com/article/2011/08/30/us-usa-campaign-spending-idUSTRE77T3ZX20110830

[59] Inside Story, "How does the US treat its homeless?" Aljazeera, 27 June, 2012 http://www.aljazeera.com/programmes/insidestoryamericas/2012/06/201262761617710509.html

[60] T.W. Farnam, "Congress won't face pay cut in sequester" Washington Post, 7 March, 2013 http://www.washingtonpost.com/politics/congress-wont-face-pay-

cut-in-sequester/2013/03/06/15dcb3e6-7795-11e2-95e4-6148e45d7adb_story.html?wpisrc=nl_fedinsider

[61] Dr. Paul Craig Roberts, "How deregulation has Resurrected American Economic Security" Global Research, 8 March, 2013 http://www.globalresearch.ca/how-deregulation-has-resurrected-american-economic-insecurity/5325738

[62] Nile Gardiner, "Barack Obama's $7 million Hawaii vacation is an insult to America's struggling middle class" The Telegraph, 4 January, 2013 http://blogs.telegraph.co.uk/news/nilegardiner/100196479/barack-obamas-7-million-hawaii-vacation-is-an-insult-to-americas-struggling-middle-class/

[63] Steven Lewis, "Capital burnout: Canberra bosses are Australia's toughest" Perth Now, 21 December, 2011 http://www.perthnow.com.au/business/canberra-bosses-are-the-toughest/story-e6frg2qc-1226227289585

[64] Jessica Wright, "Anger over MP's pay rise" The Age, 4 July, 2012 http://www.theage.com.au/federal-politics/political-news/anger-over-mps-pay-rise-20120704-21gfu.html

[65] Daniel Hurst, "MPs unite to keep pollie perks secret" The Age, 1 June, 2013 http://www.theage.com.au/federal-politics/political-news/mps-unite-to-keep-pollie-perks-secret-20130531-2nh9y.html

[66] Julian Glover, "Europeans are liberal, anxious and don't trust politicians, poll reveals" The Guardian, 14 March, 2011 http://www.theguardian.com/world/2011/mar/13/guardian-icm-europe-poll-2011?CMP=EMCGT_140311&

[67] "Dialogue 11/09/2012: Theoretical groundwork for CPC leadership" CNTV, 10 October, 2012 http://english.cntv.cn/program/dialogue/20121110/100759.shtml

[68] George Friedman, "The Election, the Presidency and Foreign Policy" Statfor, 31 July, 2012 http://www.stratfor.com/weekly/election-presidency-and-foreign-policy#ixzz22CAXTIUp

[69] "Public Trust in Government: 1958-2013" PEW Research Center for the People & the Press, 31 January, 2013 http://www.people-press.org/2013/01/31/trust-in-government-interactive/

[70] "Trust in government and CEOs low in the 2012 Edelman Trust Barometer" Edelman, 7 February, 2011

http://www.scribd.com/fullscreen/80679434?access_key=key-1krg0ahq8q5lbe2ebp6z

[71] "Black Saturday bushfires" Wikipedia: http://en.wikipedia.org/wiki/Black_Saturday_bushfires

[72] Brendan Nicholson, "We'll rebuild: Rudd" Brisbane Times, 11 February, 2009 http://www.brisbanetimes.com.au/news/national/well-rebuild-rudd/2009/02/10/1234028083598.html

[73] John Ferguson, "Slow and steady but no promise of winning race" Herald Sun, 4 February, 2010 http://www.heraldsun.com.au/archive/old-news-pages/slow-and-steady-but-no-promise-of-winning-race/story-fn4xbx59-1225826551245

[74] Perla Astudillo, "Australian bushfire royal commission: Survivors expose "stay or go" policy" WSWS, 28 May, 2009 http://www.wsws.org/en/articles/2009/05/royc-m28.html

[75] Herald Sun, "Black Saturday: Leaders faltered as Victoria burned" News, 28 May, 2010 http://www.news.com.au/national-news/black-saturday-leaders-faltered-as-victoria-burned/story-e6frfkvr-1225872289816

[76] Norrie Ross, "Police Minister and three most senior police officers absent when most deaths occurred on Black Saturday, commission hears" Herald Sun, 7 May, 2010 http://www.heraldsun.com.au/news/bob-cameron-surprised-christine-nixon-left-at-6pm-on-black-saturday/story-e6frf7jo-1225863571852

[77] Margaret Rees, "Australia: Government culpability in 2009 Victoria bushfires" WSWS, 17 May, 2010 http://www.wsws.org/en/articles/2010/05/bush-m17.html

[78] AAP, "Brumby defends bushfire rebuilding delays" Herald Sun, 7 February, 2010 http://www.heraldsun.com.au/news/victoria/brumby-defends-bushfire-rebuilding-delays/story-e6frf7kx-1225827512111

[79] Farrah Tomazin, "Labor accuses Coalition of reneging on fires vow" The Age, 26 June, 2011 http://www.theage.com.au/victoria/labor-accuses-coalition-of-reneging-on-fires-vow-20110625-1gkzq.html

[80] Chris Johnston, "Ashes to Ashes: forgotten fire town mourns again" The Age, 19 May 2012

http://www.theage.com.au/victoria/ashes-to-ashes-forgotten-fire-town-mourns-again-20120518-1ywba.html

[81] Courtney Trenwith, "'Forgotten' bushfire victims still in limbo" WA Today, 14 November, 2012 http://www.watoday.com.au/wa-news/forgotten-bushfire-victims-still-in-limbo-20121114-29c00.html

[82] Russell Skelton, "Out of the fire" The Age, 31 March, 2009 http://www.theage.com.au/national/out-of-the-fire-20090330-9h6k.html

[83] "Effects of Hurricane Katrina in New Orleans" Wikipedia http://en.wikipedia.org/wiki/Effects_of_Hurricane_Katrina_in_New_Orleans

[84] "Video shows Bush Katrina warning" BBC, 2 March, 2006 http://news.bbc.co.uk/2/hi/americas/4765058.stm

[85] Peter Grier, "Video of 2007 Obama speech: Will it affect 2012 election? (+Video)" Christian Science Monitor, 3 October, 2012 http://www.csmonitor.com/USA/DC-Decoder/Decoder-Wire/2012/1003/Video-of-2007-Obama-speech-Will-it-affect-2012-election-video

[86] Cain Burdeau, "Corps' negligence caused Katrina flooding" Brisbane Times, 20 November, 2009 http://www.brisbanetimes.com.au/world/corps-negligence-caused-katrina-flooding-20091120-ipc0.html

[87] "The Facts: The Right to Return – Rebuilding the Gulf through the framework of International Human Rights" Amnesty International http://www.amnestyusa.org/sites/default/files/pdfs/therighttoreturn.pdf

[88] Fair, "How Corporate Media Are Washing Away Katrina From America's Mind" AlterNet, 10 September, 2009 http://www.alternet.org/story/142552/how_corporate_media_are_washing_away_katrina_from_america%27s_mind

[89] Patrik Jonsson, "New Orleans' razing craze aims to clear way for post-Katrina recovery" Christian Science Monitor, 24 February, 2012 http://www.csmonitor.com/USA/2012/0224/New-Orleans-razing-craze-aims-to-clear-way-for-post-Katrina-recovery

[90] AP, "Policeman 'fired at wounded men' in aftermath of Hurricane Katrina" The Independent, 8 July, 2011 http://www.independent.co.uk/news/world/americas/policeman-fired-at-wounded-men-in-aftermath-of-hurricane-katrina-

2308802.html

[91] Chris McGreal, "Five New Orleans police officers sentenced in hurricane Katrina killings" Guardian, 5 April, 2012 http://www.theguardian.com/world/2012/apr/04/new-orleans-police-officers-katrina

[92] "Supporting Post-earthquake Recovery in China" The World Bank, 4 December, 2012 http://www.worldbank.org/en/news/feature/2012/12/04/supporting-post-earthquake-recovery-in-china

[93] AP, "Chrischurch earthquake collapse building was substandard" Guardian, 9 February, 2012 http://www.theguardian.com/world/2012/feb/09/christchurch-quake-ctv-building-substandard?CMP=EMCNEWEML1355

[94] "Ai Weiwei (Contemporary Chinese Artist)" Rise of Civilization, Spring 2013 http://anthropology.msu.edu/anp363-ss13/2013/03/27/ai-weiwei-contemporary-chinese-artist/

[95] "Deadly collapsed wall in Melbourne was 'significantly' cracked" The Australian, 4 April, 2013 http://www.theaustralian.com.au/news/nation/deadly-collapsed-wall-in-melbourne-was-riddled-with-cracks/story-e6frg6nf-1226612290406

[96] AFP, "China marks anniversary of killer Sichuan quake" Google, 11 May, 2013 http://www.google.com/hostednews/afp/article/ALeqM5iaNsAiE035vAOrCEEmaGaCCvy7QQ?docId=CNG.c61c8fd1b4791c92c28c21f9c85e385b.471

[97] Tom Phillips, "The Children airbrushed from the story of China's devastating quake" The Telegraph, 11 May, 2013 http://www.telegraph.co.uk/news/worldnews/asia/china/10051077/The-children-airbrushed-from-the-story-of-Chinas-devastating-quake.html

[98] Choi Chi-yuk, "The shame of Sichuan's tofu schools" South China Morning Post, 6 May, 2013 http://www.scmp.com/news/china/article/1230807/shame-sichuans-tofu-schools

[99] Carmen Lawrence, "Ideas to save our withering democracy" Project SafeCom Inc., 1 January, 2007 http://www.safecom.org.au/lawrence03.htm

[100] AP, "Two years later, Christchurch earthquake recovery remains slow"

News, 20 February, 2013 http://www.news.com.au/world-news/two-years-later-christchurch-quake-recovery-slow/story-fndir2ev-1226582311033

101 Michael Wright, "Christchurch rebuild inches towards recovery" Stuff, 22 February, 2013 http://www.stuff.co.nz/business/rebuilding-christchurch/8338782/Christchurch-rebuild-inches-towards-recovery

102 Sara Miller Llana, "How 'socially inclusive' is Latin America? New indicator ranks countries" Christian Science Monitor, 12 April, 2012 http://www.csmonitor.com/World/Americas/Latin-America-Monitor/2012/0412/How-socially-inclusive-is-Latin-America-New-indicator-ranks-countries

103 "Hu: China firmly follows socialism with Chinese characteristics" CNTV, 8 November, 2012 http://english.cntv.cn/20121108/102226.shtml

104 "CPC pledges to keep improving people's wellbeing" CNTV, 8 November, 2012 http://english.cntv.cn/20121108/103179.shtml

105 "Full text of Xi's address to the media" China Daily, 16 November, 2012 http://www.chinadaily.com.cn/china/2012cpc/2012-11/16/content_15934514.htm

106 "Results Profile: China Poverty Reduction" World Bank, 19 March, 2010 http://www.worldbank.org/en/news/feature/2010/03/19/results-profile-china-poverty-reduction

107 Anup Shah, "Poverty Around The World" Global Issues, 12 November, 2011 http://www.globalissues.org/article/4/poverty-around-the-world

108 "昨天胡锦涛的重要讲话，我最欣赏这一句"Sou Fun, 20 December, 2008 http://honghuhuayuan0851.soufun.com/bbs/3314178186~-1/53039670_53039670.htm

109 Lenore Taylor, "The Rudd gang of four" Australian, 9 November, 2009 http://www.theaustralian.com.au/news/features/the-rudd-gang-of-four/story-e6frg6z6-1225795556696

110 Phillip Hudson, "Shattered leader Kevin Rudd deserted by those he led to power" Herald Sun, 25 June, 2010 http://www.heraldsun.com.au/news/shattered-leader-kevin-rudd-deserted-by-those-he-lead-to-power/story-e6frf7jo-1225884032074

111 Simon Benson, "Kevin Rudd coup cost taxpayers millions in separation

payments for staff" Courier Mail, 12 November, 2010 http://www.couriermail.com.au/news/national/kevin-rudd-coup-cost-taxpayers-millions-in-separation-payments-for-staff/story-e6freooo-1225952331434

[112] Troy Bramston, "Rare peek inside the factory of faceless men as Labor replaces loyalist with a legend" Australian, 7 March, 2012 http://www.theaustralian.com.au/national-affairs/rare-peek-inside-the-factory-of-faceless-men-as-labor-replaces-loyalist-with-a-legend/story-fn59niix-1226291261992#

[113] Simon Kearney, "Julia Gillard rewards the plotters" News, 12 September, 2010 http://www.news.com.au/breaking-news/julia-gillard-rewards-the-plotters/story-e6frfkp9-1225918720500

[114] Michelle Grattan, "Gillard rewards her henchmen" The Age, 13 December, 2011 http://www.theage.com.au/national/gillard-rewards-her-henchmen-20111212-1orn9.html

[115] Simon Benson, "Secret pro-Kevin polling buried by Labor" Herald Sun, 21 March, 2013 http://www.heraldsun.com.au/news/national/secret-pro-kevin-rudd-polling-buried-by-labor/story-fncynkc6-1226601992690#

[116] "Foreign policy not my thing, says Gillard" ABC, 6 October, 2010 http://www.abc.net.au/news/2010-10-05/foreign-policy-not-my-thing-says-gillard/2286744

[117] AAP, "Crean sacked as minister" Australian, 21 March, 2013 http://www.theaustralian.com.au/news/latest-news/crean-sacked-as-minister/story-fn3dxiwe-1226602630819

[118] AAP, "PM Julia Gillard admits she has moments of self-doubt on 'Q and A'" The Telegraph, 7 May, 2013 http://www.dailytelegraph.com.au/news/national/pm-admits-she-has-moments-of-self-doubt/story-fncvk70o-1226636394763

[119] Dennis Shanahan, "Kevin Rudd ALP's best hope: Newspoll" Australian, 25 February, 2012 http://www.theaustralian.com.au/archive/national-affairs/kevin-rudd-alps-best-hope-newspoll/story-fnccyr6m-1226281089887

[120] Gemma Jones, "Voters reaching out to yesterday's men Kevin Rudd and Malcolm Turnbull" The Telegraph, 3 December, 2012 http://www.dailytelegraph.com.au/voters-reaching-out-to-yesterdays-men-kevin-rudd-and-malcolm-turnbull/story-e6freuy9-

1226528450903

[121] Michael Gordon, "Gillard stands firm" The Age, 11 June, 2013 http://www.theage.com.au/federal-politics/political-news/gillard-stands-firm-20130610-2o09e.html

[122] Stephanie Peatling, "Shorten 'believes' Gillard will lead to poll' Sydney Morning Herald, 12 June, 2013 http://www.smh.com.au/federal-politics/political-news/shorten-believes-gillard-will-lead-to-poll-20130612-2o36k.html

[123] Jonathan Swan, "Rudd ends speculation of another tilt" The Age, 22 March, 2013 http://www.theage.com.au/federal-politics/political-news/rudd-ends-speculation-of-another-tilt-20130322-2gjn6.html

[124] Patrick Lion, "Bill Shorten emerged as turncoat kingmaker to return Kevin Rudd to the Labor leadership" The Telegraph, 27 June, 2013 http://www.dailytelegraph.com.au/news/bill-shorten-emerged-as-turncoat-kingmaker-to-return-kevin-rudd-to-the-labor-leadership/story-fni0cx4q-1226670518132

[125] Simon Benson, "Poll reveals voters don't believe Kevin Rudd has changed since first stint as PM" The Telegraph, 1 July, 2013 http://www.dailytelegraph.com.au/news/national/galaxy-daily-telegraph-poll-reveals-voters-dont-believe-kevin-rudd-has-changed-since-first-stint-as-pm/story-fni0xqrc-1226672232561#

[126] AAP, "Coalition would still win election, finds poll following Kevin Rudd's comeback" The Telegraph, 28 June, 2013 http://www.dailytelegraph.com.au/news/special-features/coalition-would-still-win-election-finds-poll-following-kevin-rudd8217s-comeback/story-fnho52jp-1226671201393#

[127] Mark Kenny, "Rudd gets his revenge" Sydney Morning Herald, 27 June, 2013 http://www.smh.com.au/federal-politics/political-news/rudd-gets-his-revenge-20130626-2oxsw.html

[128] Amanda Vanstone, "Presenting the Labor leopard: spot the difference" The Age, 1 July, 2013 http://www.theage.com.au/federal-politics/political-opinion/presenting-the-labor-leopard-spot-the-difference-20130630-2p58l.html

[129] Mark Kenny, "Beware one-man show: warning for Labor" Sydney Morning Herald, 2 July, 2013 http://www.smh.com.au/federal-politics/federal-election-

2013/beware-oneman-show-warning-for-labor-20130701-2p7lk.html

[130] Richard Norton-Taylor, "MI6 and CIA were told before invasion that Iraq had no active WMD" Guardian, 18 March, 2013 http://www.theguardian.com/world/2013/mar/18/panorama-iraq-fresh-wmd-claims?CMP=EMCNEWEML6619I2

[131] "Hans Blix: The Iranian threat" Aljazeera, 27 March, 2012 http://www.aljazeera.com/news/middleeast/2012/03/201232316145 8267958.html

[132] David A. Fahrenthold, "Sen. Rand Paul: Congress has become 'an irrelevancy' on war powers" Washington Post, 9 June, 2011 http://www.washingtonpost.com/politics/sen-rand-paul-congress-has-become-an-irrelevancy-on-war-powers/2011/06/08/AGV2lyLH_story.html?wpisrc=nl_politics

[133] Joshua Keating, "Actually, US presidents have been going to war without Congress since the beginning" Foreign Policy, 9 May, 2013 http://ideas.foreignpolicy.com/posts/2013/05/09/actually_us_presidents_have_been_going_to_war_without_congress_since_the_beginning

[134] "Obama moves to keep kill list memos secret forever" RT, 21 February, 2013 http://rt.com/usa/obama-moves-to-keep-kill-list-memos-secret-forever-224/

[135] Scott Shane, "White House Tactic for CIA Bid Holds Back Drone Memos" New York Times, 20 February, 2013 http://www.nytimes.com/2013/02/21/us/politics/strategy-seeks-to-ensure-bid-of-brennan-for-cia.html?pagewanted=all&_r=2&

[136] Henry M. Paulson, Jr. "A Strategic economic Engagement – Strengthening US-China Ties" Foreign Affair, Vol. 87, No 5. September/October, 2008 http://www.jstor.org/discover/10.2307/20699304?uid=3737536&uid=2&uid=4&sid=21102728004541

[137] Christopher R. Hill, "How to Move China" Project Syndicate, 24 April, 2013 http://www.project-syndicate.org/commentary/understanding-chinese-concerns-about-north-korea-by-christopher-r--hill

[138] "China 'will not have democracy'" BBC, 9 March, 2009 http://news.bbc.co.uk/2/hi/7932091.stm

[139] Robert J. Samuelson, "The dysfunction of American politics" Washington Post, 25 October,2010

http://www.washingtonpost.com/wp-dyn/content/article/2010/10/24/AR2010102402217.html?wpisrc=nl_opinions

[140] "Australian Prime Minister Julia Gillard Sets Up Watergate Style Dirt Unit For Opposition Politicans" Kangaroo Court Australia, 17 June, 2012 http://kangaroocourtofaustralia.com/2012/06/17/australian-prime-minister-julia-gillard-sets-up-watergate-style-dirt-unit-for-opposition-politicians/

[141] "Gillard Stands by Maligned Advisers" SBS, 21 September, 2012 http://www.sbs.com.au/news/article/1694723/Gillard-stands-by-maligned-advisers

[142] Tony Moore, "Dirt file furore spreads to Brisbane City Council" Brisbane Times, 13 October, 2011 http://www.brisbanetimes.com.au/queensland/dirt-file-furore-spreads-to-brisbane-city-council-20111013-1lmd8.html

[143] Steven Wardill, "Justin Bold lashes out at Labor's 'dirt-finding machine" Courier Mail, 10 October, 2011 http://www.couriermail.com.au/news/newman-associate-blasts-muck-raking/story-e6freon6-1226163380279

[144] Tony Moore, "Dirty talk a turn-off for voters" Brisbane Times, 13 October, 2011 http://www.brisbanetimes.com.au/queensland/dirty-talk-a-turnoff-for-voters-20111012-1llbz.html

[145] Rachel Weiner, "Mitt Romney ad mocks 'historian' Newt Gingrich" Washington Post, 23 January, 2012 http://www.washingtonpost.com/blogs/the-fix/post/mitt-romney-ad-mocks-historian-newt-gingrich/2012/01/23/gIQASFZMLQ_blog.html

[146] Mitch McConnell, "The IRS scandal and Obama's culture of intimidation" Washington Post, 23 May, 2013 http://www.washingtonpost.com/opinions/mitch-mcconnell-the-irs-scandal-and-obamas-culture-of-intimidation/2013/05/22/9c4b7de6-c2f8-11e2-914f-a7aba60512a7_story.html?wpisrc=nl_politics

[147] David A. Stockman, "State-Wrecked: The Corruption of Capitalism in America" New York Times, 30 March, 2013 http://www.nytimes.com/2013/03/31/opinion/sunday/sundown-in-america.html?nl=todaysheadlines&emc=edit_th_20130331&_r=1&

[148] Sarah Seltzer, "26 killed at Connecticut Elementary School, 20 of them children: Can we ever talk about gun control? AlterNet, 14 December,

2012
http://www.alternet.org/news-amp-politics/18-or-more-children-killed-connecticut-elementary-school-can-we-ever-talk-about?akid=9801.267042.SFeWj-&rd=1&src=newsletter760998&t=2

[149] Ed Pilkington, "Obama: 'We can't tolerate this anymore, these tragedies must end'" Guardian, 17 December, 2012
http://www.theguardian.com/world/2012/dec/17/obama-newtown-speech-gun-control?CMP=EMCNEWEML1355

[150] "How many people get shot by someone using a gun each day in the US?" Answers
http://wiki.answers.com/Q/How_many_people_get_shot_by_someone_using_a_gun_each_day_in_the_US&altQ=How_many_people_get_shot_by_guns_each_day_in_the_US

[151] Richard W. Painter, "The NRA Protection Racket" New York Times, 19 December, 2012
http://www.nytimes.com/2012/12/20/opinion/the-nra-protection-racket.html?nl=todaysheadlines&emc=edit_th_20121220&_r=0

[152] Laura Gottesdiener, "The US has Averaged More than 18 Gun Deaths every Day Since the Newtown School Shooting" AlterNet, 3 January, 2013
http://www.alternet.org/news-amp-politics/us-has-averaged-more-18-gun-deaths-every-day-newtown-school-shooting?akid=9891.267042.lF0k3p&rd=1&src=newsletter770775&t=4

[153] Sari Horwitz, "States move to restrict gun magazines as federal proposal stalls in Congress" Washington Post, 11 April, 2013
http://www.washingtonpost.com/world/national-security/states-move-to-restrict-gun-magazines-as-federal-proposal-stalls-in-congress/2013/04/10/82f04dde-9d61-11e2-a2db-efc5298a95e1_story.html?wpisrc=nl_headlines

[154] Carl Campanile, "White House releases photo of Obama skeet shooting amid gun-control push" New York Post, 2 February, 2013
http://nypost.com/2013/02/02/white-house-releases-photo-of-obama-skeet-shooting-amid-gun-control-push/

[155] "Assault weapons ban dropped from Senate gun control bill" Fox News, 19 March, 2013
http://www.foxnews.com/politics/2013/03/19/reid-cuts-assault-weapons-ban-from-senate-gun-control-bill-amid-waning-support/

[156] Ed O'Keefe, "Gun-control overhaul is defeated in Senate" Washington

Post, 18 April, 2013 http://www.washingtonpost.com/politics/gun-control-overhaul-is-defeated-in-senate/2013/04/17/57eb028a-a77c-11e2-b029-8fb7e977ef71_story.html?wpisrc=nl_politics

[157] Gordon Rupe, "Woops! Obama Ordered Gun Report Reveals Guns Actually Save Lives" Infowars, 27 June, 2013 http://www.infowars.com/woops-obama-ordered-gun-report-reveals-guns-actually-save-lives/

[158] AFP, "Voters oust politicians who promoted tighter gun controls after Aurora massacre" Sydney Morning Herald, 12 September, 2013 http://www.smh.com.au/world/voters-oust-politicians-who-promoted-tighter-gun-controls-after-aurora-massacre-20130912-2tljo.html

[159] John Garnaut, "Rudd policy on China 'set by BHP'" Brisbane Times, 15 October, 2009 http://www.brisbanetimes.com.au/business/rudd-policy-on-china-set-by-bhp-20091015-gxqm.html

[160] Heath Aston, "Coalition lets miners write lands policy" Sydney Morning Herald, 20 January, 2011 http://www.smh.com.au/nsw/coalition-lets-miners-write-lands-policy-20110119-19wq7.html

[161] Wei Ling Chua, "Democracy needs reform – The cruelty of poll driven politics" Outcast Journalist, 28 June, 2010 http://outcastjournalist.com/index_files/democracy_need_reform_the_cruelty_of_poll_driven_politics.htm

[162] AAP, "Mining firms spent more than $20 million to bury Rudd's tax" WA Today, 1 February, 2011 http://www.watoday.com.au/business/mining-firms-spent-more-than-20-million-to-bury-rudds-tax-20110201-1ac4z.html

[163] Scott Murdoch, "Government accepts 98 recommendations from mining tax review" Australian, 24 March, 2011 http://www.theaustralian.com.au/business/mining-energy/government-accepts-mrrt-recommendations/story-e6frg9df-1226027474907

[164] Simon Cullen, "Mining tax raises $126m in first six months" ABC, 9 February, 2013 http://www.abc.net.au/news/2013-02-08/mining-tax-details-released/4508632

[165] AAP, "mining tax deeply flawed, Garnaut says" WA Today, 29 April,

2013 http://www.watoday.com.au/business/mining-and-resources/mining-tax-deeply-flawed-garnaut-says-20130429-2io7u.html

[166] Tuck Thompson and Sue Dunlevy, "New Redcliffe GP super clinic an empty shell" Courier Mail, 13 February, 2013 http://www.couriermail.com.au/news/queensland/new-redcliffe-gp-super-clinic-an-empty-shell/story-e6freoof-1226576557846#

[167] "Another GP super clinic pledged for Wynnum as four others yet to open" Courier Mail, 20 February, 2013 http://www.couriermail.com.au/news/queensland/another-gp-super-clinic-pledged-for-wynnum-as-four-others-yet-to-open/story-e6freoof-1226581767372

[168] Peter Martin, "Hey, big spender: Howard the king of the loose purse strings" Sydney Morning Herald, 11 January, 2013 http://www.smh.com.au/federal-politics/political-news/hey-big-spender-howard-the-king-of-the-loose-purse-strings-20130110-2cj32.html

[169] Phil Lewis, "Howard's End: how the coalition's last budget created the ground for the current deficits" Conversation, 8 May, 2013 http://theconversation.com/howards-end-how-the-coalitions-last-budget-created-the-ground-for-the-current-deficits-13848

[170] Sinclair Davidson, "Swan's budget is a lame effort from a dying government" Conversation, 16 May, 2013 http://theconversation.com/swans-budget-is-a-lame-effort-from-a-dying-government-14279

[171] Adele Ferguson, "Lies, damned lies ... and budgets" The Age, 14 May, 2013 http://www.theage.com.au/business/federal-budget/lies-damned-lies--and-budgets-20130514-2jknw.html

[172] Ross Gittins, "Budget becomes Canberra's con job" Sydney Morning Herald, 13 May, 2013 http://www.smh.com.au/business/federal-budget/budget-becomes-canberras-con-job-20130512-2jg4j.html

[173] Admin, "Tony Abbott's 12 biggest budget reply porkie pies" Independent Australia, 19 May, 2013 http://www.independentaustralia.net/2013/politics/tony-abbotts-budget-reply-porkie-pies/

[174] "Obama promises to cut the deficit in half in four years" PolitiFact, 24 March, 2009

http://www.politifact.com/truth-o-meter/statements/2009/mar/25/barack-obama/obama-promises-cut-deficit-half-four-years/

[175] Mark Knoller, "National debt up $6 trillion since Obama took office" CBS News, 1 March, 2013 http://www.cbsnews.com/8301-250_162-57572177/national-debt-up-$6-trillion-since-obama-took-office/

[176] "Dissolution of Czechoslovakia" Wikipedia http://en.wikipedia.org/wiki/Dissolution_of_Czechoslovakia

[177] Andres Cala, "Catalonia declares intent to hold independent referendum" Christian Monitor Science, 23 January, 2013 http://www.csmonitor.com/World/Europe/2013/0123/Catalonia-declares-intent-to-hold-independence-referendum

[178] same as reference no 161

[179] John Masanauskas, "Federal Government set to maintain record high immigration levels" Herald Sun, 3 September, 2009 http://www.heraldsun.com.au/news/federal-government-set-to-maintain-record-high-immigration-levels/story-e6frf7jo-1225768970486#

[180] Tim Colebatch, "City to top 7m people" The Age, 23 October, 2009 http://www.theage.com.au/national/city-to-top-7m-people-20091022-hbg7.html

[181] Kevin Rudd, "Kevin Rudd's speech in full" The Advertiser, 20 January, 2010 http://www.adelaidenow.com.au/news/kevin-rudds-speech-in full/story-e6freo8c-1225821744119

[182] Ellen Whinnett, "Poll shows Aussies want immigration capped" News, 24 January, 2010 http://www.news.com.au/national-news/poll-shows-aussies-want-immigration-capped/story-e6frfkvr-1225823001150

[183] Geoff Maslen, "Australia: Exporting education worth billions" University World, 24 January, 2010 http://www.universityworldnews.com/article.php?story=2010012309 163040

[184] Wendy Carlisle, "Holy Cash Cows" ABC Four Corner, 27 July, 2009 http://www.abc.net.au/4corners/content/2009/s2637255.htm

[185] Sushi Das, "College in gross breach of standards" The Age, 23 July, 2009 http://www.theage.com.au/national/education/college-in-gross-breach-of-standards-20090722-dtl2.html

---

[186] "UNE accused of allowing plagiarists to graduate" Australian, 29 July, 2009 http://www.theaustralian.news.com.au/story/0,25197,25849064-12332,00.html

[187] PTI, "Australian govt ignores advice on Indian students: Report" Times of India, 23 January, 2010 http://articles.timesofindia.indiatimes.com/2010-01-23/india/28118899_1_indian-students-student-safety-overseas-students

[188] AAP, "Migration U-turn: 'caught between a rock and a hard place'" Sydney Morning Herald, 8 February, 2010 http://www.smh.com.au/national/migration-uturn-caught-between-a-rock-and-a-hard-place-20100208-nlri.html

[189] Katharine Murphy, "Crackdown on skilled migrants" WA Today, 7 February, 2010 http://www.watoday.com.au/national/crackdown-on-skilled-migrants-20100208-nlf1.html

[190] Mark Metherell, "Australia rejects 20,000 migrants" Brisbane Times, 8 February, 2010 http://www.brisbanetimes.com.au/national/australia-rejects-20000-migrants-20100207-nkxh.html

[191] Ray Clancy, "Australia facing challenges to attract overseas students" Australia Forum, 7 January, 2011 http://www.australiaforum.com/information/education/australia-facing-challenges-to-attract-overseas-students.html

[192] Bernard Lane, "Visa rule reforms give universities a lifeline" Australian, 23 September, 2011 http://www.theaustralian.com.au/national-affairs/visa-rule-reforms-give-unversitieis-a-lifeline/story-fn59niix-1226144082762

[193] Dennis Atkins, "Now it is Julia Gillard's turn to stir fear" Courier Mail, 6 March, 2013 http://www.couriermail.com.au/news/now-it-is-julia-gillards-turn-to-stir-fear/story-e6frerc6-1226591048868#

[194] Stephen King, "Political opportunism, not economics, drives the attack on 457 visas" Conversation, 10 March, 2013 http://theconversation.com/political-opportunism-not-economics-drives-the-attack-on-457-visas-12731

[195] Michelle Grattan, "Gillard and Abbott bet on Australia's xenophobia" Conversation, 5 March, 2013

https://theconversation.com/gillard-and-abbott-bet-on-australias-xenophobia-12639

[196] Staff, "Nicolas Sarkozy joins David Cameron and Angela Merkel view that multiculturalism has failed" Mail Online, 11 February, 2011 http://www.dailymail.co.uk/news/article-1355961/Nicolas-Sarkozy-joins-David-Cameron-Angela-Merkel-view-multiculturalism-failed.html

[197] Adriana Garcia, "Whites to become minority in US by 2050" Reuters (US edition), 12 February, 2008 http://www.reuters.com/article/2008/02/12/us-usa-population-immigration-idUSN1110177520080212

[198] "Minorities expected to be majority in 2050" CNN, 13 August, 2008 http://edition.cnn.com/2008/US/08/13/census.minorities/

[199] Genaro C. Armas, "America's Face Is Changing" CBS News, 11 February, 2009 http://www.cbsnews.com/2100-201_162-607022.html

[200] Sam Roberts, "Projections Put Whites in Minority in US by 2050" New York Times, 17 December, 2009 http://www.nytimes.com/2009/12/18/us/18census.html?_r=5&WT.mc_id=fb_nyt967&WT.mc_ev=click&

[201] Rich Benjamin, "Pockets of White America Are in the Throes of an Existential Crisis" AlterNet, 18 December, 2009 http://www.alternet.org/story/144672/pockets_of_white_america_are_in_the_throes_of_an_existential_crisis

[202] AP, "Whites in US Edge Toward Minority Status" CBS News, 10 March, 2010 http://www.cbsnews.com/2100-201_162-6284387.html

[203] AP, "Census: Whites make up minority of babies In US" USA Today, 23 June, 2011 http://usatoday30.usatoday.com/news/nation/2011-06-23-Census-babies-minority_n.htm

[204] Jeffrey S. Passel, "Explaining Why Minority Births Now Outnumber White Births" PEW Research, 17 May, 2012 http://www.pewsocialtrends.org/2012/05/17/explaining-why-minority-births-now-outnumber-white-births/

[205] AP, "Census: More minority US births than white now" CBS News, 17 May, 2012 http://www.cbsnews.com/8301-201_162-57435957/census-more-minority-u.s-births-than-white-now/

[206] Sabrina Tavernise, "Whites Account for Under half of Births in US" New

York Times, 17 May, 2012 http://www.nytimes.com/2012/05/17/us/whites-account-for-under-half-of-births-in-us.html?pagewanted=all

[207] Matt Taibbi, "Pat Buchuan: GOP Imperiled by Decline of White Population" Rolling Stone, 27 July, 2012 http://www.rollingstone.com/politics/blogs/taibblog/pat-buchanan-gop-imperiled-by-decline-of-white-population-20120727

[208] Stephanie Siek, "Most US children under 1 are minorities, Census says" CNN, 17 May, 2012 http://edition.cnn.com/2012/05/17/us/census-population-diversity

[209] Ruy Teixeira, "When Will Your State Become Majority-Minority?" Think Progress, 8 May, 2013 http://thinkprogress.org/election/2013/05/08/1978221/when-will-your-state-become-majority-minority/?mobile=nc

[210] AP, "Census: Immigration Surpassing US Births, White Children a Minority by 2018" CBS DC, 15 May, 2013 http://washington.cbslocal.com/2013/05/15/census-immigration-surpassing-us-births-white-children-a-minority-by-2018/

[211] AP, "Whites losing majority in US in under-5 group" CBS News, 13 June, 2013 http://www.cbsnews.com/8301-201_162-57589109/whites-losing-majority-in-u.s-in-under-5-group/

[212] Sam Roberts, "Census Benchmark for White Americans: More Deaths Than Births" New York Times, 13 June, 2013 http://www.nytimes.com/2013/06/13/us/census-benchmark-for-white-americans-more-deaths-than-births.html?nl=todaysheadlines&emc=edit_th_20130613&_r=0

[213] Hope Yen, "Census: White majority in US gone by 2043" NBC News, 13 June, 2013 http://usnews.nbcnews.com/_news/2013/06/13/18934111-census-white-majority-in-us-gone-by-2043?lite

[214] Daivd Anderson, "Meet America's emerging minority group – whites" CNN, 22 August, 2013 http://edition.cnn.com/2013/08/22/opinion/anderson-white-minority/index.html

[215] Aaron Blake, "Another race-tinted showdown in Hawaii" Washington Post, 23 April, 2013 http://www.washingtonpost.com/blogs/the-fix/wp/2013/04/23/race-often-influences-politics-in-hawaii/?wpisrc=nl_pmpolitics

[216] Kate Zernike, "Poll Finds Tea Party Backers wealthier and More Educated" New York Times, 14 April, 2010 http://www.nytimes.com/2010/04/15/us/politics/15poll.html?_r=0

[217] Lydia Saad, "Blacks, Postgrads, Young Adults Help Obama Prevail" Gallup Politics, 6 November, 2008 http://www.gallup.com/poll/111781/blacks-postgrads-young-adults-help-obama-prevail.aspx

[218] Jonathan Martin, "Black pols stymied in Obama era" Politico, 29 April, 2013 http://www.politico.com/story/2013/04/black-pols-stymied-in-obama-era-90727.html

[219] Mark J. Magyar, "Mapping out New Jersey's minority representation' NJ Spotlight, 11 march, 2011 http://www.njspotlight.com/stories/11/0311/0055/

[220] Marie Diamond, "Perry Accused of Distorting redistricting Map To Weaken The Latino Vote In Texas" AlterNet, 7 September, 2011 http://www.alternet.org/newsandviews/article/662720/perry_accused_of_distorting_redistricting _map_to_weaken_the_latino_vote_in_texas/

[221] Todd Eberly, "Md. redistricting's big losers: minorities" Washington Post, 14 October, 2011 http://articles.washingtonpost.com/2011-10-14/opinions/35279130_1_majority-minority-district-1st-congressional-district-6th-district

[222] Callin Tong, "Redistricting away seattle's minority representation" Crosscut News, 7 November, 2011 http://crosscut.com/2011/11/07/washington-legislature/21516/Redistricting-away-Seattles-minority-representatio/

[223] Kimberly Reeves, "Redistricting GOP Was "Very, Very Clever" in Limiting Minorities' Voting Power, Expert Testifies" Houston Press, 9 September, 2011 http://blogs.houstonpress.com/hairballs/2011/09/redistricting_gop_texas.php

[224] Thomas Kaplan, "Albany Redistricting Plan Faulted as Unfair to Minorities" New York Times, 30 January, 2012 http://www.nytimes.com/2012/01/31/nyregion/new-york-redistricting-faulted-for-unfair-representation-of-minorities.html?nl=nyregion&emc=ura1

[225] "Voter redistributing disadvantages for minorities" MSNBC News, 15

February, 2012
http://video.msnbc.msn.com/now/46400042#46400042

226 Melanie Hunter, "Holder: Texas Electoral redistricting Maps 'Manipulated' to Minimize 'Minority Electoral Strength' CNS News, 30 May, 2012 http://cnsnews.com/news/article/holder-texas-electoral-redistricting-maps-manipulated-minimize-minority-electoral

227 David W. Chen, "New York's Proposed Council Map Is Called Unfair to Minority Groups" New York Times, 2 October, 2012 http://www.nytimes.com/2012/10/03/nyregion/new-york-city-redistricting-map-is-called-unfair.html?_r=1&nl=nyregion&emc=edit_ur_20121003

228 Trip Gabriel, "Redistricting in Virginia Hurts Blacks, Democrats Say" New York Times, 23 January, 2013 http://www.nytimes.com/2013/01/24/us/politics/virginia-senates-redistricting-is-protested.html?nl=todaysheadlines&emc=edit_th_20130124&_r=0

229 Ari Berman, "Texas Redistricting Fight Shows Why Voting Rights Act Still Needed' The Nation, 5 June, 2013 http://www.thenation.com/blog/174652/texas-redistricting-fight-shows-why-voting-rights-act-still-needed#

230 Brenda Wright, "Minority Vote Dilution Is Still Illegal" Southern Change, Vol.22, No. 4, 2000 pp. 7 to 10 http://beck.library.emory.edu/southernchanges/article.php?id=sc22-4_004

231 Jonathan Cook, "Bedouins in Israel denied elections" The National, 7 December, 2009 http://www.thenational.ae/news/world/middle-east/bedouins-in-israel-denied-elections

232 Jonathan Cook, "Arab Politicians Face Tide of 'Persecution' in Israel" Global Research, 2 February, 2010 http://www.globalresearch.ca/arab-politicians-face-tide-of-persecution-in-israel/17355

233 Xinhua, "Watery assault steams Israel lawmakers" China Daily, 10 January, 2010 http://www.chinadaily.com.cn/world/2012-01/10/content_14416004.htm

234 Lawrence Davison, "Israel's Persecution of Haneen Zoabi" Global Research, 7 January, 2013

http://www.globalresearch.ca/israels-persecution-of-haneen-zoabi/5318064

[235] Eric Waddell, "The United States' Global Military Crusade (1945-)" Global Research, 11 February, 2007 http://www.globalresearch.ca/the-united-states-global-military-crusade-1945/4610

[236] Amrit Singh, "Globalizing Torture – CIA secret detention and extraordinary rendition" Open Society Justice Initiative, 2013 http://www.opensocietyfoundations.org/sites/default/files/globalizing-torture-20120205.pdf

[237] Xinhua, "China's CPC membership exceeds 85 million" ECNS, 7 January, 2013 http://www.ecns.cn/2013/07-01/70845.shtml

[238] 人民网，"统战部：3.2 万名非中共人士担任县处级以上职务"凤凰网，29 June, 2011 http://news.ifeng.com/mainland/special/jiandang90nian/content-2/detail_2011_06/29/7325690_0.shtml?_from_ralated

[239] Yu Keping, "A shift towards social governance in China" East Asia Forum, 9 September, 2011 http://www.eastasiaforum.org/2011/09/09/a-shift-towards-social-governance-in-china/

[240] Xinhua, "Chinese government's NGO funding peaks in 2012" China Daily, 13 February, 2013 http://www.chinadaily.com.cn/china/2013-02/13/content_16221162.htm

[241] Robert Fogel, "$123,000,000,000,000 – China's estimated economy by the year 2040. Be warned" Foreign Policy, January/February, 2010 http://www.foreignpolicy.com/articles/2010/01/04/123000000000000

[242] AAP, "Canberra doesn't get mining tax: Forrest" WA Today, 22 June, 2011 http://www.watoday.com.au/business/canberra-doesnt-get-mining-tax-forrest-20110622-1gemd.html

[243] Peter Ker, "Mining Tax embarrassment as Rio funds returned" Sydney Morning Herald, 9 August, 2013 http://www.smh.com.au/business/mining-tax-embarrassment-as-rio-funds-returned-20130808-2rku4.html

[244] Felicia Sonmez, "At Illinois GOP dinner, a gloomy Gingrich bemoans

'methodically and deliberately stupid' political system" Washington Post, 13 March, 2012 http://www.washingtonpost.com/blogs/post-politics/post/at-illinois-gop-dinner-a-gloomy-gingrich-bemoans-methodically-and-deliberately-stupid-political-system/2012/03/14/gIQAeSc6CS_blog.html?wpisrc=nl_pmpolitics

245 David Hayes, "Britain's economic tunnel" Inside Story, 3 December, 2012 http://inside.org.au/britains-economic-tunnel/

246 "Editorial: Our governance has yet to enter the 21st century" The Independent, 18 September, 2012 http://www.independent.co.uk/voices/editorials/editorial-our-governance-has-yet-to-enter-the-21st-century-8145118.html

247 Oliver Duggan, "Politicians 'should face performance review' The Independent, 24 May, 2011 http://www.independent.co.uk/news/uk/politics/politicians-should-face-performance-reviews-2288236.html

248 Print edition of The Economist, front page title 'The Hopeless Continent', 13 May, 2000 http://www.economist.com/printedition/2000-05-13

249 "The hopeful continent – Africa rising" The Economist, 3 December, 2011 print edition http://www.economist.com/node/21541015

250 Nick Turse, "Tomgram: Nick Turse, The Pentagon's Planet of Bases" TomDispatch, 9 January, 2011 http://www.tomdispatch.com/archive/175338/nick_turse_empire_of_bases_2.0?utm_source=TomDispatch&utm_campaign=d027c16bb5-TD_Vine7_15_2012&utm_medium=email

251 Chris Cole, "Mapping drone proliferation: big business vs. the MTCR" Drone Wars UK, 18 September, 2012 http://dronewars.net/2012/09/18/mapping-drone-proliferation-big-business-vs-the-mtcr/

252 Dave Lindorff, "Your Tax Dollars at War: More Than 53% of Your Tax Bill Goes to the Military" Global Research, 14 April, 2010 http://www.globalresearch.ca/your-tax-dollars-at-war-more-than-53-of-your-tax-bill-goes-to-the-military/18659

253 Arvind Virmani, "Global Economic Governance: IMF Quota Reform" International Monetary Fund, July 2011 http://www.imf.org/external/pubs/ft/wp/2011/wp11208.pdf

---

254 Sjamsu Rahardja, "What China's economic prospects mean for Indonesia" East Asia Forum, 9 August, 2012 http://www.eastasiaforum.org/2012/08/09/what-china-s-economic-prospects-mean-for-indonesia/

255 Sean Jacobs, """Is PNG's Westminster system worth keeping?" East Asia Forum, 5 October, 2013 http://www.eastasiaforum.org/2013/10/05/is-pngs-westminster-system-worth-keeping/

256 Graham Davis, "Australia's humiliating backdown over failed foreign policy on Fiji" Scoop, 1 August, 2012 http://pacific.scoop.co.nz/2012/08/australias-humiliating-backdown-over-failed-foreign-policy-on-fiji/

257 "Switzerland's Political System and Government" All About Switzerland http://swiss-government-politics.all-about-switzerland.info/

258 Kurt Nimmo, "Bush the First, Hating saddam, Selling Him Weapons" Counter Punch, 19 September, 2002 http://www.counterpunch.org/2002/09/19/bush-the-first-hating-saddam-selling-him-weapons/

259 Sherwood Ross, "US Sponsored Genocide Again Iraq 1990-2012. Killed 3.3 million, Including 750,000 Children" Global Research, 6 December, 2012 http://www.globalresearch.ca/us-sponsored-genocide-against-iraq-1990-2012-killed-3-3-million-including-750000-children/5314461

260 "Australian referendum, 1967 (Aborigine), Wikipedia http://en.wikipedia.org/wiki/Australian_referendum,_1967_%28Aboriginals%29

261 "Voting Rights of Australian Aborigine" Wikipedia http://en.wikipedia.org/wiki/Voting_rights_of_Australian_Aborigines

262 "White Australia policy" Wikipedia http://en.wikipedia.org/wiki/White_Australia_policy

263 Laura Tomlinson, "Constitution must change, say indigenous leaders" In My Community, 4 January, 2013 http://www.inmycommunity.com.au/news-and-views/local-news/Constitution-must-change-say-indigenous-leaders/7638512/

264 "Royal Commission into Aboriginal Deaths in Custody" Indigenous Law Resources Reconciliation and Social justice Library, 29 April, 1998 http://www.austlii.edu.au/au/other/IndigLRes/rciadic/

265 Martin Cuddihy, "Aboriginal deaths in custody numbers rise sharply over past five years" ABC, 24 May, 2013

---

http://www.abc.net.au/news/2013-05-24/sharp-rise-in-number-of-aboriginal-deaths-in-custody/4711764?section=nt

[266] Jane Lee, "Disadvantaged Aboriginal background now a factor in court rulings" The Age, 3 October, 2013 http://www.theage.com.au/national/disadvantaged-aboriginal-background-now-a-factor-in-court-rulings-20131002-2uswz.html

[267] "Aborigine 'cooked' to death in prison van" The Telegraph, 28 June, 2010 http://www.telegraph.co.uk/news/worldnews/australiaandthepacific/australia/7858877/Aborigine-cooked-to-death-in-prison-van.html

[268] John Anderson, "Shock new evidence in Palm Inquest" Townville Bulletin, 9 March, 2010 http://www.townsvillebulletin.com.au/article/2010/03/09/120855_news.html

[269] George Waters, "Doomadgee compo details stay secret" Brisbane Times, 24 May, 2011 http://www.brisbanetimes.com.au/queensland/doomadgee-compo-details-stay-secret-20110523-1f0cy.html

[270] Katherine Fenech, "Pregnant woman 'Tasered up to eight times'" WA Today, 5 October, 2010 http://www.watoday.com.au/wa-news/pregnant-woman-tasered-up-to-eight-times-20101005-165e8.html

[271] Aja Styles, "Court of Appeal quashes Spratt conviction" WA Today, 24 February, 2011 http://www.watoday.com.au/wa-news/court-of-appeal-quashes-spratt-conviction-20110224-1b6h7.html

[272] Rania Spooner, "Police charged over taser incident: Police Minister" WA Today, 11 April, 2013 http://www.watoday.com.au/wa-news/police-charged-over-taser-incident-police-minister-20130411-2hnct.html

[273] AAP, "Doomadgee family wins 'victim of crime' compensation" Brisbane Times, 21 May, 2011 http://www.brisbanetimes.com.au/queensland/doomadgee-family-wins-victim-of-crime-compensation-20110520-1ex1d.html

[274] "UN report paints grim picture of conditions of world's indigenous people" UN News Centre, 14 January, 2010 http://www.un.org/apps/news/story.asp?NewsID=33484&Cr=indigenous&Cr1#.UlfnclOf-Sp

[275] Joel Orenstein, "Being Nobody – The Difficulties faced by Aboriginal

Victorians in Obtaining Identification" Conference Paper, NACLC Conference Perth, 18 September, 2009 http://orenstein.com.au/NACLC%20conf%20paper.pdf Summary: http://www.law.monash.edu.au/castancentre/events/2009/orenstein-pres.pdf

276 "Ferdinand Marcos" Wikipedia https://en.wikipedia.org/wiki/Ferdinand_Marcos

277 "Iranian Revolution" Wikipedia https://en.wikipedia.org/wiki/Iranian_Revolution

278 "Egyptian Revolution of 2011" Wikipedia https://en.wikipedia.org/wiki/2011_Egyptian_revolution

279 "Dissolution of the Soviet Union" Wikipedia http://en.wikipedia.org/wiki/Dissolution_of_the_Soviet_Union

280 James Corbett, "The Death of Dr. David Kelly" GRTV, 13 October, 2011 http://tv.globalresearch.ca/2011/10/death-dr-david-kelly

281 Steve Friess, "Edward Snowden: Google, Facebook disclosures deceiving" Politico, 17 June, 2013 http://www.politico.com/story/2013/06/edward-snowden-google-facebook-92937.html

282 Joshua Bickel, "How the Faithful Voted: 2012 Preliminary Analysis" PEW Research,7 November, 2012 http://www.pewforum.org/2012/11/07/how-the-faithful-voted-2012-preliminary-exit-poll-analysis/

283 Paul Taylor, "The Growing Election Clout of Blacks Is Driven by Turnout, Not Demographics" PEW Research, 26 December, 2012 http://www.pewsocialtrends.org/2012/12/26/the-growing-electoral-clout-of-blacks-is-driven-by-turnout-not-demographics/

284 Scott Clement, "2012 voters: The deepest racial split since' 88" Washington Post, 25 October, 2012 http://www.washingtonpost.com/blogs/the-fix/wp/2012/10/25/2012-voters-the-deepest-racial-split-since-88/

285 Steven Rosenfeld, "Supreme Court's Right-Wing Clique Guts the Voting Rights Act – After Five Decades of Protecting Minorities, Suddenly, It's 'Unconstitutional'" AlterNet, 25 June, 2013 http://www.alternet.org/news-amp-politics/supreme-court-guts-voting-rights-act?akid=10624.267042.OntzKj&rd=1&src=newsletter860315&t=6

286 Edward Taylor, "ECB in Frankfurt surrounded by thousands of debt-

crisis protesters" Independent, 31 May, 2013 http://www.independent.ie/business/ecb-in-frankfurt-surrounded-by-thousands-of-debtcrisis-protesters-29310447.html

[287] Graeme Wearden, "Europe's day of anti-austerity strikes and protests turn violent – as it happened" Guardian, 15 November, 2012 http://www.theguardian.com/business/2012/nov/14/eurozone-crisis-general-strikes-protest-day-of-action?CMP=EMCNEWEML1355

[288] "More mass riots in Europe as Slovenian protesters attempt to enter parliament_cip 1883" Before its news, 30 November, 2012 http://beforeitsnews.com/politics/2012/11/more-mass-riots-in-europe-as-slovenian-protesters-attempt-to-enter-parliament_cip1883-2473410.html

[289] Haroon Siddique, "G8 summit protest: riot police arrest 57 in raid of London HQ" Guardian, 12 June, 2013 http://www.theguardian.com/world/2013/jun/11/anti-g8-protest-headquarters-london-riot-police

[290] Agencies, "Sweden riots continue after police shooting" MWC News, 22 May, 2013 http://mwcnews.net/news/europe/27107-sweden-riots.html?utm_source=feedburner&utm_medium=email&utm_campaign=Feed%3A+mwcnews%2FXrew+%28MWC+News+Alert%29

[291] "Arrests in Brookln in 3rd night of police brutality protest [Photos]" RT, 14 March, 2013 http://rt.com/usa/police-flood-brooklyn-neighborhood-238/

[292] "Interview With President Obama" New York Times, 27 July, 2013 http://www.nytimes.com/2013/07/28/us/politics/interview-with-president-obama.html?pagewanted=all&_r=2&&gwh=BBAF3EC2FCBB6D816DC0C269F25B1D63

[293] George Friedman, "Europe, Unemployment and Instability" Stratfor, 5 March, 2013 http://www.stratfor.com/weekly/europe-unemployment-and-instability#ixzz2MfPtOfKZ

[294] Christa Case Bryant, "Before debating democracy, poor Egyptians want their stomachs filled" Christian Science Monitor, 2 August, 2013 http://www.csmonitor.com/World/Middle-East/Olive-Press/2013/0802/Before-debating-democracy-poor-Egyptians-want-their-stomachs-filled

[295] "Europe Stalling intergration" Stratfor, 6 March, 2013

http://www.stratfor.com/sample/geopolitical-diary/europes-stalling-integration

296 Gordon N. Bardos, "Spectre of Separatism Haunts Europe" National Interest, 17 January, 2013 http://nationalinterest.org/commentary/spectre-separatism-haunts-europe-7979

297 Emily Uliya, "The UK sends warships to Gibraltar because that's how they deal with things" Scrape TV, 12 August, 2013 http://scrapetv.com/News/News%20Pages/Everyone%20Else/pages-23/The-UK-sends-warships-to-Gibraltar-because-thats-how-they-deal-with-things-Scrape-TV-The-World-on-your-side-2013-08-12.html#.Ulf2b1Of-Sp

298 David Hayes, "A politics out of time" Inside Story, 25 July, 2013 http://inside.org.au/a-politics-out-of-time/

299 Oliver Wright, "British politics at the crossroads: Tory membership plummets over disenchantment with Westminster" The Independent, 9 August, 2013 http://www.independent.co.uk/news/uk/politics/british-politics-at-the-crossroads-tory-membership-plummets-over-disenchantment-with-westminster-8753054.html

300 "Prime Ministers during the Heisei period (1989 – present)" Wikipedia http://en.wikipedia.org/wiki/List_of_Prime_Ministers_of_Japan#Prime_Ministers_during_the_Heisei_period_.281989.E2.80.93present.29

301 Julian Ryall, "Hurry up and die, Japan's deputy PM tells old folk" Sydney Morning Herald, 23 January, 2013 http://www.smh.com.au/world/hurry-up-and-die-japans-deputy-pm-tells-old-folk-20130123-2d5uf.html

302 Mitsuru Obe, "Japan Fin Min Aso: Want To Retract Use of Nazi Example In Monday Speech" Wall Street Journal, 31 July, 2013 http://online.wsj.com/article/BT-CO-20130731-722191.html

303 "Obama Administration Notifies the Congress on Including Japan in the trans-Pacific Partnership (TPP) Negotiation" Ex-SKF, 24 April, 2013 http://ex-skf.blogspot.com.au/2013/04/obama-administration-notifies-congress.html

304 Michale Cucek, "Japan's nothing' election" East Asia Forum, 16 December, 2012 http://www.eastasiaforum.org/2012/12/16/japans-nothing-election/

305 "Chinese Dissident Visits Taipei, Says Taiwan Can Be Political Model for

China" VOA, 24 June, 2013 http://www.voanews.com/content/chinese-dissident-visits-taipei-says-taiwan-can-be-political-model-for-china/1687822.html

306 Maia Huang, "China Times: Taiwan struggling with democracy" Focus Taiwan News Channel, 30 June, 2013 http://focustaiwan.tw/news/asoc/201306300018.aspx

307 "Ma the bumbler" The Economist, 17 November, 2012 http://www.economist.com/news/asia/21566657-former-heart-throb-loses-his-shine-ma-bumbler

308 年代民调中心 Survey http://survey.eracom.com.tw/item/i24.xml

309 Bob Drogin, "'Guns, Goons, Gold' Time in Philippines: Elections: Authorities brace for traditional violence and cheating campaigns get under way" Los Angeles Times, 10 February, 1992 http://articles.latimes.com/1992-02-10/news/mn-1347_1_national-election-campaign

310 John McLean, "Democracy Philippines-style" BBC, 30 January, 1998 http://news.bbc.co.uk/2/hi/programmes/from_our_own_correspondent/52070.stm

311 David Gorman, "The Philippine politics: Guns, goons, gold and the war on terror" Jakarta Post, 1 December, 2009 http://www.thejakartapost.com/news/2009/12/01/the-philippine-politics-guns-goons-gold-and-war-terror.html

312 Michael Tan, "The 4th G to guns, goons, gold: Glitches" Inquirer, 5 November, 2010 http://newsinfo.inquirer.net/inquirerheadlines/nation/view/20100511-269338/The-4th-G-to-guns-goons-gold-Glitches

313 Leandro DD Coronel, "Guns, goons and gold are back!" Balita, 15 February, 2013 http://www.balita.ca/2013/02/guns-goons-and-gold-are-back/

314 Wenfang Tang, Michael S. Lewis-Beck, and Nicholas F. Martini, "Government for the People in China?" The Diplomat, 17 June, 2013 http://thediplomat.com/2013/06/17/government-for-the-people-in-china/

315 Wenfang Tang, Michael S. Lewis-Beck, and Nicholas F. Martini, "A Chinese Popularity Function: Sources of Government Support" Sage Journals, Political Research Quarterly, 30 April, 2013 http://prq.sagepub.com/content/early/2013/04/29/1065912913486196.abstract

---

316 Austin Ramzy, "Haiti and China: A Tale of Two Earthquakes" Time, 19 January, 2010 http://content.time.com/time/world/article/0,8599,1954644,00.html

317 Peter Foster, "China v India: Two kinds of people power" The Telegraph, 15 April, 2009 http://blogs.telegraph.co.uk/news/peterfoster/9507086/China_v_India_two_kinds_of_people_power_/

318 "Galileo Galilei" Wiki http://en.wikipedia.org/wiki/Galileo_Galilei

319 Steven Hill, "China's tentative steps towards democracy" Guardian, 20 January, 2011 http://www.theguardian.com/commentisfree/cifamerica/2011/jan/19/china-barack-obama

320 Damien Ma, "Young Chinese People May Just Not Be That Into Western-Style Democracy" The Atlantic, 18 July, 2013 http://www.theatlantic.com/china/archive/2013/07/young-chinese-people-may-just-not-be-that-into-western-style-democracy/277885/

321 "Upbeat Chinese Public May Not Be Primed for a Jasmine revolution" PEW Research, 31 March, 2011 http://www.pewglobal.org/2011/03/31/upbeat-chinese-public-may-not-be-primed-for-a-jasmine-revolution/

322 CCTV, ""洗脚妹"代表：长期分居致大量农民工结成临时夫妻" 凤凰网, 10 March, 2013 http://news.ifeng.com/mainland/special/2013lianghui/yanlun/detail_2013_03/10/22939380_0.shtml

323 新京"90 后女孩：2 月中旬得知自己当选代表 非常惊讶(图)" 大公报, 28 February, 2013 http://news.takungpao.com/mainland/2013-02/1463662.html

324 人民网，"广东新兴县要求乡镇干部每周在镇里至少住宿 3 晚 - 住镇新规管得了"走读干部"吗" 人民网，4 May, 2012 http://society.people.com.cn/GB/17804237.html

325 Svenja O'Donnell, "Afghan Army May Need NATO Support Unitl 2020, UK Official Says" Bloomberg Business Week, 29 June, 2013 http://www.businessweek.com/news/2013-06-29/afghan-army-may-need-nato-support-until-2020-u-dot-k-dot-official-says

326 "Bush Doctrine – Democratization" Wikipedia http://en.wikipedia.org/wiki/Bush_Doctrine#Democratization

327 Peter Van Buren, "Why the invasion of Iraq Was the Single Worst

---

Foreign policy Decision in American History" The Nation, 7 March, 2013 http://www.thenation.com/article/173246/why-invasion-iraq-was-single-worst-foreign-policy-decision-american-history?rel=emailNation#

[328] "UN: July deadliest month in Iraq since 2008" Aljazeera, 1 August, 2013 http://www.aljazeera.com/news/middleeast/2013/08/20138192433716965.html

[329] Same as reference no 324

[330] "2006-07 economic sanctions against the Palestinian national Authority" Wikipedia http://en.wikipedia.org/wiki/2006%E2%80%9307_economic_sanctions_against_the_Palestinian_National_Authority

[331] Keith Ablow, "A nation can be a democracy and still be a mortal enemy of the US" Fox News, 9 July, 2013 http://www.foxnews.com/opinion/2013/07/09/nation-can-be-democracy-and-still-be-mortal-enemy-us/

[332] Walter Pincus, "US intervention in Egypt is not the solution" Washington Post, 22 August, 2013 http://www.washingtonpost.com/world/national-security/us-intervention-in-egypt-is-not-the-solution/2013/08/21/1a91ec7c-09b6-11e3-8974-f97ab3b3c677_story.html?wpisrc=nl_fed

[333] Robert D. Kaplan, "The Tragedy of US Foreign Policy" National Interest, 1 August, 2013 http://nationalinterest.org/commentary/the-tragedy-us-foreign-policy-8810?page=show

[334] Thom Hartmann, "America Didn't "End" Slavery After the Civil War – We Simply Exported It" AlterNet, 27 November, 2012 http://www.alternet.org/labor/america-didnt-end-slavery-after-civil-war-we-simply-exported-it?paging=off¤t_page=1#bookmark

[335] Kevin Phillips, "Wealth and Democracy: A Political of the American Rich" Foreign Affairs, January/February Issue http://www.foreignaffairs.com/articles/58523/derek-lundy/wealth-and-democracy-a-political-history-of-the-american-rich

[336] Noam Chomsky, "Chomsky: The US behaves nothing like a democracy" Salon, 17 August, 2013 http://www.salon.com/2013/08/17/chomsky_the_u_s_behaves_nothing_like_a_democracy/

[337] Jason Groves, "Nightmare vision for Europe as EU chief warns

'democracy could disappear' in Greece, Spain and Portugal" Mail Online, 15 June, 2010 http://www.dailymail.co.uk/news/article-1286480/EU-chief-warns-democracy-disappear-Greece-Spain-Portugal.html

[338] James Jay Carafano, "Obama's Sloppy History Problem" National Interest, 4 August, 2013 http://nationalinterest.org/commentary/obamas-sloppy-history-problem-8830

[339] Brian Costar, "Political donations: the real-time disclosure option" Inside Story, 8 August, 2013 http://inside.org.au/political-donations-the-real-time-disclosure-option/

[340] James Cusick, "Exclusive: David Cameron condemned over 'ridiculous' reforms to lobbying" The Independent, 19 August, 2013 http://www.independent.co.uk/news/uk/politics/exclusive-david-cameron-condemned-over-ridiculous-reforms-to-lobbying-8773473.html

[341] Adam Liptak, "Justice, 5-4, Reject Corporate Spending Limit" New York Times, 21 January, 2013 http://www.nytimes.com/2010/01/22/us/politics/22scotus.html?pagewanted=all&_r=2&&gwh=30BCCA259D10B2212944189FBAED1962

[342] Ray Henry, "Jimmy Carter: Unchecked campaign contributions are 'legal bribery'" Christian Science Monitor, 18 July, 2013 http://www.csmonitor.com/USA/Latest-News-Wires/2013/0718/Jimmy-Carter-Unchecked-campaign-contributions-are-legal-bribery

[343] Dave Johnson, "Multinationals Are Plotting to Steamroll What's Left of Our Democracy to Make Huge Profits" AlterNet, 20 August, 2013 http://www.alternet.org/economy/huge-multinationals-are-plotting-steamroll-our-democracy-their-hunt-profits?akid=10841.267042.U01D10&rd=1&src=newsletter886570&t=6

[344] Nile Bowie, "The Trans-Pacific Partnership (TPP), An Oppressive US-Led Free trade Agreement, A Corporate Power –Tool of the 1%" Global Research, 2 April, 2013 http://www.globalresearch.ca/the-trans-pacific-partnership-tpp-an-oppressive-us-led-free-trade-agreement-a-corporate-power-tool-of-the-1/5329497

[345] David Uren, "Half RBA board absent on rates" Australian, 20 October,

2010 http://www.theaustralian.com.au/business/economics/half-rba-board-absent-on-rates/story-e6frg926-1225940903029

[346] Dean Henderson, "The Federal Reserve Cartel: The Eight Families" Global Research, 1 June, 2011 http://www.globalresearch.ca/the-federal-reserve-cartel-the-eight-families/25080

[347] Rajeev Syal, "One in five passholders in the House of Lords linked to lobbying" Guardian, 9 November, 2011 http://www.theguardian.com/politics/2011/nov/08/house-of-lords-passholders-lobbying?CMP=EMCNEWEML1355

[348] "Swiss canton backs burqa ban" Euronews, 23 September, 2013 http://www.euronews.com/2013/09/23/swiss-canton-backs-burqa-ban/

[349] "Exercising US Leadership: Democracy Funding in a Time of Global Change" Freedom House, 15 May, 2012 http://www.freedomhouse.org/sites/default/files/Exercising%20U.S.%20Leadership%20%20Democracy%20Funding%20in%20a%20Time%20of%20Global%20Change.pdf

[350] Admin, "China must follow world trend of democracy: Dalai lama" Zakat Foundation of India, 17 september, 2013 http://twocircles.net/2013sep17/china_must_follow_world_trend_democracy_dalai_lama.html

[351] Klaus Jansen, "German anxieties over China's rise" DW, 20 July, 2013 http://www.dw.de/german-anxieties-over-chinas-rise/a-16963665

[352] Krishore Mahbubani, "America's Blinders" Project Syndicate, 24 May, 2013 http://www.project-syndicate.org/commentary/the-denial-of-american-decline-by-kishore-mahbubani

[353] Gerard Lemos, "What Keeps the Chinese Up at Night" New York Times, 9 September, 2012 http://www.nytimes.com/2012/09/10/opinion/what-keeps-the-chinese-up-at-night.html?pagewanted=all&_r=0&gwh=3B9450629822086BBEF72F6ACC391D96

[354] Michael S Wilson, "Noam Chomsky: The Kind of Anarchism I Believe in, and What's Wrong with Libertarians" AlterNet, 28 May, 2013 http://www.alternet.org/civil-liberties/noam-chomsky-kind-anarchism-i-believe-and-whats-wrong-

libertarians?akid=10511.267042.Fr8s6j&rd=1&src=newsletter848598&t=5

[355] Paul Joseph Watson, "Paulson Was Behind Bailout Martial Law threat" Infowars, 20 November, 2008 http://www.infowars.com/paulson-was-behind-bailout-martial-law-threat/

[356] Newt Gingrich, "A Rising Anti-Government Tide" Washington Post, 22 May, 2009 http://www.washingtonpost.com/wp-dyn/content/article/2009/05/21/AR2009052103724.html?wpisrc=newsletter&wpisrc=newsletter

[357] "Occupy Arrests Near 8,000 As Wall Street Eludes Prosecution" Huffington Post, 23 May, 2013 http://www.huffingtonpost.com/2013/05/23/occupy-wall-street-arrests_n_3326640.html

[358] Dan Cassino, "Beliefs About Sandy Hook Cover-up, Coming Revolution Underlie Divide On Gun Control" Fairleigh Dickinson University's Public Mind Poli, 1 May, 2013 http://publicmind.fdu.edu/2013/guncontrol/

[359] Jia Qinglin, "The Development of Socialist Consultative Democracy in China" Qiushi, English Edition of Qiushi Journal, Vol.5 No.1, 1 January, 2013 http://english.qstheory.cn/leaders/201302/t20130227_213720.htm

[360] Luisa Kroll, "Inside The 2013 Forbes 400: Facts And Figures On America's Richest" Forbes, 16 September, 2013 http://www.forbes.com/sites/luisakroll/2013/09/16/inside-the-2013-forbes-400-facts-and-figures-on-americas-richest/

[361] Matt Stoller, "Economic Shock Wave: 1 in 7 Americans Pursued by Debt Collectors" AlterNet, 28 February, 2012 http://www.alternet.org/story/154329/economic_shock_wave%3A_1_in_7_americans_pursued_by_debt_collectors?akid=8324.267042.t55ECr&rd=1&t=8

[362] Shan Li, "Nearly half of Americans are one emergency from ruin" Los Angeles Times, 30 January, 2013 http://articles.latimes.com/2013/jan/30/business/la-fi-mo-savings-financial-emergency-20130130

[363] "Poverty sours in US despite economic recovery" MWC News, 18 September, 2013 http://mwcnews.net/news/americas/31455-poverty-soars-in-

us.html?utm_source=feedburner&utm_medium=email&utm_campaign=Feed%3A+mwcnews%2FXrew+%28MWC+News+Alert%29

364 Sam Roberts, "Poverty Rate is Up in New York City, and Income Gap is Wide, Census data Show" New York Times, 19 September, 2013 http://www.nytimes.com/2013/09/19/nyregion/poverty-rate-in-city-rises-to-21-2.html?nl=nyregion&emc=edit_ur_20130919&_r=0

365 Mireya Navarro, "In New York, Having a Job, or 2, Doesn't Mean Having a Home" New York Times, 17 September, 2013 http://www.nytimes.com/2013/09/18/nyregion/in-new-york-having-a-job-or-2-doesnt-mean-having-a-home.html?nl=nyregion&emc=edit_ur_20130918

366 Editorial Board, "Tips and Poverty" New York Times, 14 September, 2013 http://www.nytimes.com/2013/09/15/opinion/sunday/tips-and-poverty.html?_r=0&gwh=23E72EF50341C0C1CEEC7A96F86C94FC

367 Christie Thompson,"To Cope with Sequenster, Justice Department Staffs Unpaid Attorney" ProPublica, 28 June, 2012 http://www.propublica.org/article/to-cope-with-sequester-justice-department-staffs-unpaid-attorneys

368 H. Luke Shaefer, "Rising Extreme Poverty in the United States and the response of Federal Means-Tested transfer Programs" National Poverty Center Working Paper Series #13-06, May 2013 http://npc.umich.edu/publications/u/2013-06-npc-working-paper.pdf

369 Richard Fry, "A Rise in Wealth for the Wealthy; Declines for the lower 93%" PEW Research, 23 April, 2013 http://www.pewsocialtrends.org/2013/04/23/a-rise-in-wealth-for-the-wealthydeclines-for-the-lower-93/

370 Peter Whiteford, "Poverty in a time of prosperity" Inside Story, 15 September, 2013 http://inside.org.au/poverty-in-a-time-of-prosperity/

371 Noel Towell, "Tough call on 1200 jobs at Centrelink" The Age, 18 September, 2013 http://www.theage.com.au/federal-politics/political-news/tough-call-on-1200-jobs-at-centrelink-20130917-2txdc.html

372 Karina Barrymore, "Millions of Aussies missing out on financial help" Courier Mail, 4 November, 2012 http://www.couriermail.com.au/money/missing-out-on-financial-help/story-e6freqoo-1226510695517

373 Heath Aston, "Kill poor to fix budget, writes lobbyist with Liberal links"

Sydney Morning Herald, 17 April, 2013 http://www.smh.com.au/federal-politics/political-news/kill-poor-to-fix-budget-writes-lobbyist-with-liberal-links-20130416-2hygv.html

[374] Michelle Grattan, "Coalition targets welfare 'bludgers'" The Age, 6 July, 2012 http://www.theage.com.au/federal-politics/political-news/coalition-targets-welfare-bludgers-20120705-21k44.html

[375] Helen Davidson, "Food relief: 65,000 Australians a month ask for help but get nothing" Guardian, 16 October, 2013 http://www.theguardian.com/world/2013/oct/16/food-relief-65000-australians-a-month-ask-for-help-but-get-nothing

[376] Renee Viellaris, "WorkCover review could strip workers of right to compensation" Courier Mail, 23 September, 2013 http://www.couriermail.com.au/news/queensland/workcover-review-could-strip-workers-of-right-to-compensation/story-fnihsrf2-1226724844008

[377] Kim Stephens, "Retirees' home ownership set to plummet to 2 percent" Brisbane Times, 22 August, 2013 http://www.brisbanetimes.com.au/queensland/retirees-home-ownership-set-to-plummet-to-2-per-cent-20130821-2sbmu.html

[378] Robyn Ironside, "Struggling consumers can't pay souring power bills with some presioners being left in the dark" Courier Mail, 25 March, 2013 http://www.couriermail.com.au/news/queensland/struggling-consumers-cant pay soaring-power-bills-with-some-pensioners-being-left-in-the-dark/story-e6freoof-1226604578716#

[379] Rachel Wells, "Power struggle: homes cut off" The Age, 10 December, 2012 http://www.theage.com.au/victoria/power-struggle-homes-cut-off-20121210-2b5qu.html

[380] Reema Rattan, "Children's well-being report captures Australia's growing inequality" The Conversation, 15 March, 2013 http://theconversation.com/childrens-well-being-report-captures-australias-growing-inequality-12841

[381] Gerry Georgatos, "Human Rights Allance media release: WA minning boom and record poverty and homeless rates" Independent media Australia, 23 July, 2012 http://indymedia.org.au/2012/07/23/human-rights-allance-media-release-wa-mining-boom-and-record-poverty-and-homelessness-rat

[382] Matthew Thompson, "Almost 3 million adult Aussies lack basic financial services" The Conversation, 29 May, 2013 http://theconversation.com/almost-3-million-adult-aussies-lack-basic-financial-services-7335

[383] "1 in 100 homeless in past year" ABC, 30 April, 2010 http://www.abc.net.au/news/2010-04-30/1-in-100-homeless-in-past-year/416336?section=justin

[384] Brigit Busicchia, "The average Australian wastes 200kg of food a year – yet two million of us also go hungry. Why? The Conversation, 14 February, 2012 http://theconversation.com/the-average-australian-wastes-200kg-of-food-a-year-yet-two-million-of-us-also-go-hungry-why-5278

[385] Natalie Savino, "Melbourne Airport fee hikes to cripple small bus and parking businesses" Herald Sun, 8 October, 2013 http://www.heraldsun.com.au/leader/north/melbourne-airport-fee-hikes-to-cripple-small-bus-and-parking-businesses/story-fnglenug-1226734121737

[386] Steven Wardill, "Double-digit shock as electricity bills set to surge by 21.4 percent" Courier Mail, 22 February, 2013 http://www.couriermail.com.au/news/queensland/electricity-bill-shock/story-e6freoof-1226583094724#

[387] Neil Keene, "Huge profit for CTP insurers in NSW as premium prices skyrocket" The Telegraph, 24 June, 2013 http://www.dailytelegraph.com.au/news/nsw/huge-profit-for-ctp-insurers-in-nsw-as-premium-prices-skyrocket/story-fni0cx12-1226668456669

[388] Courtney Trenwith, "Census reveals extent of souring mortgages, rent" WA Today, 22 June, 2012 http://www.watoday.com.au/wa-news/census-reveals-extent-of-soaring-mortgages-rent-20120621-20qul.html

[389] Clancy Yeates, "Ian Narev defends CBA record profit" Sydney Morning Herald, 14 August, 2013 http://www.smh.com.au/business/banking-and-finance/ian-narev-defends-cba-record-profit-20130814-2rwlm.html

[390] Stephen McMahon, "NAB on track to hit $6bn profits" Courier mail, 7 February, 2013 http://www.couriermail.com.au/business/companies/nabs-profit-continues-to-fall-cash-earnings-up/story-fndfrjq1-1226572414651?from=public_rss#

[391] News, "Australians slapped $4 billion in bank fees, RateCity finds" The Telegraph, 21 June, 2011 http://www.dailytelegraph.com.au/money/australians-slugged-4-billion-in-bank-fees-ratecity-finds/story-fn300aev-1226078965557

[392] Ben Grubb, "Virgin's call rates increase by up to 1289%" Sydney Morning Herald, 19 February, 2013 http://www.smh.com.au/digital-life/mobiles/virgins-call-rates-increase-by-up-to-1289-20130219-2eoue.html

[393] Glenda Kwek, "Airport car park prices go sky high" Sydney Morning Herald, 24 August, 2012 http://www.smh.com.au/travel/travel-news/airport-car-park-prices-go-sky-high-20120823-24oxl.html

[394] Sarah Whyte, "Australia Post faces backlash over increased delivery charges" WA Today, 8 April, 2013 http://www.watoday.com.au/business/australia-post-faces-backlash-over-increased-delivery-charges-20130408-2hglc.html

[395] Michelle Hele, "Unit owners fight huge increases in body corporate charges" Courier Mail, 3 April, 2012 http://www.couriermail.com.au/lifestyle/unit-owners-fight-huge-increases-in-body-corporate-charges/story-e6frequ6-1226316889662#

[396] Bill Lindsay, "Caltex Australia profit up 33pc" Australian, 22 April, 2010 http://www.theaustralian.com.au/archive/business/caltex-australia-profit-up-33pc/story-e6frg9ef-1225856760803#

[397] "Westfield Group posts lift in FY profit" Business Spectator, 27 February, 2013 http://www.businessspectator.com.au/news/2013/2/27/retail/westfield-group-posts-lift-fy-profit

[398] "Supermarket duopoly blamed for soaring food prices" WA Today, 9 November, 2009 http://www.watoday.com.au/business/supermarket-duopoly-blamed-for-soaring-food-prices-20091109-i3tn.html

[399] Peter Ker, "Mining tax embarrassment as Rio funds returned" Sydney Morning Herald, 9 August, 2013 http://www.smh.com.au/business/mining-tax-embarrassment-as-rio-funds-returned-20130808-2rku4.html

[400] Paddy manning, "Magnate's company paid no tax" WA Today, 12 April, 2012 http://www.watoday.com.au/business/magnates-company-paid-no-tax-20120411-1wsl2.html

---

[401] Georgia Wilkins, "Tax system at risk: Treasury" Brisbane Times, 24 July, 2013 http://www.brisbanetimes.com.au/business/tax-system-at-risk-treasury-20130723-2qhkr.html

[402] Susannah Moran, "BHP has a victory in its $2.2bn tax case" Australian, 18 March, 2010 http://www.theaustralian.com.au/business/bhp-has-a-victory-in-its-22bn-tax-case/story-e6frg8zx-1225842069888#

[403] "Man slapped with $750 fine for swearing at police" The Queensland Times, 1 October, 2013 http://www.qt.com.au/news/man-slapped-with-750-fine-for-swearing-at-police/2036982/

[404] Tim Colebatch, "Millionaires snub taxman" The Age, 7 May, 2013 http://www.theage.com.au/business/millionaires-snub-taxman-20130506-2j3pr.html

[405] Abrahm Lustgarten, "Unfair Share: How Oil and Gas Drillers Avoid Paying Royalties" ProPublica, 13 August, 2013 http://www.propublica.org/article/unfair-share-how-oil-and-gas-drillers-avoid-paying-royalties

[406] Simon Bowers, "US bloacks crackdown on tax avoidance by net firms like Google and Amazon" Guardian, 15 July, 2013 http://www.theguardian.com/business/2013/jul/14/us-tax-avoidance-google-amazon?CMP=EMCNEWEML6619I2

[407] Yues Smith, "Noble Prize-Winner joe Stiglitz Blasts America's 1 Percent-Coddling Tax System" AlterNet, 15 April, 2013 http://www.alternet.org/economy/nobel-prize-winner-joe-stiglitz-blasts-americas-1-percent-coddling-tax-system?akid=10339.267042.35PQP2&rd=1&src=newsletter826895&t=6

[408] Ben Protess, "Inside the End of the US Bid to Punish Lehman Executive" New York Times, 8 September, 2013 http://dealbook.nytimes.com/2013/09/08/inside-the-end-of-the-u-s-bid-to-punish-lehman-executives/?nl=todaysheadlines&emc=edit_th_20130909&_r=2

[409] Michael Sallah, "Left with nothing" Washington Post, 8 September, 2013 http://www.washingtonpost.com/sf/investigative/2013/09/08/left-with-nothing/?wpisrc=al_excl

[410] Mu Chunshan, "'Cooking the Books'? China's Data Dilemma" The

Diplomat, 17 August, 2012 http://thediplomat.com/china-power/cooking-the-books-chinas-data-dilemma/

[411] Keith Bradsher, "China's Unemployment swells as Exports Falter" New York Times, 5 February, 2009 http://www.nytimes.com/2009/02/06/business/worldbusiness/06yuan.html?pagewanted=all&_r=1&

[412] Ben Collins, "Wealth gap narrows in China" Financial Standard, 2 November, 2012 http://www.financialstandard.com.au/news/view/23825969

[413] Qiu Quanlin, "'Lost' Staff prompt a headache" China Daily, 4 April, 2012 http://www.chinadaily.com.cn/bizchina/2012-02/04/content_14536730.htm

[414] Wang Xinye, "Migrant workers in shortage after Spring Festival holiday" CNTV, 19 February, 2013 http://english.cntv.cn/program/china24/20130219/102398.shtml

[415] "China puts people before banks" Aljazeera, 14 August, 2009 http://www.aljazeera.com/focus/chinabuystheworld/2009/08/2009810844187407 60.html

[416] CCTV, "习近平：使我们的红色江山永远不变色" 凤凰网, 12 July, 2013 http://news.ifeng.com/mainland/special/qunzhongluxian/content-3/detail_2013_07/12/27455823_0.shtml

[417] 人民网, "专家解读李克强总理经济理念：落脚点都是民生"人民网, 19 July, 2013 http://finance.people.com.cn/n/2013/0719/c1004-22255711.html

www.ingramcontent.com/pod-product-compliance
Lightning Source LLC
Chambersburg PA
CBHW071038290526
45795CB00004B/1216